D1561628

Chicago Public Library

REFERENCE

Form 178 rev. 1-94

Reptile Journalism

Reptile Journalism

The Official Polish-Language
Press under the Nazis,
1939-1945

Lucjan Dobroszycki

Translated by
Barbara Harshav

Yale
University
Press
New Haven
and
London

Published with assistance from Warren Grover,
Lawrence Newman, George M. and Shirley M.
Szabad, and Yeshiva University's Fund for East
European Jewry Research created by Dr. Laszlo
N. Tauber.

Designed by Sonia L. Scanlon
Set in Times Roman type by Keystone
Typesetting, Inc., Orwigsburg, Pennsylvania.
Printed in the United States of America by
BookCrafters, Inc., Chelsea, Michigan.

Library of Congress Cataloging-in-Publication
Data
Dobroszycki, Lucjan.
    [Legale polnische Presse im
Generalgouvernement, 1939–1945. English]
    Reptile journalism : the official Polish-
language press under the Nazis, 1939–1945 /
Lucjan Dobroszycki ; translated by Barbara
Harshav.
        p. cm.
    Includes bibliographical references and index.
    ISBN 0-300-05277-4
    1. Press — Poland — History — 20th century.
2. World War, 1939–1945 — Poland. I. Title.
PN5355.P6D613   1994
073'.8'09044 — dc20   94-17013
                                        CIP

A catalogue record for this book is available
from the British Library.

The paper in this book meets the guidelines for
permanence and durability of the Committee on
Production Guidelines for Book Longevity of the
Council on Library Resources.

10 9 8 7 6 5 4 3 2 1

For Felicja and Joanna

For your hands are defiled with crime

And your fingers with iniquity.

Your lips speak falsehood,

Your tongue utters treachery.

—Isaiah 59:3

Contents

Contents
viii

Preface to the
English Edition

My study of reptile journalism in Poland during World War II has its own peculiar history. From the start it was an unintentional, if not to say fortuitous, subject of inquiry, yet, for all that, one fraught with unforeseen consequences.

At the end of the 1950s, while working on the *Central Catalog of the Polish Clandestine Press, 1939–1945* and preparing several essays for publication, I embarked on the writing of an extended monograph about the Polish clandestine press. I began, as usual, by drafting a general outline, the first section of which was to discuss Nazi press policy in occupied Poland. In the place of a single section there emerged an entire book.

This came about because I was quickly able to establish that nothing had been written on this topic heretofore, if one discounted a few articles of scant significance that were, on the whole, error-filled or misleading into the bargain. Their conclusion was that the reptile press, like the film industry, had been boycotted by Polish society, in response to the appeals of the resistance movement. "Only swine sit in the cinema," declared one of the numerous illustrated flyers distributed in Poland. The same sort of thing was said of the readership of the reptile press. Such views persisted after the war, especially during the 1960s, when they were promoted as part of the state's official, ultra-patriotic propaganda.

The preliminary results of my archival research indicated, however, that the reptile press was well nigh universally bought and read, despite being published by the detested occupying power. It was no easy task to convince even my friends, who indeed had never touched these newspapers, of this fact.

Fortunately, the Institute of History at the Polish Academy of Sciences, where I was employed starting in 1954, was one of a handful of oases in postwar Poland where intellectual freedom and unfettered scholarly research were preserved. My immediate superior and research director was Dr. Stanisław Płoski, head of the Historical Bureau of the Home Army during the war. The director of the institute was the renowned historian of the early Middle Ages, Professor Tadeusz Manteuffel; during the occupation he was one of the founders of the clandestine university in Warsaw. Dr. Płoski's department employed several former members of the Bureau of Information and Propaganda of the Home Army (the so-called BIP, or Sixth Section of the Home Army GHQ), together with its former chief, Colonel

Jan Rzepecki. The BIP was unquestionably one of the most liberal sections in the Home Army, since it gave employment to the flower of the Polish intelligentsia, including persons of Jewish origin. Another member of the BIP was Jan Karski, prior to his secret departure from occupied Warsaw on his historic mission to England and the United States.

It goes without saying that among my colleagues at the Institute of History I found full support and understanding for the subject I had raised. Towards the end of 1967 I submitted a typescript of the book to the State Scholarly Publishing House (PWN). It was rejected out of hand. One of the readers reportedly stated that either the author had to be writing about the German press or the book was, in reality, a covert critique of the current Polish press. Soon thereafter, following the Six-Day War in the Middle East, the official campaign of anti-Semitism was unleashed in Poland. All publishing houses were forbidden to publish books written by Jewish authors.

In November 1969 I left Poland with my family, but only after I managed, with the help of friends, to send the typescript of my book out to the West.

In the spring of 1970, en route to Denmark, where, I had been awarded a fellowship at the Royal Library in Copenhagen, I stopped off in Munich. There I visited the Institut für Zeitgeschichte. Following a conversation I had with the director, Dr. Martin Broszat, the institute expressed an interest in the manuscript of my book. A short time later, Dr. Broszat informed me that the institute would translate and publish the work. Bearing the title *Die legale polnische Presse im Generalgouvernement* (ed. Wolfgang Jacobmeyer), the book appeared under the auspices of the institute in Munich in 1977.

Today, more than twenty-five years after it was written, the book is coming out in an English translation. I can assuredly say that nothing has been written, either in Poland or elsewhere, that is capable of casting the slightest doubt on my version of events. In recent years, especially during the Solidarity period and following the change of regimes, a variety of works on the subject of the reptile press have appeared, but all of them are based on my research or on the sources that I brought to light.

The present English edition is in essence identical to the text published in 1977 in Munich. I have made only a few minor changes and added some explanatory footnotes addressed primarily to American readers.

This is the place to thank Dr. Leon Kilbert and Mark Winchester, my two friends who, as volunteers at the Yivo Institute for Jewish Research, assisted me in preparing this volume for publication. I wish also to express my heartfelt thanks to Mark Getter, my colleague and friend of many years' standing from the Institute of History at the Polish Academy of Sciences, for his help in collecting the reproductions of reptile newspapers that illustrate the English edition.

While preparing the English edition for publication, I enjoyed the support and encouragement of several friends: Andrea and Warren Grover, Pamela and Jeffrey Gurock, Elaine and Larry Newman, Susie and Henry Orenstein, Ludwik Seidenman, George and the late Shirley Szabad. Their friendship has been an inspiration in my work from the time my family and I arrived on these shores. David Margolick, who has constantly initiated me in the arcana of the English language, was also always ready to lend a hand.

I warmly thank Barbara Harshav, my translator.

It is my great pleasure to express special gratitude to Yale University Press, from whose editorial assistance I have benefited since the days in 1984 when *The Chronicle of the Łódź Ghetto* was published. I owe particular thanks to Jonathan Brent, senior editor, and Richard Miller, manuscript editor, for the quality and final shape of this book.

L.D.

New York City

May 1994

Abbreviations

AAN	Archiwum Akt Nowych, Warsaw
AGKBZH[1]	Archiwum Głównej Komisji Badania Zbrodni Hitlerowskich w Polsce, Warsaw
APW	Archiwum Panstwowe m.St. Warszawy i Wojewodztwa Warszawskiego
AWIH	Archiwum Wojskowego Instytutu Historycznego
AZHP[2]	Archiwum Zakladu Historii Parti
CAMSW[3]	Centralne Archiwum Ministerstwa Spraw Wewnetrznych, Warsaw
DTgb Hans Frank,	*Diensttagebuch*
DZA-Potsdam	Deutsches Zentralarchiv I, Potsdam
GG	Generalgouvernement
IHPAN	Instytut Historii Polskiej Akademii Nauk, Warsaw
OKW	Wehrmacht headquarters
PK	Propagandakompanien
RMVP	Reich Ministry for Public Enlightenment and Propaganda
WAP-Łódź	Wojewodzkie Archiwum Panstwowe, Łódź

[1]The name has been changed to Główna Komisja Badania Zbrodni Przeciwko Narodowi Polskiemu.

[2]The holdings have been transferred to the AAN.

[3]The holdings have been transferred to the Archive of the Military Historical Institute.

Reptile Journalism

The division of Poland during World War II.

Introduction

There is an extensive literature on the history of the Nazi occupation of Poland: accounts of the actions of the German authorities and of the Polish resistance movement fill countless anthologies, monographs, popular and scholarly works, memoirs, and published archival sources. These works have treated general subjects as well as extremely specific problems and issues. An inclusive bibliography would run to several volumes.

Although the struggles and the sufferings of the Polish people both in the areas incorporated into the Reich and in those in the Generalgouvernement (GG) have been widely researched, there is a surprising paucity of work concerned with the assumptions, methods, and special practices used by the Nazis to influence public opinion. The lack is especially striking on the topic of so important a means of modern communication as the press. While there are several valuable contributions on the clandestine press in occupied Poland, there is no work on the press published in Polish territories by the occupation force itself, on its orders, or with its approval — that is, on the "legal" press for the subjugated population. It is difficult to attain a complete picture of occupation policies without considering this area. Yet the subject of Nazi press policy in Poland has not been treated either in Polish historiography or in any other. Within the 1939 borders of Poland, newspapers and journals designated for specific national groups were published from the start of the occupation. First there was a German-language press for the Germans of the Reich and for *Volksdeutsche* who lived in the annexed areas and in the GG. There was also a press in Ukrainian for the relatively privileged Ukrainian population of the GG; a press in Polish, primarily for the indigenous populations of the so-called Nebenland (that is, the GG); a short-lived newspaper in Polish for the residents of the closed ghettos;[1] and finally a press in Byelorussian and Lithuanian for the national minorities in the so-called Ostland and the Białystok district. Although these different presses shared the goal of reinforcing German control, each had a defined function; each was distinguished from the others in many respects, and each was tailored to specific objectives of the occupier.

The subject of this work is restricted to the press for the Polish population in the GG, which included the District of Galicia after mid-1941. It is not concerned with the press in the East, which for all practical purposes was limited to Vilna, or with the Polish-language press that appeared in the territories annexed by the Reich, including, from 1941 on, the Białystok district. Polish-language press in these areas was quite rudimentary. Except perhaps for the *Nowy Kurier Białystocki* (New Białystok Courier) and the

Vilna *Gazeta Codzienna* (Daily Gazette), the few official gazettes that appeared there in Polish were insignificant. They are comparable to the newspapers published by the Germans for forced laborers in the Reich (such as *Pod Stropem* for Polish laborers, *Holos* for the Ukrainians, and *Trud* for the Russians) rather than to the press in the GG or to the German-language Nazi press.[2] Significantly, Polish-language Nazi newspapers from the GG were not circulated in the annexed area. Publishers in the GG and propaganda officials in the annexed territories of Silesia and Wartheland carried on a long and almost amusing paper war over this issue. For commercial reasons, the publishers were interested in selling their newspapers there, while the propaganda officials, whose principal purpose was pursuit of the relentless struggle against Polish nationalism, did everything to prevent them. At last Goebbels decided the quarrel, and the sale of newspapers from the GG was forbidden in the annexed areas.[3]

The occupiers intended the GG press to serve various political and propagandistic purposes with respect to the Polish population. Unlike the Nazi tactics in the territories annexed to the Reich, the propaganda and press policy conducted by the occupational force was uniform in principle, with only insignificant deviations necessitated by the changing situation. It was enacted in the "legal" press — encompassing Polish-language newspapers, periodicals, and information gazettes, as well as specialized and professional journals — as opposed to the extensive, well-organized, and dynamically developing clandestine press that existed in the GG, the only authentic expression of social opinion under the German occupation. The underground press, published by almost all the military resistance organizations, parties, and political, social, and cultural groups — and even by especially active individuals — successfully performed in occupied Poland the informative and political function the press usually plays in society. It exercised a freedom of expression seldom found in Poland even in peacetime. The publication of a clandestine paper depended only on the abilities of individuals or groups in the underground society. The newspapers published by the occupying force, in contrast to the clandestine papers, were generally called "reptile press" (*prasa gadzinowa*).

In Polish literature on World War II, one usually reads that the designation "reptile press" stemmed from a peculiar distortion of the name of the newspaper *Godzina Polski* (Polish Hour), which appeared during the German occupation in World War I, first in Łódź and later in Warsaw. Its nominal owner was Adam Napieralski, but in fact the paper, which supported the policy of Governor-General Hans Hertwig von Beseler, was initiated and subsidized by the Germans.[4] What was initially supposition soon became an open secret and gave rise to mockery and an appropriate scorn for this anti-Polish publication. The change of a single letter produced the desired effect: instead of *godzina* (hour), people generally said and wrote *gadzina* (reptile).

The designation "reptile press" has another, older origin: it was coined in Prussia in the last century to characterize organs of the press that derived their money from secret funds, or *Reptilienfonds*. Bismarck used it to stigmatize the allies of the Hanover court who were hostile to Prussia. However, after the battle of Langensalza in 1866 and the annexation of Hanover, when it became known that Bismarck himself was bribing editors to support Prussian policy, their newspapers became known as the reptile press. By the same principle, Polish-language publications in the Prussian area whose attitudes and objectives were counter to Polish interests were also called the reptile press.[5]

Bad as the reptile press of the nineteenth century was, it cannot be compared to the daily and weekly newspapers that appeared in the GG from 1939 to 1945. An essential feature of the old reptile press was the secrecy of its ownership. But neither Hans Frank, governor-general of the occupied Polish territory, nor his administration seemed concerned that it was clear who was doing the publishing and editing. For a long time, the Germans did not even try to win over Polish publishers, editors, and journalists but built their own press, obtaining staff by following the method they used to recruit informants. Furthermore, the press in the GG had a monopoly, while Bismarck's and Beseler's reptile press had to compete with other, albeit censored newspapers. In short, despite certain features in common, these cannot be compared—just as Hitler cannot be compared to Bismarck, Frank to Beseler, or Wilhelm Ohlenbusch, head of the propaganda department in the GG, to the well-known journalist Georg Cleinow, head of the press department in the Ober-Ost.

The exceptional status of the GG and its regime of terror determined the special role of the press for the Poles. In a conquered country condemned to misery, the pen does not destroy what the sword has captured, as the *Krakauer und Warschauer Zeitung* (Kraków and Warsaw Newspaper) so graphically wrote.[6] Because the nature of the press in the GG was obvious, "rag press" became a common pejorative description, like "reptile press." The popular weekly *Biuletyn Informacyjny* (Information Bulletin) of the resistance wrote on January 9, 1941, " 'Reptile press' is what people call the journals of the serpents who treacherously slip into the cloak of the Polish language in order to poison the organism of the Polish people. The language is Polish but the brain and the guiding hand are German. Its goal is to work for Germany."

This view, shared by all the clandestine publications, refers to the newspapers and journals published by the Germans that were concerned with political information and propaganda. These dominated the publishing market of the GG and reflected the character and direction of German press policy. But the "legal" press did not end with periodicals of this type. In addition, a few newspapers and journals published legally by Poles, both before and after the establishment of the GG, appeared for longer or shorter periods. And it is difficult to designate as reptile or rag press such purely professional journals as *Medycyna Współczesna* (Modern Medicine), published by the Serological Institute of Warsaw; *Weterynaryjne Wiadomości Terapeutyczne* (Veterinary Therapeutic News), a periodical of the Bayer (Pharmaceutical) Company; or *Wiadomości Międzyzwiązkowej Spółdzielni Powierniczej* (Communication of the Trustee Society), which was published for a time by the former association of cooperative societies, then under German control.

I intend to discuss legal press in the GG against the background of the German occupation policy. Although in my presentation I focus on several specific problems, I nevertheless proceed chronologically, distinguishing what I see as three periods: (1) from the occupation of individual Polish areas by the German army in September 1939 to the establishment of the GG in November 1939; (2) from the establishment of the GG to spring 1943; and (3) from the German defeats on the various fronts (especially on the eastern front), beginning in spring 1943, to the end of the occupation in January 1945.

The first period includes the German-Polish war, the German military administration, and the first Nazi attempt to form a so-called rump state out of part of central Poland. Two closely linked factors characterize the beginning of the occupation. The procedure of the occupation force was predominantly local, limited in time, and often only improvised, which might indicate the lack of clearly defined goals. On the Polish side, there was the deceptive hope for the reestablishment or continued existence of at least a few newspapers and journals, a hope expressed in the partly but briefly fruitful efforts of Polish publishers, as well as in a memorandum put forward by the Association of Newspaper and Journal Publishers that was rejected by the German authorities.

In the second period the Polish press was eliminated and an extensive propaganda apparatus and press service was created whose main goal was to

humiliate the Polish people, make them obedient, and convince them of the invincibility of the Third Reich and of the continuance of German rule in Poland.

The fiasco of the Nazi press policy became clear to the occupiers in the third period. Consequently, they took pains to change the profile of the press and — following the model employed in other occupied countries — tried to create a legal, censored Polish press. As a result, the collaborationist journal *Przełom* (Breakthrough) appeared in Kraków. In an unrelated move, the occupation force circulated a few pseudo-underground gazettes that imitated the Polish underground press, including *Nowa Polska: Organ Organizacji Niepodległościowej Nowa Polska* (New Poland: Organ of the Organization Favoring the Independence of New Poland), *Gazeta Narodowa* (National Gazette), and *Głos Polski* (Voice of Poland). This campaign, undertaken in the final months of the occupation, was primarily calculated to win over Polish society for the battle against the Soviet Union and against Communist groups in the GG.

This study is based primarily on analysis of the "legal" press itself. Although firsthand accounts have also been used, they are of limited value here — as they often are in studies of recent history — especially since those Poles who collaborated with the German press did not boast of it. I was able to make extensive use of the actual publications of the legal press since most of them have been preserved in public and private collections. I examined more than a hundred titles, including about thirty that appeared during the September 1939 campaign, twenty from the time of the German military administration, and fifty that came out in the GG. I also used the underground press so as to highlight the contrast.

The availability of archival sources leaves much to be desired. Such significant files as those of the GG's press secretary, of the main department of propaganda, and of the publishing house of the *Krakauer und Warschauer Zeitung* either have not been preserved or exist only in minuscule remnants. This is true also of the editorial records of the individual newspapers and journals that appeared in the GG. Among the surviving editorial archives, the material currently preserved in the Archiwum Głównej Komisji Badania Zbrodni Hitlerowskich w Polsce (renamed, after the demise of communism, Główna Komisja Badania Zbrodni Przeciwko Narodowi Polskiemu [Main Commision to Investigate Crimes against the Polish Nation]) proved especially valuable. Most important are two files containing the correspondence of the editorial staff and the management of the *Kurier Częstochowski* (Częstochowa Courier), as well as a few notebooks and documents from the main department of propaganda (correspondence, guidelines, elaborate programs, accounts, circulars, personal and official printed matter).

Since the basic documentation of the press secretary and the main department of propaganda is lacking, I have taken pains to substitute other material, primarily from both higher and subordinate officials. Among the files of the former, those of the government of the GG, especially of the finance and personnel departments, were fruitful sources; they contained extensive correspondence with press and propaganda offices, lists of employees, work plans, and structural and organizational schemes of the press secretary, and of the main department of propaganda. I also had access to certain parts of periodic accounts prepared by the main department of propaganda in Kraków for the Reich Ministry for Public Enlightenment and Propaganda in Berlin. Hans Frank's diary, as well as the extensive documentation in the records of the trial of Joseph Bühler, the state secretary in the GG, were excellent additional sources. From the documents of subordinate officials, I used, among others, the files of the propaganda department of the District of Radom, those of the head of the District of Warsaw, and those of the heads of the regions of Kielce, Jędrzejów, and Busko.

Among the German central military and government sources, especially for the beginning of the occupation, the files of the head of the civil administration of the Eighth German Army are of great interest; these are in the Wojewódzkie Archiwum Państwowe (Provincial State Archive) in Łódź. In the extensive collection of documents of the Reich Ministry of Propaganda (Potsdam), I used those concerning the press and radio in occupied Poland.

The Polish sources I consulted were materials from the Departament Informacji Delegatury Rządu RP na Kraj (Information Department of the Governing Delegation), as well as from the Biuro Informacji i Propagandy Komendy Głównej Armii Krajowej (Information and Propaganda Office of the Supreme Command of the Home Army). These materials (including firsthand accounts of the legal press, analysis of the mood of the population, and spy reports on the activities of German publishing houses and propaganda institutions) were in the Instytut Pamięci Narodowej until 1948 and, after the liquidation of that institute, were transferred to the Zakład Historii Partii (Institute of the History of the Communist Party) in Warsaw.

Other documents that proved helpful for particular problems or journals were in the files of the Rada Główna Opiekuńcza (Main Welfare Council), Polski Związek Wydawców Dzienników i Czasopism (Polish Association of Newspaper and Journal Publishers), Polski Czerwony Krzyż (Polish Red Cross), Związek Pracowników Prasy Tajnej 1939–1944 (Association of Employees of the Clandestine Press) and the archive of I. Paderewski. I also used the reports of the Interior Ministry of the Polish government-in-exile in London on the situation in occupied Poland.

A separate group of sources includes legal files from the trials of former staff members of the German press in Polish. These files, dating from 1946 to 1949, comprise the records of the criminal cases against Stanisław Homan and other staff members of the *Kurier Częstochowski*; Helena

Wielgomasowa and other staff members of the legal Warsaw journals including Józef Sierzputowski of the *Nowy Kurier Warszawski*; Stanisław Wasylewski of the *Gazeta Lwowska*; and Feliks Burdecki and Emil Skiwski, editors of *Przełom,* as well as other staff members of the legal Kraków press and the German press agency Telepress. Despite the obvious bias against the defendants and the clear preponderance of proof in the testimony presented by the prosecution in these cases, these files turn out to be exceptionally valuable for research on the composition and activities of the editorial staffs of the reptile press and the German press agency. Numerous German documents attached to the trial records as corpus delicti also shed some light.

Part 1
Nazi Press Policy
in Poland,
September–
November 1939

1

The First
Measures

As readily available media of mass propaganda, the press and the radio played a considerable role in preparations for the attack on Poland. Hitler's Germany kept its comprehensive war propaganda machinery ready in both the military and the governmental spheres. On April 1, 1939, the Wehrmacht's propaganda program, in preparation since 1937, was finally formed. Authority for supervising propaganda in the event of war had been defined by an agreement reached earlier in 1939 between the Reich Ministry for Public Enlightenment and Propaganda (RMVP) and Wehrmacht headquarters (OKW). One of the points of the agreement read: "Propaganda is recognized as an essential means of war, equal to the armed struggle. The Wehrmacht is responsible for conducting the armed struggle; the propaganda war will be conducted by the RMVP. In the home district, the RMVP carries it out completely independently; in the operations area, in coordination with the OKW."[1]

Shortly before the outbreak of war, provisional decisions were also made concerning the organizational structure of every country Germany intended to conquer. In Poland, the Germans originally planned to surrender executive power to the military administration and to those heads of the civil administration who were active on Germany's behalf with the corresponding army commanders-in-chief. In fact, however, the military administration simply served in the brief transitional phase before the final division of Polish areas into those annexed by the Reich and those incorporated into the Generalgouvernement (GG).[2]

The civil administration was responsible for the management of an office of civil administration as well as for social and political life in the occupied areas. Thus, it also had to liquidate the Polish press and radio and set up its own information network, in conformance with the agreement between the RMVP and the OKW and the guidelines of the RMVP. As the German troops advanced, Goebbels's machinery took over the press and the radio, according to preparations that had been made even before the invasion of Poland.[3] On Goebbels's orders, independent propaganda departments were established in the civil administration offices in Poznań (Reich Propaganda Office Łódź (Reich Propaganda Office II), and Kraków (Reich Propaganda Office III), as well as in subbranches or field posts in Warsaw, Radom, and Lublin.

These posts were occupied by propaganda functionaries from the Reich and by *Volksdeutsche* who had been in Nazi service for some time. They included Heinz Strozyk, who had served before the war as a noncommissioned officer in the Kraków Railroad Bridge Building Battalion and was later director of printing institutions in the Generalgouvernement; Adolf Kargel, who had been the acting chairman of the journalists' association in Łódź until 1933; Eugeniusz Riedel, the former literary director of the Dom Prasy (Press House) in Warsaw, who was the personnel and administrative director of the *Nowy Kurier Warszawski* (New Warsaw Courier) during the occupation; Feliks Rufenach, a grammar-school teacher before the war and, afterward, organizer of the reptile press in Radom, Częstochowa, and Lemberg (Lwów); and Dr. Karol Grundmann, former assistant to Prof. Zygmunt Łempicki in the department of Germanistics at Warsaw University, and later a staff member of the propaganda department of the Warsaw district.[4] The management of the press in the occupied territory was taken over by Wilhelm Ohlenbusch, who was later head of the Warsaw district propaganda department and, from February 1, 1941, in charge of the Main Department of Propaganda in the GG.[5]

Special propaganda units (*Propagandakompanien*, or PK) were formed in the headquarters of the attacking armies — PK 501 in the Third Army, PK 689 in the Fourth, PK 670 in the Tenth, and PK 621 in the Fourteenth. In addition, there were two units in the headquarters of the Luftwaffe, LW PK 1 and LW PK 4.[6] These units had a double function: to supply their troops with information and propaganda material and to undermine the enemy's morale through the use of mass media — the press, leaflets, and radio. Their training included instruction in the Polish language.

At the end of August 1939, newspapers had begun to be printed for the invading units in Breslau, Moravska Ostrava, and Allenstein, where the Eighth, Fourteenth, Third, and Fourth Armies were headquartered. The *Nachrichtenblatt für die Ostpreussische Armee* (News Gazette for the East Prussian Army) and the *Schlesische Frontschau* (Silesian Front Review) were followed, after the crossing of the Polish border, by the *Soldatenzeitung der Schlesischen Armee* (Soldiers' Newspaper of the Silesian Army). After mid-September, military newspapers also appeared in Kraków and Łódź.[7] The RMVP did not want PK writings to appear in Polish.

The Nazi press in Poland began with the soldiers' newspapers. Because they were in German, however, their effectiveness was limited; they served, however, as the official press organs of the invaders and were delivered as such to the local Polish authorities, especially to the ad hoc citizens' committees. Soon they appeared in Polish, under the supervision of the original newspapers' staffs. The Polish versions not only drew their information from the soldiers' newspapers but also reprinted whole articles from them. The editorial staffs and technical equipment of the soldiers' newspapers later took part in the creation of the main German propaganda organ, the *Krakauer und Warschauer Zeitung* (Kraków and Warsaw Newspaper).[8]

Along with the soldiers' newspapers, Nazi propaganda made ample use of radio.[9] By early September 1939 German radio transmitters had taken over Polish airwaves in violation of international law, broadcasting misleading news to confuse Polish defense forces and to promote a defeatist mood among the people. The Germans later used the experience acquired during the September campaign in other theaters of war. German broadcasting came to specialize in such diversionary tactics, transmitting special broadcasts for Polish soldiers in English and American units and for independent Polish forces in the West. German broadcasters falsely announced their programs in the names of the Western radio stations; during the Warsaw uprising of August and September 1944, one German program was transmitted via the rebel station *Blyskawica* (Lightning).[10] At the beginning of the war, Kraków and Warsaw broadcasts were primary targets of this method of usurpation. For greater effect, the Germans also used official call signs: the *Hejnał* (Reveille) of the tower of the Church of the Virgin in Kraków, and *My, Pierwsza Brygada* (We, the First Brigade), the theme song of Piłsudski's legions as well as of Warsaw I.[11]

As soon as a Polish city was captured, its radio stations were commandeered by technical units specifically formed for the purpose. Wherever equipment had been destroyed or dismantled by the retreating Polish units, the Germans created fake transmitters.[12] Thus, for example, after the occupation of Katowice and Kraków, German transmitters began broadcasting in Polish in the name of those cities' stations. Since it was generally known that the Katowice transmitter had been evacuated and the Kraków transmitter destroyed, the effect was quite the opposite of what was intended, as shown by a memorandum dated September 13, 1939, from Dagobert Dürr, director of the propaganda office in Kraków, to the Reich Ministry of Propaganda: "For a few days now, the transmitters in Gliwice and Kraków have announced themselves as 'Branch Station Kraków.' I consider this announcement misguided since the people of Kraków know that the transmitter isn't working and can always check it with a few receivers. Such a false announcement provokes in the population the idea that other German news is also false. Broadcasts from Kraków must be given in good Polish and must be aimed at the mollification and guidance of the local population."[13]

The memorandum also mentions the Katowice transmitter, which did not even exist anymore, having been dismantled before the Polish authorities had left the city, and taken to Baranowicze. Although Dagobert Dürr was undoubtedly one of the most intelligent staff members of the German propaganda machinery in Poland, the problem he addressed was not taken seriously in Berlin.[14] No doubt the decision to seize Polish radio transmitters, a decision that had been made in early September, was already known in the central office.[15] Initially, it was considered a temporary war measure, and in the final days of the campaign, confiscated radio equipment was even returned.[16] However, the threat of draconian punishment (fifteen years in prison or the death penalty) for listening to foreign broadcasts and disseminating their news remained in effect.[17] Hitler himself decided what was to happen with the radio equipment as reflected in this special order of October 10, 1939, from the headquarters of the Eighth army: "The Führer has ordered that throughout the Ober-Ost, that is, in the entire area occupied by our troops, the Polish population, including Jews, is to be deprived immediately of all radio equipment. Germans and *Volksdeutsche* are not afected by this measure. The Führer demands immediate execution."[18]

The distribution of the confiscated property was also decided: 75 percent of the commandeered equipment was allotted to the army, 25 percent to the German civil administration.[19]

In greater Poland, Pomerania, and Polish Silesia, the occupying force abolished Polish journalism. From the first day of the occupation — even before Hitler had announced its annexation — these areas were considered by the local Wehrmacht and civil authorities to be permanent acquisitions and components of the greater German Reich. An official proclamation to that effect was signed by Captain Goede, commandant of the Włocławek (Leslau) region, and published in Polish and German in the September 29 issue of the *Leslauer Boten* (Leslau Messenger).[20] After announcing that Warsaw had surrendered unconditionally, Goede wrote: "Thus, the fate of Poland is finally sealed. In accordance with the wishes of the Führer a line demarcating the border of the Reich in the East, agreed upon by the Russians, has been drawn. Thus, the Leslau area is, and will forever remain, a territory of the German Reich." All extant orders issued by the heads of the civil administration and, later, by the Gauleiter of Warthegau, Danzig, and Silesia, are in the same spirit.

By September 15, the head of the civil administration of Upper Silesia (Border Guard — Section Command 3), O. Fitzner, issued an order stipulating that both the continuation of previously published newspapers and journals, and the appearance of new titles, required special authorization. Publishers, printers, even newspaper vendors were threatened with fifteen-year prison sentences for not observing this injunction. Fitzner's order merely "legalized" the de facto condition. An order of October 10, 1939, from Arthur Greiser, the *Gauleiter* of Warthegau during the occupation, also had the character of legislation ex post facto. It dealt with the takeover of the real estate and movable goods of Poznań publishers like Drukarnia Polska (Polish Printing Press) and its *Kurier Poznański* (Poznań Courier), the printing press of the *Dziennik Poznański* (Poznań Daily Gazette), and the publishing house Św. Wojciecha (St. Adalbert). This order concerning the confiscation of the property of publishers who served Polish culture had propaganda value, too, since it was explained that the presses were expropriated because they had published "inflammatory" writings against the Germans, and were to be placed in the custody of German ownership so as to create a Nazi publishing house.[21] After Poznań had been captured by German troops, a group of local publishers petitioned Greiser for permission to publish Polish newspapers, but they were told that such a thing would not even be considered; finally, their companies were seized.[22]

Eventually, the Germans confiscated all printing presses owned by either Poles or Jews in Pomerania, greater Poland, and Polish Silesia. Large corporations were liable to be expropriated directly for the German state or the Nazi party, while smaller enterprises were turned over to *Volksdeutsche* and German colonists. In the course of the expropriation campaign, much of the equipment and many of printing presses were deliberately damaged and declared rubbish, while valuable equipment was sent to the Reich. In the territories incorporated into the Reich, the Germans took over about 3,000 printing presses, or almost half the number in the Polish state.[23]

Obviously, a Polish press could no longer survive under such conditions. Moreover, even a German press in the Polish language was banned.[24] In the territory of the future Generalgouvernement and in Łódź things were somewhat different, even if here, too, the Polish language remained forbidden in many places. In an area of more than a hundred thousand square kilometers, with a population of about fifteen million, the occupation force permitted a few insignificant newspapers to be published by the Poles. These appeared in Kraków, Częstochowa, Radom, Kielce, Radomsk, Lublin, Warsaw, and Łódź. It should not be surprising that Łódź is included here, since the decision to incorporate the city into the Reich took place later.[25] As the conditions and circumstances under which newspapers came into being differed from place to place, I deal with them separately according to their cities of publication.

2

The Emergence of
Polish Newspapers

Kraków

The first Polish newspaper to appear after the invasion of German troops was the *Dziennik Krakowski* (Kraków Daily). The prewar daily news-papers — *Ilustrowany Kurier Codzienny* (Illustrated Daily Courier), *Tempo Dnia* (Daily Rhythm), *Głos Narodu* (Voice of the Nation), and *Nowy Dziennik* (New Daily) — had ceased publication on September 3, 1939, the day the civil and military authorities had left the city in accordance with the evacuation order. The IKC Company, publisher of *Ilustrowany Kurier Codzienny,* was also evacuated to the East; its founder and editor in chief, Marian Dąbrowski, a Sejm deputy, had gone to Paris a few days before the outbreak of the war.[1]

Against the background of these events, Kazimierz Dobija, manager of the IKC, along with a group that had remained in Kraków — Ludwik Szczepański, Dr. Kazimierz Szczepański, Dr. Józef Flach, Włodzimierz Długoszewski, Stanisław Stwora, and Stanisław Mróz — decided with staff members of the *Dziennik Krakowski* to put out a new newspaper. But the citizens' committee of Kraków, chaired by Cardinal Adam Sapieha, decided on September 4 to publish a newspaper called the *Gazeta Krakowska* (Kraków Gazette), in which all Polish editorial staffs would be represented. The IKC editors accepted the decision and agreed not to publish the almost completed issue of their *Dziennik Krakowski*. On September 5, the first and last edition of the *Gazeta Krakowska* appeared on the streets of Kraków; the managing editor was a priest, Jan Piwowarczyk, director of the department of press propaganda of the citizens' committee.[2]

On September 7, one day after the occupation of Kraków by units of the German Fourteenth Army, Ludwik Szczepański and Stanisław Rymar, on behalf of the IKC staff, presented the German deputy city commandant, Colonel Delhuber, with a proposal to publish a newspaper again in Kraków. They received immediate permission, but on condition that they promise to submit the text for preliminary censorship and to print German communiqués.[3] On Friday, September 8, the first issue of *Dziennik Krakowski* appeared for sale. The masthead read: "Published by the Publishing House of the IKC Press in Kraków, Editor Ludwik Szczepański." A publisher's note emphasized that *Dziennik Krakowski* would work closely with the citizens' committee. Although such a formulation could be taken to mean that *Dziennik Krakowski* was continuing the publishing activity of the committee, this was not the case. A clarification was not issued, however, until September 11, when a notice from the editorial staff announced that the newspaper was not an organ of the citizens' committee but did print all communiqués submitted by the committee and, naturally, relied primarily on information from the committee and the city council.[4]

Between September 8 and September 13, seven issues of *Dziennik Krakowski* appeared; number 4 (September 12) appeared in two different editions. Aside from Szczepański (a former editor of the *Ilustrowany Kurier Codzienny* and the author of anti-Nazi feuilletons published in it before the war in the form of angry letters to Goebbels), the staff included Flach, former president of the Kraków journalists' association; Długoszewski, former editor of the weekly *Raz-Dwa-Trzy* (One, Two, Three); Stwora, Mieczysław Zielenkiewicz, Tadeusz Malek, and Dr. Kazimierz Szczepański.[5] On September 14, the *Dziennik Krakowski* changed its name back to *Ilustrowany Kurier Codzienny* and largely restored its prewar format. The first issue of the new IKC continued the prewar numbering and listed on the masthead all branches except Kraków, from Warsaw to Gdynia, Poznań, Lwów (Lemberg), Vilna, and Zakopane. The reversion to the old title, however, was illegitimate because immediately after the evacuation of the IKC from Kraków, a few of its staff — including Jan Stankiewicz, Jadwiga Harasowska, and Zygmunt Nowakowski — reestablished the paper in Lwów and, starting on September 8, again published *Ilustrowany Kurier Codzienny* in successive numbers. As an editorial in the first issue stated: "The editorial staff of Ilustrowany Kurier Codzienny, driven out of its workplace at this time, has decided not to stop its information work, not to give up its service to the public, strengthening the spirit of its fellow countrymen and imparting to their souls the belief that what is not lost can never be lost and must emerge triumphant from oppression."[6]

On the title page of the new Kraków IKC, however, the words "Printed in Poland" were removed, but the name of the founder of the company, Marian Dąbrowski, appeared, and Ludwik Szczepański was listed as deputy editor in chief. On September 18, though, Szczepański withdrew from editorial work on the pretext of illness.[7] An IKC journalist, Jan Lankau, surmised that Szczepański feared German reprisals because of his prewar articles.

The conditions under which *Dziennik Krakowski* was reorganized into *Ilustrowany Kurier Codzienny* were unusual, even for the early days of the occupation. The Germans, who had occupied Kraków only for just over a week, had already settled in solidly. The editorial staff of the soldiers' newspaper had been housed in the Kraków IKC building and had even found time to go through piles of prewar *IKC*s carefully, especially through those issues that had appeared right before the outbreak of the war and were strongly anti-Nazi in tone. At the same time, Polish journalists were summoned to a conference by the German authorities, who received them very politely, almost as equals.

Unfortunately, as with other aspects of this subject, we do not have access to the minutes of this meeting and can learn of the discussion only from the testimony of the participating Polish journalists, in the files of the 1949 criminal trial in absentia of Feliks Burdecki and Emil Skiwski in the district court in Kraków. Witnesses for the prosecution included Kazimierz Dobija, former manager of the IKC, and Zofia Lewakowska, an editor. A former president of the Kraków journalists' association, Lankau appeared at the trial as an expert witness, and his book *The Kraków Press in the Critical September Days* contains parts of the reports of editors Stanisław Rymar and Mieczysław Zielenkiewicz. The testimony of all witnesses, with the exception of Dobija, concurs even in insignificant details:

> After the Germans had occupied Kraków, a conference called by the propaganda department took place. . . . At this conference, a propaganda official read a report on the relation of the Hitler regime to the journalists. In essence, it said that the occupation authorities dispensed with the Polish journalists' services and would carry out the work according to their own principles. (Testimony of Kazimierz Dobija)[8]
>
> No one foresaw the purpose of the summons. Everything indicated that the first act of oppression would now begin. Then we were welcomed with due respect. The propaganda chief read a speech in which he greeted us as "colleagues." He assured us that he considered previous sins against the Germans as canceled, and he asked that the newspaper be administered in the Polish spirit. (Report of Mieczysław Zielenkiewicz)[9]
>
> On September 9 or 10, all members of the editorial staff were called to the district building.[10] There, a German who introduced himself as press secretary, delivered an address in a conciliatory spirit. He assured us that the freedom of the purely Polish newspaper run by us would be preserved and that articles by Polish authors would appear on the front page, the German communiqués only on the following ones. (Testimony of Zofia Lewakowska)[11]

Finally, Stanisław Rymar reported on the working conditions enumerated for the Polish journalists: "in general the normal conditions of an occupation, but they gave us a great deal: Be free, Polish journalists, serve your people! We demand from you no praise of the Germans or of the principles of Nazism"[12] After the meeting, the director of the Kraków propaganda department (Reich Propaganda Office III), Dagobert Dürr, ordered the *Dziennik Krakowski* dissolved; the *Ilustrowany Kurier Codzienny* was allowed to resume publication.[13]

From September 14 to October 26, 1939, thirty-seven issues of the *IKC* appeared in Kraków. During that time, the format did not change significantly from that of the first issue (nominally no. 246). The only noticeable change was undertaken after Hitler signed the decree of October 8 concerning the administration of the so-called annexed areas. Henceforth, the offices in the annexed cities (Gdynia, Bydgoszcz, Toruń, Katowice, and Poznań) were omitted from the masthead, except for Łódź. The paper also refrained from citing branches in Vilna and Lwów.[14]

Częstochowa

Events preceding the resumption of newspaper publication in Częstochowa were completely different from those in Kraków. As units of the German Tenth Army captured Częstochowa on September 3, the city immediately became a scene of murder and violence against the defenseless population. The worst horrors came on September 4 and the following days. After provocative shootings, of which the Germans suspected everyone, terror, violence, pillage, and murder erupted. In the first two days after the occupation of Częstochowa, the Germans murdered 227 persons, including 194 men, 25 women, and 8 children.[15] In this situation, there was no illusion as to the real intentions of the occupation force.

For twelve days the population was without newspapers. The *Goniec Częstochowski* (Częstochowa Messenger), published by Franciszek D. Wilkoszewski, which had appeared for thirty-four years, ceased publication on September 3. The German authorities immediately occupied the publisher's offices at 52 N. Marii Panny (Virgin Mary Street). There was no question of *Goniec*'s remaining in the hands of the editorial staff; the newspaper was characterized as explicitly anti-German, national-Catholic, and — to make things complete — under Jewish influence.[16] Wilkoszewski was arrested in the series of preventive measures taken before the national holiday in November.[17]

On September 15, the head of the civil administration of the Tenth Army, Hans Rüdiger, reported in a secret order of the day that the German authorities had succeeded in establishing a newspaper that the Nazi mayor could use for his announcements.[18] Although *Goniec Częstochowski* went on sale the same day, it had been in preparation by an unknown editorial staff since September 9.[19]

Goniec was really a bilingual paper: the headlines of the Polish articles and all the news columns were printed in German. To preserve appearances, the old name was maintained, along with the claim of thirty-four years of publication and the earlier format. To the name were added, though, the words "with official announcements of the authorities." Supervision of the editorial staff of the revived *Goniec* was assumed by Paul Majunke-Lange of the Breslau propaganda department, who was a German from the Reich and a member of the party. On September 22, there first appeared on the masthead the notice, "Overall Direction as Trustee, Paul Majunke-Lange." The front listed, as both publisher and editor in chief, a previously unknown person with the very Polish name of Franciszek Sowiński, a name that later appeared as that of the editor-in-chief of *Nowy Kurier Warszawski* (New Warsaw Courier). In all probability, he was a fictitious person. On the other hand, it can be ascertained that someone called Otrębski, who claimed to be a Polish journalist, played a considerable role on the editorial staff of *Goniec Częstochowski*. He defrayed most of the cost of the issues himself, and almost all Polish articles passed through his hands. These articles might be submitted by anyone: for example, an important article titled "Germans and Poles" was written by the daughter of a Polish typesetter for the paper.[20]

Goniec Częstochowski was printed in Wilkoszewski's plant. Initially it appeared three times a week (Tuesday, Thursday, and Saturday, with the following day's date; from October 3 on, it appeared daily. Thirty-four issues, with circulations of ten to twelve thousand, were published. The last issue appeared on November 3, 1939, a date that coincided with the takeover of the GG by Frank from the Military Administration.

Radom, Chełm, Kielce, Radomsk, Lublin

Unfortunately, archival sources on the inception of the press are very meager for these five cities, which, like Częstochowa, were under the control of the head of the civil administration of the Tenth Army. For Kielce, Radomsk, and Lublin, no trace of copies has been found that would allow us to determine even a few details about publication — let alone to undertake a textual analysis. Nevertheless, it is possible to construct at least a general picture of the press in this region from those copies that are available and from the fragments of documents and reports.

In his September 15 order of the day, Rüdiger expressly established newspapers in all the big cities under his command; informing the population by means of placards had proved unsatisfactory. He indicated that these newspapers were to be in Polish but that the announcements of the authorities were to be printed in a bilingual version, and he emphasized that Polish journalists would be supervised.[21]

As a result of this order, new newspapers began appearing in the district under Rüdiger's supervision. Thus, on October 10, the first issue of *Kurier Radomski* (Radom Courier) was published in the Radom printing plant and bookbindery of Czesław Oziemek. Initially it appeared twice a week, and later — from November 15, on — three times a week, on Tuesday, Thursday, and Saturday; it presented news and articles in Polish and announcements in bilingual form. Oziemek was named publisher; Bolesław Słupiecki and, later, R. Moszczeński were listed as editors. Fifty-five issues appeared through February 28, 1940, when it was discontinued.[22]

The bilingual weekly *Chelmer Nachrichten-Wiadomości Chełmskie* (Chelm News), began publication on October 22. It was openly published by the local commander in Chełm, and its editors were commissioned and non-commissioned officers of the Wehrmacht (in succession, Rausmeyer, Wischeropp, H. Freund, and Wischeropp again). *Chelmer Nachrichten* was printed in the local printing plant of the *Zwierciadło* (Mirror), where, in the first and last days of the September campaign, the *Kronika Nadbużańska* (Bug Chronicle) had also been printed, as well as the *Kurier Poranny* (Morning Courier), which had been evacuated from Warsaw.[23] Nine issues and a special edition appeared, each four to twelve pages. On December 24, the following editorial note ran: "By order of the Ministry of Propaganda, *Wiadomości Chełmskie* ceases publication with this issue."

Information about other newspapers that appeared in the area occupied by the Tenth Army must be gleaned from various sources. For Kielce, we have the draft of a memorandum to the editor Władysław Jackowski preserved in the files of the propaganda office there; previous negotiations or correspondence with him about the publication of a Polish press organ probably took place. In this memorandum, Jackowski was informed that as of September 25, 1939, the daily newspaper *Kielcer Zeitung* could appear in Polish and German and that the guidelines of the army headquarters and of the head of the civil administration were to be strictly followed.[24] We learn of a Polish newspaper published in Radom from files of the propaganda department of the District of Radomsk, which indicate that after the fighting ended, the German authorities in Radom agreed to the continuation of a regional newspaper that had previously appeared in Radomsk.[25] Its publisher was Zdzisław Rudowski, former editor in chief of the weekly *Gazeta Radomskowska* (Radomsk Gazette). The newspaper began publication on October 10, and 6,000 copies were produced by the printing plant of M. & J. Pański in Radomsk.[26] Although every edition was censored by the local district administrator before leaving the plant, in January 1940 Rudowski was arrested for anti-German bias in the newspaper he edited.

Information about the newspapers published in Lublin comes from Władysław Gralewski, editor in chief of the prewar *Express Lubelski* (Lublin Express), who served during the occupation as head of the Information and Propaganda Office of the Armia Krajowa (Home Army) of the Lublin region. During the September campaign, the *Express,* still edited by Gralewski, was both the press organ of the Information and Propaganda Ministry and later, after the evacuation of the ministry, the newspaper of the Citizens' Committee of Lublin. Gralewski reports that on September 19, the day Lublin was captured by German troops, the authorities summoned him to the city's military command post and suggested he continue publishing the *Express Lubelski.* Initially, Gralewski refused, since they demanded that the paper appear in two languages. But later, in early October, he and Bruno Morzyński, editor of the *Głos Lubelski* (Lublin Voice), the organ of the *Stronnictwo Narodowe* (National party), successfully appealed to Lublin Mayor Krüger for permission to publish their newspapers and received it on the spot. *Express* and *Głos* did not last long, even though they too were subject to German censorship. After the publication of an article in the *Express* titled "So — War," which commented on England and France's negative reaction to to Hitler's "peace" proposals, both newspapers were banned and Gralewski, the author, was prosecuted for public incitement. Gralewski himself does not give a precise date for the liquidation of the newspapers in Lublin, but Zygmunt Klukowski notes in his diary on October 24, 1939: "Today, through acquaintances, I was sent the *Głos Lubelski* of October 22. This is a sheet (2 pages) in the usual layout of the *Głos L.* A few news items of minor significance, a few official announcements, price lists valid in Lublin, an excerpt from a story or novel about the current war, a few advertisements for missing persons. That is all, but it is enough for a person who has not seen a newspaper since September to pick up even such a rag with a special feeling."[27]

Łódź

All Łódź newspapers — *Głos Poranny* (Morning Voice), *Kurier Łódzki* (Łódź Courier), *Express Ilustrowany* (Illustrated Express), *Echo,* and *Republika* — ceased publication three or four days before the city was captured. The same is true of the German-language newspapers — *Volkszeitung* (People's Newspaper), *Neue Lodzer Zeitung* (New Łódź Newspaper), and *Der Deutsche Wegweiser* (German Guide) — for those resident Germans who had officially declared loyalty to the Polish state. None of these newspapers reappeared after the capture of the city on September 9, 1939. Instead, there were the weekly *Der Volksfreund* (Friend of the People) and the daily *Die Freie Presse* (Free Press), both organs of the Łódź Nazis that had been banned by the Polish authorities at the outbreak of the war. In addition, as noted above, the Germans published the *Soldatenzeitung der Schlesischen Armee* in Łódź.

As in Kraków, the first days of the occupation in Łódź were relatively calm. Not until much later did the Germans carry out mass arrests and executions as in other Polish cities.[28] The citizens' committee, active in Łódź since September 6, had been instrumental in maintaining order; its members included the diocesan bishop Dr. Kazimierz Tomczak, Prof. Zygmunt Lorentz, and Włodzimierz Graliński, along with well-known citizens of German origin such as the prominent industrialists Arno Kindermann, Otto John, and Stefan Ender.[29]

In this situation, one of two initiatives to publish Polish newspapers had a measure of success. A few days after the invasion, a makeshift newspaper appeared for general sale. It was called *Przyjaciel Narodu: Bezpartyjne pismo codzienne m. Łodzi* (Friend of the People: Nonpartisan Daily Newspaper of the City of Łódź). The publisher and editor in chief was Henryk Rabczyński, who had been the representative of the Łódź center of AEG in Kalisz during World War I, a member of the Łódź press during the Second Polish Republic, a representative of the Trade Corporation, and general secretary of the Narodowe Zjednoczenie Mieszczańskie (National Federation of the Middle Class), an organization he had founded in March 1938. Rabczyński, who was married to a German, had tried to insinuate himself into German minority in Łódź even before the war and had aimed at Polish-German cooperation. In this spirit, he appealed to the field command office in Łódź and received permission to publish and distribute the first edition of the *Przyjaciel Narodu*. In prewar Łódź, he had written for *Rozwój* (Development), *Hasło Łódzkie* (Łódź Word), and *Ilustrowany Kurier Poznański* (Poznań Illustrated Courier); and in May 1938 he had founded his own journal. Only one issue appeared, but he continued the title in September 1939: *Przyjaciel Narodu: Miesięcznik Polityczny Społeczny i Literacki Poświęcony Idei Skonsolidowania Stanu Średniego* (Friend of the People: Monthly of Politics, Society, and Literature for the Consolidation of the Middle Class). Although further issues of the *Przyjaciel Narodu* were planned in 1939, for some unknown reason this remained the only one. All that is known is that Rabczyński negotiated with the military authorities for weeks in an effort to attain a change of German policy toward the Polish population. Later he was registered on the German national list and changed his name to von Rabe. He died during the occupation without playing any political role.[30]

The citizens' committee asked Arno Kindermann to publish a bulletin in Polish. He apparently received temporary permission from the military authorities, since on September 16 the already completed first issue of the *Biuletyn,* which presented general news of the city, was submitted to the field command office for censorship. The authority did not agree, however, to the publication of a newspaper by a Polish organization. The commissar of the city of Łódź, Dr. Leister, and SS Sturmbannführer Grosskopf raised objections to the publication of the *Biuletyn.*[31]

A German propaganda office was established in Łódź, directed by the former head of propaganda for the province of Silesia, Dr. Ludwig Fischer. On his orders, the editor of the *Soldatenzeitung der Schlesischen Armee,* Erdmann, began publishing a newspaper in Polish. By September 14 he reported to his chief: "The preparations for the publication of a Polish newspaper are as good as done. The projected name: *Gazeta Łódzka.* Printers and publishers: *Kurier Łódzki.*"[32] He also proposed the following editorial staff: provisional director, Dr. Heinz Schulz; managing editor, Michał Walter; deputy editor, Fryderyk Nathelt; translators Willi Agather and Lotte Braun; proofreader, Helena Lisowa.The technical staff was to consist of Edmund Opoliński, Ludwik Lewy, Bronisław Knobloch, Emil Has, Stanisław Wiśniewski, Jan Adamski, Antoni Lewandowski, and Mieczysław Dąbrowski. Erdmann's memorandum to Fischer contains a few handwritten remarks. "From Königsberg" is appended to the name Heinz Schulz, "unknown" to Michał Walter; Fryderyk Nathelt is annotated only with a question mark (he was a Łódź journalist of German origin who worked on *Republika* and *Mały Głos* before the war). Erdmann's proposal was accepted by Wilhelm Ohlenbusch, the head of the civil administration, who was in charge of the press. The first issue of the *Gazeta Łódzka* appeared after a one-week delay, on September 22.

To give the impression of having a Polish publisher, the paper assumed the title of a newspaper published in Łódź during the German occupation in World War I. Its readers were thus left in the dark about the composition of the editorial staff. The well-known journalist Michał Walter, former manager of the cultural staff of the *Kurier Łódzki,* was officially appointed "provisional" editor in chief. After a few issues of the *Gazeta Łódzka* had appeared, Walter was arrested in the editorial office; late he was executed. According to Mieczysław Jagoszewski, a journalist from Łódź, "Walter wanted to avoid the painful task of managing a Polish newspaper under German control and did not reply to the first summons to the newspaper; afterward he was brought there by the police." In addition to Walter and Nathelt, the Polish journalists Dembowski and Bartoszek also worked on the *Gazeta Łódzka.*[33]

The German daily *Die Freie Presse* was renamed the *Deutscher Lodzer Zeitung* (German Łódź Newspaper). It featured the orders of the German military and civil authorities and appeared a few hours before the *Gazeta Łódzka*. The timing was not accidental, since the German paper served as a source of news for the *Gazeta*.[34]

The *Gazeta Łódzka* appeared six times a week in an edition of 50,000 copies and was distributed in the zone of the civil administration of the German Eighth Army. In accordance with the guidelines of the RMVP, the propaganda department retained the right to forbid publication of another newspaper in the region.[35] Forty-two issues of the *Gazeta Łódzka* appeared, the last on November 9, two days after Artur Greiser's formal proclamation integrating Łódz into the Warthegau, one of the Polish territories incorporated into the Reich.[36]

Warsaw

Despite enemy air raids on the capital, the Warsaw press continued working with no major disruptions during the first five days of the Polish-German war. About thirty daily newspapers appeared regularly, some with morning and afternoon editions.[37] The situation changed quickly and fundamentally, however. On September 4, a decision was made to partially evacuate the government to Lublin and the surrounding area. At a press conference the next day, the newly appointed propaganda minister, the former governor of Silesia, Michał Grażyński, announced that the retreating government wanted to take with it the leaders of the political parties, press representatives, and necessary technical equipment. After the conference Warsaw journalists convened in the editorial office of the *Kurier Poranny* to discuss details. The train reserved for the press was to travel that night. The representatives of the socialist press, Rafał Praga and Zygmunt Zaremba, opposed the plan in the name of the Polish Socialist Party and, with the support of the editor in chief of *Robotnik* (Worker), Mieczysław Niedziałkowski, declared that they would remain in the city. The Journalists Association of the Republic of Poland also debated whether the press should stay in the capital or leave it but did not come to any binding conclusion, leaving the decision to the individual newspapers.[38] But the next day, September 6, the situation of the press was shaken by setbacks on the front, and after Colonel Roman Umiastowski's radio address calling on all able-bodied men to leave Warsaw immediately, it was clear that the press would be affected. Though able to function to that point, it now shared the fate of the entire capital.

Most editorial staffs, along with the majority of journalists, left Warsaw. Witold Giełżyński, the vice president of the Journalists Association, estimated that of the four hundred journalists employed in Warsaw, more than two hundred left the capital. Although it is difficult to determine how many newspapers appeared in Warsaw between September 7 and September 9, the notion that Warsaw was completely without newspapers in the days of the evacuation is not true, for such papers as the *Czas* (Times), *Kurier Codzienny,* and *Kurier Warszawski* have come down to us from the period of the great evacuation panic.[39] The entire news service, however, either was removed or had collapsed. The Polish Telegraph Agency evacutated with the government to the East. The Raszyn radio transmitter was silenced and, lest it fall into enemy hands, was destroyed at the last minute. The equipment of the other transmitter, Warsaw II, was dismantled on September 5, and the employees were dismissed. The radio managers, led by their director, Konrad Libicki, left the city. After the night of September 6–7, Warsaw radio was silenced.[40]

A turning point for Warsaw's press and radio was the decision to defend the capital and to form a headquarters for that defense. As commander in chief, Brig. Gen. Walerian Czuma had stated in an appeal on September 7 that Warsaw would be defended, and he had called on the citizens for help and for an immediate return to their normal activity. On September 8, the civil commissar of the headquarters for the defense of Warsaw, Maj. Stefan Starzyński, the mayor, made a similar appeal, stating: "The goal of my work is to satisfy all concerns of the military and to guarantee the normal course of daily life for the civilian population."[41]

One of the first measures enacted by the headquarters was the restoration of the Warsaw radio transmitter to organize the defense and prevent the chaos expected in the evacuation of a city of a million. Under the management of a newly appointed director, Edward Rudnicki, the radio was "deliberately and purposefully placed at the disposal of the struggle and life of the fighting city."[42]

No less important for the defense of Warsaw was the full resumption of press activity. The *Kurier Warszawski,* which, along with *Robotnik,* had begun the rebirth of the September press, wrote on the eighth: "The juggernaut of the war machine has deeply corroded the organism of our society and destroyed or cut off the roots of the most important cultural and educational institutions. . . . The noisy wheels of the gigantic rotary press have stopped in their rapid course, the metallic staccato of the typesetters is silenced, the printer's ink in the barrels is drying, the editorial pens no longer grate. . . . *E pur si muove.* And yet it moves! The Polish press does not want to die. It knows that it need not die. To rouse and nourish life — that is its holy duty to nation and society."

Almost all the Warsaw dailies reappeared on the streets of the defended capital: *ABC, Czas — 7 wieczór* (Time — 7 p.m.), *Dobry Wieczór* (Good

Evening), *Kurier Czerwony* (Red Courier), *Express Poranny* (Morning Express), *Dziennik Ludowy i Powszechny* (General People's Newspaper), *Dziennik Polski* (Polish Daily News), *Goniec Warszawski* (Warsaw Messenger), *Hajnt* (Today; Yiddish), *Kurier Codzienny* (Daily Courier), *Kurier Poranny* (Morning Courier), *Kurier Warszawski*, *Moment* (Yiddish), *Nasz Przegląd* (Our View; a Jewish paper in Polish), *Polska Zbrojna* (Armed Poland), *Robotnik*, *Unzer Express* (Our Express; Yiddish), *Warszawski Dziennik Narodowy* (Warsaw National Newspaper), *Wieczór Warszawski* (Warsaw Evening). Along with these Warsaw newspapers, which appeared relatively regularly, small spontaneous papers emerged in the surrounding localities, which had no electricity and therefore no access to the radio. These papers were posted on fences as news sheets.[43]

Within a few days, through the efforts of journalists, publishers, and printers, as well as with the considerable help and financial support of the civil commissar in the headquarters for the defense of Warsaw, eighteen to twenty daily newspapers were revived in Warsaw, and other journalistic organizations emerged. The Polish Telegraph Agency did not return to Warsaw, however, and the Ministry of Information and Propaganda was evacuated before it was formed. Similarly, the executive committee of the Journalists Association of the Republic of Poland and the Union of Warsaw Journalists practically ceased to exist because most of their members were gone. The press office of the city administration and headquarter's the civil commissariat under the management of Czesław Nusbaum, assumed journalistic functions. At an assembly on September 17 in the building of the Society of Writers and Journalists, the journalists elected a provisional management for the Union of Warsaw Journalists.[44]

Thanks to the initiative of Stanisław Kauzik, the director of the Polish Association of Newspaper and Journal Publishers, and of a group of publishers and journalists (Jan Kuczabiński, Witold Giełzyński, Stanisław Goryński, Halszka Buczyńska, Jadwiga Krawczyńska, and Bohdan Skąpski), a provisional press agency was organized. From September 11 to September 20, it published the *Biuletyn dla Użytku Pism Warszawskich* (Press Bulletin for the Warsaw Newspapers), one hundred copies of which were mimeographed and distributed gratis to the editorial boards of all Warsaw newspapers as well as to military and civil institutions (military headquarters, citizens' defense groups, Polish Red Cross, city administration). Information from the city was gathered by a single network of correspondents; news from the interior and from abroad was based on the broadcasts of Paris Mondial, the BBC, Radio Roma, and Radio Moscow and on broadcasts from Lwów and Vilna. A bulletin from the press office of city hall, edited by Antoni Bidar, was published on October 8, 1939.[45]

During the siege of the city, the Warsaw press was more reminiscent of frontline newspapers than of normal dailies. Given the difficult working conditions and a shortage of paper, each newspaper limited itself to at most two columns, in which it tried to present the most important news, a brief communiqué, or an appeal.

Political barriers tumbled. Without the traditional titles, it would have been hard to tell who published any particular newspaper. Moreover, many newspapers helped one another by pooling typesetting services. The identity of each newspaper was to be found in its style, the audience it addressed, and the tradition it espoused. Characteristic press, polemics and mutual reproaches for mistakes and misunderstandings ceased. An unlimited commitment to the defense of the city set the dominant tone.

Having joined the defense of the capital, the press was affected by the military situation, whose deterioration, however, did not influence the content of the newspapers as much it did their production. The interruption of the gas supply had shut down the typesetting machines, and printers were forced to set type by hand. The lack of electricity and the loss of telephone links, quite apart from the constant bombings, crippled the work of the editorial staffs and the printing presses. The first victim of the enemy air raids on the capital was the publishing house of the *Dziennik Ludowy i Powszechny*. The next to suffer were the oldest editorial facilities, including the *Kurier Warszawski* and the *Kurier Poranny,* and the building of the Polish Telegraph Agency, which were completely destroyed. On September 18, a bomb fell on the offices of the *Biuletyn Prasowy;* two days later the building was decimated, and the press agency ceased to exist. The incessant bombing of September 23–26, the final days before the surrender of Warsaw, destroyed the municipal electric company, the radio stations, and the *Robotnik* building on Warecka Street. The last independent Warsaw newspaper was dated September 23. The edition for Sunday, September 24, had been prepared but could no longer be printed. A few copies were hung in galleys on the doors of the print shop.[46]

On September 27, after the beginning of the truce and during the negotiations for the surrender, publishers and journalists of the Warsaw press agreed to combine forces to publish at least one more paper: *the Gazeta Wspólna*. This was a newspaper composed of five independent editorial staffs, and the contributions of each were identified by name: *Goniec Warszawski, Kurier Poranny, Czas, Wieczór Warszawski*, and *Poranny*. For this purpose, a common editorial committee was established, composed of representatives of the following newspapers: *Goniec Warszawski, Kurier Poranny, Czas, Wieczór Warszawski, Express*.[47] The five formed a common editorial committee and saw as their purpose to inform the population of the capital, which had been without news for four days, but also to show the German authorities that a Polish press still existed.

The first edition of the *Gazeta Wspólna,* edited by Marian Grzegorczyk, appeared on September 28 after the surrender of Warsaw, but — like the following issues — before the entrance of German troops into the city. The *Gazeta Wspólna,* especially the early issues, and the *Kurier Warszawski,* which was independent of it and reappeared on September 28 after an interruption of several days, were the last true newspapers of fighting Warsaw. The first issue of the *Gazeta Wspólna* (Sept. 27) still expresses the belief that the city, "despite everything, did not despair of receiving help in response to its sos signals and that it would ultimately be freed, so that its sacrifices, unprecedented in history, would not have been in vain."[48] This was a repeat of the last communiqué of Radio Warsaw.

In the first days of the occupation, the life of the city was governed by the conditions of the surrender agreement of September 28, which banned all activities of political parties or similar organizations, but did not mention the press.[49] Thus, no formal obstacles existed for the continuation of newspapers, and in accordance with an order, the Poles did not have the right to leave the jobs they had had previously.[50] Hence, the various editorial staffs of the *Gazeta Wspólna,* in agreement with Stefan Starzyński, set out to compose the third issue on September 29. This time, too, the newspaper was prepared at Szpitalna Street 12. But, before they could finish the composition, German soldiers accidentally passing by pushed into the print shop and arrested the members of the editorial staff there — Marian Grzegorczyk, Hieronim Wierzynski, and Medard Kozłowski.[51] The matter was quickly cleared up, however, and they were released. At this opportunity, the *Gazeta Wspólna* obtained its approval from the German military authorities.

Beginning the next day, the newspaper was published in a somewhat different form. It no longer appeared as the *Gazeta Wspólna.* Instead, each participant published the same paper under its own banner, namely, *Czas, Express Poranny, Kurier Warszwaski,* and *Wieczoar Warszawski.* The decision was made suddenly and at the last minute, since the fourth issue of *Gazeta Wspólna* had been prepared for September 30. Two party-affiliated newspapers that also appeared in Warsaw attracted attention: the *Dziennik Ludowy* (People's Newspaper), the former organ of the central committee of the Polish Socialist party; and the *Warszawski Dziennik Narodowy* (Warsaw National Newspaper), the prewar local right-wing paper of the municipal committee of the National Democratic party. Next to their titles the newspapers listed the names of the managing editors as well as those of their publishing houses.[52] They also returned to their previous numbering to emphasize their continuity. Warsaw, it appeared, was once again a city with a multitude of newspapers. But in reality all these newspapers were copies of the same one-page newssheet, *Gazeta Wspólna.* "It was an unusually interesting phase in the history of the Polish press," said one report a few years later. "All the newspapers in the capital were printed in the same print shop, set by the same typesetters, and edited by the same staff, without regard for the various political affiliations. They were distinguished only by their titles; contents, arrangement of news, and format were the same in all of them."[53]

Under the circumstances, the appearance of newspapers was regarded as a positive omen. The publishers hoped that in time the situation might somehow be stabilized. For in the first days of the occupation hardly anyone knew what the real intentions of the Germans were. This uncertainty can be seen in the following statements of various publishers and journalists: "Naturally, we cannot expect that the Germans will allow all the prewar newspapers. But a few will be permitted (Antoni Lewandowski, vice-president of the Association of Newspaper and Journal Publishers); "During the last German occupation, all prewar Warsaw papers appeared and a few new sheets were even added" (Stefan Krzywoszewski). "If we are lucky, we can count on five or six daily newspapers. They will not allow more, and they will use a paper shortage as an excuse" (Stanisław Kauzik).[54] The current situation was explained by temporary difficulties — the lack of electricity, telephone communication, radio, water, and space. "Technical conditions make it impossible for us to guarantee the normal circulation of our newspaper," wrote *ABC-Nowiny Codzienne* on October 4. "But the return to normal working conditions is only a matter of a few days. Then our newspaper will also appear for sale in the street."[55] Three days later, this advance notice proved partially true. With water and electric lines repaired, the printing machines in the Polish Press House were working again, and the press run could be increased from 1,500 to 10,000 copies.[56] On October 7, 8, and 9, the newspapers could be purchased easily (for the nominal price of ten groszy). The content, however, remained the same for all newspapers and was subject to censorship by the military authorities. At the same time, on October 8, the *Dziennik Urzędowy Miasta Stołecznego Warszawy* (Official Warsaw Daily) appeared, edited by Antoni Bida, the press secretary. It contained notices and orders of Mayor Starzyński and the German military

authorities.[57] Relations seemed to have normalized. The newspaper publishers and distributors, however, did not yet know that the fate of the Warsaw press had been sealed: the German propaganda office (a branch of the RMVP), under the direction of the former press secretary, Wilhelm Ohlenbusch, had decided to take over the Polish publishing houses in Warsaw. On October 8 the head of the civil administration in the AOK Warsaw Branch had informed the central office in Łódź that his office was preparing a special edition of the *Gazeta Łódzka* for Warsaw.[58]

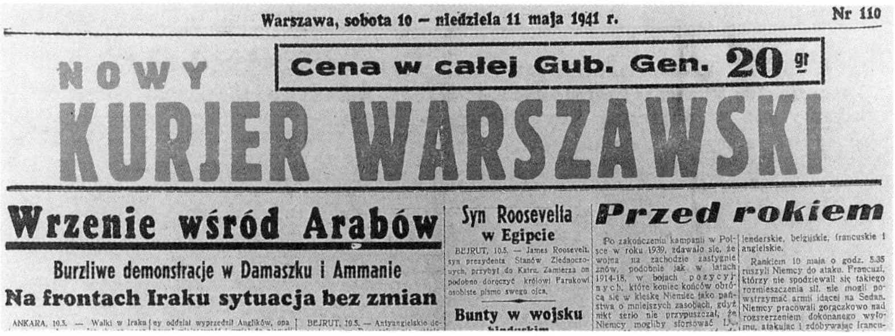

Warszawa, sobota 10 – niedziela 11 maja 1941 r. Nr 110

NOWY

Cena w całej Gub. Gen. 20 gr

KURJER WARSZAWSKI

Wrzenie wśród Arabów

Burzliwe demonstracje w Damaszku i Ammanie

Na frontach Iraku sytuacja bez zmian

ANKARA, 10.5. — Walki w Iraku ... ny oddział wyprzedził Anglików, opa ...

BEJRUT, 10.5. — Antyangielskie de- ...

Syn Roosevelta w Egipcie

BEJRUT, 10.5. — James Roosevelt, syn prezydenta Stanów Zjednoczonych, przybył do Kairu. Zamierza on podobno doręczyć królowi Farukowi osobiste pismo swego ojca.

Bunty w wojsku ...

Przed rokiem

Po zakończeniu kampanii w Polsce w roku 1939, zdawało się, że wojna na zachodzie zastygnie znów, podobnie jak w latach 1914-18, w bojach pozycyjnych, które koniec końców obrócą się w klęskę Niemiec jako państwa o mniejszych zasobach, gdyż nikt serio nie przypuszczał, że Niemcy mogliby sforsować L... lenderskie, belgijskie, francuskie i angielskie.

Rankiem 10 maja o godz. 5.35 ruszyli Niemcy do ataku. Francuzi, którzy nie spodziewali się takiego rozmieszczenia sił, nie mogli powstrzymać armii idącej na Sedan. Niemcy pracowali gorączkowo nad rozszerzeniem dokonanego wyłomu, atakując i zdobywając francu-

Fig. 1. *Nowy Kurjer Warszawski,* Warsaw (May 10/11, 1941), the major Nazi Polish-language newspaper.

In the early morning of October 10, 1939, the Gestapo summoned Stanisław Kauzik and informed him that all Polish newspapers and journals in Warsaw were banned.[59] At the same time, German security police conducted thorough searches of Warsaw editorial offices; the journalists present were arrested and the rooms sealed. Konrad Olchowicz describes how this operation proceeded at the *Kurier Warszawski*: "We were all . . . taken out of the editorial offices to the police car, which was later known in the streets of Warsaw as a *buda* (hut). The car drove back and forth through the streets for an hour, as if, in the chaos of the first days of the occupation, the German police escorting it didn't know where they were to deliver us. After they had evidently deliberated, we were all sent home and given a stern warning against unnecessary meetings; for the newspaper, at any rate, was not allowed to appear anymore."[60] Indeed, Polish newspapers were no longer distributed.

The next day, October 11, the first issue of the *Nowy Kurier Warszawski* (New Warsaw Courier) appeared on the streets; in fact, this was number 17 of the *Gazeta Łódzka*. The distributor had not even bothered to inform readers where this "new" newspaper came from. The paper listed as managing editor the same Franciszek Sowiński who was purportedly the publisher and editor-in-chief of the *Goniec Częestochowski*. Not until the second and third issues of the *Nowy Kurier Warszawski* did a notice assure readers that it was a Polish newspaper published in Warsaw. The text of the announcement was simply copied from the first issue of the *Gazeta Łódzka,* only the words *Łódź* and *mieszkańcy Łódzi*" (inhabitants of Łódź) were changed to *Warszawa* and *mieszkańcy Warszawy*.

Polish publishers and journalists, surprised by these events, tried to fathom the reasons for the sudden decision of the German authorities. At first glance, they thought the ban on publishing newspapers in Warsaw had to do with some specific misdeed. They assumed — without basis — that the last issue of the newspaper had given the German authorities cause for dissatisfaction. In particular, the newspaper's reference to an article and commentary in the *Soldatenzeitung der Schlesischen Armee* about Hitler's October 6 "peace" speech in the Reichstag was presumed to have prompted the ban.[61] People sought concrete reasons and were reluctant to give up hope that everything would be clarified.

Soon after the liquidation of the Warsaw newspapers, Ohlenbusch appeared in the Polish Press House for a "friendly" talk with Polish publishers and journalists. He is reputed to have cautioned the journalist Adam Romer, whom he had known personally for a long time, against harboring any illusions. Romer and the others, he said, did not understand the totalitarian state, especially in wartime. There could be no talk of a Polish press as they understood it, that is, as it had existed before the war.[62] Ohlenbusch emphasized that he was willing to receive representatives of the Polish Association of Newspaper and Journal Publishers. A meeting probably did take place, especially since Ohlenbusch declared that he wanted to test the Polish demands. These conversations were no doubt partly reflected in a memorandum presented to the German authorities by the publishers' association. Little information about this memorandum has previously been available, and its fate should receive some attention. It actually consisted of three separate memoranda in Polish, with German translations. The first memorandum, of October 16, states demands for the publication of newspapers; the second, of the same date, concerns journals; the third, of October 20, repeats almost literally the two previous memoranda; and concerns both newspapers and journals. Since these memoranda are found in the files of the senders and not in those of the addressees,[63] we cannot be absolutely sure they were delivered to the German authorities. However, the fact that copies are included in other official correspondence of the publishers' association does allow the conclusion that they were indeed sent out. Moreover, the memoranda were "drawn up with the agreement of the director of the propaganda office"; and, finally, there is a corresponding indication in the memoirs of the well-informed Władysław Studnicki, which appeared in the London *Wiadomości* (News) after the war.[64]

Writing of the situation in Warsaw after the surrender, he notes: "At the beginning of the occupation, many persons tried to obtain a license to publish a newspaper. The director of the publishers' association tried to get permission for six weeklies. Every day another one was to appear, one was to present political news, another economic news, a third literary news, etc."[65] From this we may assume that Studnicki knew the contents of the memorandum. And it is worth noting that Kauzik never publicly challenged Studnicki's comments, even though, in letters to the editorial staff of the

Wiadmości, he corrected other errors.[66] In the early days of the occupation, when the objectives of German policy were not yet known, representatives of other liberal professions petitioned the German authorities.For example, Stefan Jaracz writes that he and Karol Adwentowicz, another famous Polish actor, "presented an application to the German authorities for the reopening of our theater, for we thought that one should do one's duty in spite of the difficult conditions of the occupation period. At that time, we didn't yet have any idea of the bestial lot the Germans had devised for us or of the perfidy they were capable of."[67]

On October 15, 1939, one day before the date of the first two memoranda of the publishers' association, six members of the central council, the main administrative board of the association, resigned: Edward Gromski of the joint-stock company Prasa Nowa (New Press), Antoni Borman of the *Wia-domości Literackie* (Literary News), Władysław Polak and Marian Nusbaum-Ołtaszewski of *Republika,* Daniel Rozencwajg of *Nasz Przegląd* (Our View), and Józef Chodak of the *Gazeta Polska.* The minutes of the meeting at which the association board members announced their resignation give no indication of their reasons, but they were probably forced to that step by the so-called Aryan paragraph; for, according to the Nuremberg laws these publishers were Jews, whose dismissal had been demanded by the Germans from the beginning of the occupation.

There is no essential difference between the memoranda of October 16 and the memorandum of October 20, except for one important detail. In the first two memoranda, which can clearly be seen as two parts of a single entity, the association, "as representative of all Polish publishers," requests permission of the German authorities to resurrect the press in Warsaw. In the third memorandum, on the other hand, the association states the need for newspaper publication in Warsaw without specifying who is to be entrusted with it. Apparently, a negative answer had been received to the first two memoranda.

Initially, the authors of the memoranda emphasized that prior to the war thirty-two daily newspapers and about eight hundred journals had appeared in Warsaw. The population of the capital felt their cessation as a great void in daily life. Moreover, the authors argued, the absence of the press had an extremely adverse general effect because it tended to facilitate the distribution of the subversive Communist propaganda leaking out of the Soviet-occupied areas of Poland. This danger was especially menacing at a time when living conditions in Poland were extraordinarily difficult. The lack of trustworthy newspapers also hindered efforts to explain the economic difficulties experienced by the Polish population. To reduce these hardships, it was important to inform the population of the measures being introduced in the economic arena; without newspapers, inhabitants were prevented from obtaining real information. Likewise, professional groups deprived of their own press organs were impeded in their efforts to coordinate their work. The one newspaper that did appear (the *Nowy Kurier Warszawski*) could not compensate for the abolition of the earlier press. As a new, hitherto unknown paper, it could not generate as much trust among the masses as could those newspapers that had existed for a long time and were well known. The people of Warsaw were used to reading various types of newspapers according to the intellectual, professional, and social needs of the population. Thus, the new paper could achieve only a very limited distribution and would not reach the majority of the population. Finally, such a newspaper simply could not substitute for the journals, with their important social role.

Thus, the publishers' association pleaded for a renewal of the periodical and daily press in Warsaw as completely and as soon as possible. If that was not feasible, the publishers indicated, at least a few newspapers would need to be published. Also needed were weekly professional and special periodicals for economics, agriculture, the popularization of the latest in science and technology, culture and literature, as well as journals of a "family" nature, mainly for women, special journals for children, and an illustrated journal. A detailed plan was enclosed.

It is significant that in the memorandum the publishers' association did not prostrate itself before the occupation powers and made no concessions in the character of the press it demanded. The paragraph discussing the Communist danger can be interpreted either as an attempt to please the Nazis or as an expression of prewar attitudes. The authors of the memorandum primarily emphasized the needs of the Polish population and the role of the press in the normalization of life. In characterizing the *Nowy Kurier Warszawski* as a newspaper that could not win the trust of the masses and could only count on a small and unsophisticated circle of readers, they rendered careful but unambiguous criticism. The memorandum had no effect.

3

The Content of
the Newspapers

What did the publications print in the early days of the occupation? What was their aim and purpose? Was the press Polish or German? These questions must be answered cautiously, for, although these newspapers appeared during the German occupation and were subject to German censorship, they did not represent a monolithic line. Some of them were direct or indirect organs of the German authorities (for example, *Goniec Czestochowski, Gazeta Łódzka, Wiadomości Chełmskie*), while others emerged at the initiative of Polish publishers and journalists (for example, *Dziennik Krakowski* and *Gazeta Wspólna*).[1] The content of different newspapers was also decisively determined by their places of publication. Finally — and this is especially important — within a short time they underwent such radical changes that they completely lost their individuality. One exception is the *Gazeta Wspólna*, which, not coincidentally, was the first to be liquidated by the Germans. Furthermore, the paper presented almost exclusively the reports and appeals of the citizens' committee and its subordinate organizations.

The *Gazeta Wspólna,* which continued the struggle of the Warsaw press of September 1939, was beyond question a Polish newspaper, as is evident from every news item and article in all eleven issues after the surrender. Mainly it provided information about the situation in the city, the problems of the inhabitants, the endeavors of city hall and Mayor Starzyński to alleviate the effects of the siege and of the war in general. It also published the commands and orders of the German authorities and, now and then, international news, although that was presented tersely and without commentary. In local news, the *Gazeta Wspólna* emphasized the enormous extent of the war's destruction, and discreetly protested the fact that the targets of enemy air attacks were hardly limited to military ones, but included artistic monuments and public institutions like the palace of King Stanisław August in Łazienki Park, the Belweder, the observatory and the botanical gardens, as well as residential areas, which (by the paper's somewhat exaggerated account) were 75 percent destroyed or damaged. In international reporting, the *Gazeta Wspólna* compiled information designed to show that the war continued despite the surrender of Poland. The editing, material, and style of this newspaper indicate a strong sense of responsibility among the editors. Every item was carefully and pragmatically weighed, and there was an absence of sensationalism and screaming headlines.

The *Dziennik Krakowski,* the future *Ilustrowany Kurier Codzienny,* took a completely different stance. According to its editorials, it wanted simply to report local events, to work closely with the citizens' committee, and to publish the orders of city hall and even, when necessary, those of the German authorities.[2] But the very first issue of the newspaper indicates that its publisher was striving for something more ambitious, that aside from news it also wanted to disseminate opinions and views. Gradually, the newspaper's leitmotifs became the break with the past, criticism of the prewar Polish government, and the attempt to find a modus vivendi with the Germans — in the hope of thus achieving a favorable status for the city and the country. The relatively liberal behavior of the German civil and military administrations at the beginning of the occupation, as well as the general mood prevailing in Kraków, had prepared the ground for such thinking.

The text of an October 25, 1939 proclamation by the Kraków city commissar, Ernst Zörner (later governor of the Lublin district), illustrates this point: "To establish the closest possible contact with the inhabitants of the city and to assure the Kraków population of a share in the tasks of city hall in this especially hard time, I have appointed a number of citizens of various professions members of a council; it will meet regularly under my direction to advise me in the responsible leadership of the city. The members of the council are acting in an honorary capacity and are completely independent politically. Their work is only to serve the commonweal."[3]

The members of the council appointed by Zörner included Prof. Tadeusz Lehr-Spławinski, rector of the Jagiellonian University; Prof. Stanisław Kutrzeba, president of the Polish Academy of Science; Dr. Zygmunt Kuliga, canon of the cathedral chapter; Henryk Maista, vice-director of the Chamber of Industry and Commerce; Izydor Sawicki-Stella, an engineer and a professor at the Mining Academy; and Ludwik Lelito, an industrialist. Zörner appointed Dr. Julian Twardowski chairman of the council.

In a study the Polish writer and social activist Halina Krahelska wrote during the war, "Postawa społeczeństwa polskiego pod okupacją niemiecką" (The behavior of Polish society under the German occupation), she describes the prevailing mood: "In Kraków, a conciliatory attitude was evident at the beginning of the occupation. . . . This placating attitude, widespread among the Kraków intelligentsia and the citizenry in general, can be attributed to the customs and traditions of the older generation, to the period of World War I, when the Kraków Poles still had extremely close relations with Vienna, the Austrian military and bureaucracy. . . . Furthermore, during the first year of the occupation, German behavior in Kraków may have created such a deception. The occupation forces in Kraków did not encounter any resistance; Kraków had capitulated in September without a shot; during the war and in the takeover, pacification of the city and the surrounding area had turned out to be unnecessary."[4] German behavior in Kraków at the beginning of the occupation did indeed contribute to the mood in the city.

Historians have shown interest in Hitler's objectives in Poland during the first two months of the war. Scholars agree that the fate of Poland had not yet been decided in the early weeks.[5] Documents from September and October 1939 indicate that exploratory conversations had been conducted among some German officials on the subject of a rump state and that there had been discussions with Polish representatives too. Rumors of these conversations, which leaked out, must have been picked up by the editorial staff of the *Dziennik Krakowski,* especially since Dagobert Dürr, director of the Kraków propaganda office and in charge of the press, had offered his services as an advocate of German-Polish understanding; moreover, he had acted as an intermediary in conversations with Władysław Studnicki and had tried to convince him of the necessity of an immediate trip to Berlin to discuss all pending questions with Goebbels. He had also put his car and driver at Studnicki's disposal in order to locate Wincenty Witos, the leader of the prewar Polish Peasant party, for the Germans would have liked to have seen Witos as the leader of a collaborationist government, if such a government had come into existence.[6]

The *Dziennik Krakowski* took these matters seriously and tried to advance them. The issue of September 11, carried a long article headlined "International Conventions of War." For occupied Kraków, it was a sensational article, and it could hardly have appeared without the knowledge of the Kraków propaganda office. In any case, German censors raised no objections, nor did they intervene when the *Dziennik Krakowski,* in almost every issue, presented pictures of the Kraków monument titled *Nasz stary Kraków* (Our Old Kraków). The article detailed international treaties and the century-old tradition of proper conduct of war. It also maintained that the occupation of a country by a hostile army did not mean the end of that country's independence. Citing each and every clause of the Hague agreement, the author raised the question of how these principles applied to Poland. He answered:

> In the final analysis, peace will determine the fate of Poland and Kraków. For the present, we find ourselves in a transition stage. During this period of occupation, a proclamation of German army headquarters, refelcting the international military conventions we cited will be in effect.[7] . . . In this proclamation, the intent to confer on Polish society self-rule and responsibility is obvious. . . . It would be regrettable if the abandoned and vanquished Polish people were to take the view that since the Germans have come to us, let them therefore think about us and for

us. . . . The division of authority in the Polish territory occupied by German troops is settled in principle. Recognized old customs and international law continue to be fully binding. The German army reserves for itself the decisions that directly concern military operations, security, and the transport and provisioning of its troops. All other questions that have to do with the daily life of the citizens and the country are issues of the provisional local Polish authorities.[8]

One indication that the article's publication was not accidental is that, somewhat later, on September 15, after the newspaper's name was changed to *Ilustrowany Kurier Codzienny,* the paper took up the question again, and printed excerpts from a book on international law — especially from the section on "The Rule of the Enemy in the Occupied Country" — by Zygmunt Cybichowski, a prominent scholar.

The Kraków paper considered a peace treaty necessary and spoke out carefully at first, but then more courageously and decisively, against the perpetuation of the Polish-German war by the "unsound policy of the Polish government." Thus, the *Dziennik Krakowski* clearly changed the position its staff had advanced prior to the outbreak of the war in the columns of the *IKC,* which was loyal to the government. To some extent, the change was an attempt to reach an understanding with the occupation forces. In its very first issue (September 14, 1939), in an article headlined "Work and Calm," the newspaper had declared unnecessary the evacuation of the city in the early days of September. The author of the article, editor in chief Ludwik Szczepański, wrote: "This is not the time to settle accounts, but in the name of truth and in justice to the suffering population, it must be stated that to a great extent the guilt for events lies with the authorities who left the city and its inhabitants without information or instructions and delivered them to rumors and panic."[9]

Two days later, the *Dziennik Krakowski* went further — once more in the name of truth and from the viewpoint of the common man. Its criticism, in the rather biting style of the old *IKC,* was now addressed to city hall, Mayor Bolesław Czuchajowski, and other authorities, who were charged with responsibility for Kraków's inadequate defense against air raids, for the belated and badly executed mobilization, and for the chaos in the evacuation and transport of "all valuable movable goods from the city." A week after the name change, the paper launched an extraordinarily vehement attack against the internal and external policy of the Polish government, holding it responsible for the outbreak of the war and the misfortune that had befallen the country. The paper immediately identified the principal guilty parties: the English, the Jews, and the Freemasons. Henceforth, the *Ilustrowany Kurier Codzienny* was unscrupulous in its methods. The following excerpts from news-agency reports and articles of September 15–19 show how the character and tone of the paper changed every day, until its style was finally reminiscent more of the later reptile press than a newspaper edited by Polish journalists.

September 15, 1939 (No. 247):

"The Polish government at the Romanian border. Wife and daughter of the Foreign Minister already in Czerniowce."

"This April, Hitler asked Poland to return the Free City of Danzig to the Reich and to permit an extraterritorial highway to be built through the [Polish] Corridor. In exchange, he offered a twenty-five-year peace treaty. Our government rejected this proposal because it overestimated our might and the help of our friends, while it underestimated the strength and determination of the German Reich. . . . A continuation of the policy of self-deception can only aggravate our situation. We consider it the duty of a responsible government to acknowledge reality soberly and clearly, and then to make whatever decisions can save whatever of the people's freedom and happiness can still be saved. If it thinks this objective can be achieved through war, let it continue to fight. No sacrifice is too great for the freedom of the people. If, however, this objective cannot be achieved through the continuation of the war, then the government must have the courage to draw the conclusions of this recognition." ("The Polish Situation")

September 16, 1939 (no. 248):

"The Polish government no longer exists. President Mościcki also in Czerniowcz. We have been abandoned and forsaken."

"It may be easy for such people to pack up their pearls and gems to go live carefree and prosperous in another country. . . . This behavior is worthy of people whose fatherland is always where they can best do business and where we *goyim* can most easily be cheated. These gentlemen in caftans have fled en masse — and if the German occupation has any advantage for Poland, perhaps it is that, at least for a while, it has put a stop to this plague and perhaps may even — for now we don't yet dare hope — free us from it completely." ("Flight or Starvation")

September 18, 1939 (no. 249)

"England profits from Poland's defeat. Great Britain transports the Polish treasury to London. The Jews and Polish high lords transfer themselves and their money to safety."

"The Jews in Poland" (article)

September 19, 1939 (no. 250):

"Poland's destroyers [Mościcki and Śmigły-Rydz] enjoy a pleasant vacation."

The German-Polish war is practically over. . . . So we have been betrayed — by our ministers and by the foreign powers that dragged them and us into the maelstrom of war. No one can expect us to feel any obligation to them. But what should we do? As things stand, it is impossible to go on fighting. Should we let the war — which also means the war in Poland itself — become a permanent condition? Thus we would certainly not do the Polish people any favor. . . . We are talking about peace, and there is no one on our side who would undertake to conclude a peace. The government has flown. For the moment, there is no new government. That was precisely the reason for the invasion of Soviet troops into our country. Germany and Soviet Russia declared their willingness to help settle the new political situation of the Polish people. Let those who consider themselves called upon to take the nation's fate in their hands become more strongly attached to the creative classes than are those who have left us now in such a cowardly way. ("What Will Be?")

The Kraków paper began its attacks against the Polish government at a time when the outcome of the war was not yet decided — at least in the awareness of the people. Despite the early defeats including the loss of a considerable part of the territory, the September campaign was still going on: two armies were still fighting on the Bzura River, Warsaw was defending itself, and there was hope of help from the western powers. The collapse of the front, the evacuation of the local authorities, the flight of the military high command and of the government provoked deep shock and disappointment. All of this was later fiercely criticized both in the Polish underground press and in the emigré press. But that criticism was rendered under completely different conditions (free of all censorship) and with a different objective (mobilization for the battle to retrieve the country's lost independence). The *Dziennik Krakowski* and the *Ilustrowany Kurier Codzienny* chose to break with the past at the most unsuitable time and place.

The content of the other daily newspapers is much easier to analyze. Some papers were under the direct influence and supervision of the Germans, but they were distinguished from one another by region and administration. In form, content, and language, the *Kurier Radomski* and *Wiadomości Chełmskie* were quite similar, basically official gazettes to which shoddy propaganda articles and meager international news items were simply tacked on. The newspapers in Łódź and Częstochowa were of a somewhat higher level and tried to preserve an appearance of independence, at least in the early days.

In the first issue, the editorial staff of the *Goniec Częstochowski* called its paper "a herald of calm and security," indicating that a new era was to begin at the foot of the Jasna Góra, the church of the Black Madonna, and that a bridge would be built between the two peoples, the Germans and the Poles, so that "understanding between them could no longer be prevented by the Warsaw and Kraków intriguers and their malicious propaganda." In the second issue, the editorial staff reported on the warm acceptance of the *Goniec* by the public and promised it would endeavor to make the paper a "true reflection of all areas of municipal life" and "an exhaustive source of objective and precise news." In fact, however, these words had no relation to reality; the *Goniec* had never been a local paper. Local news did not occupy much space, while almost all the issues were filled with shrill articles on politics and the historical mission of Nazi Germany.[10] For example, the article "The Germans: Pioneers of Culture and Civilization" declared: "We are witnesses to the way the Germans progress inexorably in their epochal victory march to fulfill their centuries-old mission as pioneers of civilization and culture. The name of Chancellor Hitler, the brilliant statesman of the Germans, will be engraved in gold letters in the book that will be written by those who have made themselves worthy of mankind and civilization."[11]

After the first few issues, the affirmations of a German-Polish understanding disappeared and were replaced by threats and orders. From its fifth issue on, the *Goniec* ran a weekly Sunday for Catholics that gave the impression it was written by priests. Subjects from Holy Scripture and the catechism, too, were to serve Nazi propaganda here. (A similar supplement had appeared in the pre-war *Goniec*.) The supplement was printed without the approval of church authorities — indeed, against their will. The church, particularly the diocese of Częstochowa, rejected the German editorial staff's invitations to participate in the editing of the paper and ignored the accompanying threats.[12]

The *Gazeta Łódzka* occupied a middle position between the Kraków and Częstochowa newspapers. At least in the first issues, there were reverent articles about the Polish people. It was also emphasized that the arrival of the Germans had absolutely no effect on the right to life and work.[13] At the same time, even in its first issue, the *Gazeta Łódzka* assumed a critical stance toward the Polish authorities, cleverly exposing all the weaknesses of pre-war Polish propaganda. Thus, for example, an article entitled "Illusion and Reality" stated: "Owing to deliberately disseminated accounts, we imagined the Germans as tattered, dirty, hungry, and whipped into battle with threats. Then we saw them: an extraordinarily well-equipped army confidently facing the future, young men blindly devoted to the Führer. The enormous mass of technical weapons astounded us. . . . So it is no wonder that, despite the bitter resistance of Poland's soldiers, the Germans won continuous victories.[14]

For comparison, the newspaper also reprinted articles from the Polish daily newspapers — for example, one by General Władysław Sikorski from the *Kurier Warszawski* of June 1, 1939 (no. 149), which discussed the weakness of the Third Reich. The article was headlined in the October 10 *Gazeta Łódzka*, "What Was Written About the Readiness of the Germans before the Outbreak of the War. How the Polish Public Was Led Astray. A Contemporary Memoir."

The *Gazeta Łódzka* soon came to resemble the *Goniec Częstochowski* and the *Ilustrowany Kurier Codzienny*. Arguments were replaced with hollow phrases, false reports were substituted for information. By late September, all three newspapers showed the characteristics they were later to demonstrate while cooperating with the propaganda department of the occupation force. Polish journalists devoted to the illusion that they could influence the content of the newspapers despite the occupation suffered a tragic fate. From the outset, their hands were bound by German censorship and the pressure of the Nazi propaganda department, and by the time they realized how far they had deviated from their original intentions, it was too late. The newspapers edited with their help were no longer Polish newspapers. Significantly, none of these journalists worked for the reptile press published by the propaganda department. Many of them were killed by the Nazis in concentration camps and prisons — including Michał Walter, the editor of the *Gazeta Łódzka,* and Stanisław Mróz of the *Dziennik Krakowski* — Włodzimierz Długoszewski, who was also interned in a concentration camp, died shortly after the liberation. The resistance fighter Józef Flach (the prewar president of the Journalists Association of Kraków) died in Kraków, on May 12, 1944.

Part 2
The Polish-Language
Press in the
Generalgouvernement

4

Aims and Organization of Press Propaganda

Hitler's decrees dated October 8 and 12, 1939, concerning future annexation and administration of the eastern regions and his decree concerning the administration of the occupied Polish territory left no doubt about his intention to eliminate the Polish state. These decrees basically divided the Polish territory occupied by the Germans into the region annexed to the Reich (Warthegau, Danzig-Westpreussen, and Bezirk Zichenau) and the Generalgouvernement, thus ending the military administration and the provisional occupation status. The concept of a rump state was also abandoned, even if it was still being considered in certain German circles.

The Führer's decrees went into effect the day they were promulgated, October 26, 1939. That same afternoon, the last issue of the *Ilustrowany Kurier Codzienny* appeared in Kraków. The first page presented in German and Polish the text of a proclamation by Hans Frank, which was followed by this statement from the editorial staff and the publisher: "As the public proclamation on the first page of our newspaper indicates, Reich Minister Hans Frank, who has been appointed governor-general of the occupied Polish territory by decree of the Führer and Reich chancellor, takes over administration of the government today. A new epoch begins. With the advent of the governor-general's administration and the new conditions, the *IKC* ceases publication today."[1]

In its place came the official *Goniec Krakowski*. This new Polish-language newspaper was supposed to publish official announcements, along with general news. The local section was to be expanded so as to provide the population with "up-to-date and reliable information." The first issue of the new paper appeared the next afternoon. At the same time, Frank issued his first order concerning publishing in the GG, which made the publishing, printing, and distribution of all material subject to approval.[2]

The announcement of the cessation of the *Ilustrowany Kurier Codzienny* as well as Frank's order concerning publishing can be understood only in connection with certain unpublished documents. One of these, the minutes of a conference between Frank and Goebbels on October 31, is essential to an understanding of the real intentions of the German occupation force.

Frank received Goebbels in his temporary residence in Łódź. The conference also included Frank's deputy, Dr. Arthur Seyss-Inquart; the head of the still provisional propaganda department of the GG, Dr. Maximilian Baron du Prel; and the gauleiter of Silesia, Dr. Fischer, who had been temporarily assigned to the propaganda department of Łódź. Discussion focused almost exclusively on cultural problems, including the deployment of press and radio in the GG, and Goebbels and Frank were in general agreement, even if the formulations of the Reich propaganda minister were much sharper and more ruthless. At the start, Frank said that the Poles should be given the kind of education that would make it clear to them that they had no future as a nation; Goebbels seconded Frank, saying that, that very morning, Hitler had told him the Poles should not have hope of restoration, and should not even think they might somehow rebuild their country. Having agreed about these general objectives, both ministers expressed the view that the entire Polish information system was to be destroyed and that radio and press would have to be taken away from the Poles. Instead of radios, loudspeakers would be set up to transmit news and orders at certain times of day. The press was to be replaced with newspapers of a purely informational character. In any case, Goebbels explicitly stressed, no opinions were to be expressed in the papers.[3]

Frank and his entourage took literally the widely accepted tenets espoused by Goebbels and made them the guiding principles of their actions. Emil Gassner, press adviser and later chief of press of the GG, admitted frankly that, following the instructions given him, he made sure that the Polish-language press became exclusively an organ of the German administration and a means of transmitting the orders of the occupier; at best, it published military reports.[4] A similar formulation came out of Frank's first working meeting on November 8, which was devoted to the questions of publishing. According to du Prel, the newspapers projected for the individual districts were to be "not opinion papers but simply official and news gazettes."[5] In other words, the Poles were to carry out obediently what the authorities demanded and were to know only as much as seemed useful to German interests.

Interestingly, neither at the meeting between Frank and Goebbels nor at subsequent discussions about press issues was there any mention of the direction and goals of German propaganda for the Poles. Instead, the Germans behaved as if no program existed. Goebbels did not mention anything either when, two days after the conversations in Łódź he reported on them to his subordinates in Berlin.[6] That was hardly accidental; indeed, the Germans really did not intend to win over any Poles for their cause. Indicative of their indifference on this point is the exchange of opinions between Frank and

Goebbels about films for the Polish population. Goebbels immediately objected to a proposal to show only films of little value or those that glorified the greatness and strength of the Third Reich, the propaganda minister was categorically opposed to allowing Polish cinemas (or theaters and cabarets) to remain open. Only in exceptional cases, he thought, when the streets had to be cleared for example — in big cities — might film screenings be organized for the Poles, and these would be regulated.[7]

Goebbels's directives conformed to Hitler's plans for the GG in the first phase. On January 19, 1940, Frank elucidated these plans, explaining that he had received the command "to establish the administration of the captured eastern territory, with a special order to impoverish the region mercilessly as a war area and country of plunder, to wreck its economic, social, cultural, and political structure."[8]

The press was indeed superfluous as an instrument of propaganda for the realization of these objectives. Thus, no new newspapers were founded in the GG and only those that Frank had taken over from the military administration were issued. It soon became clear that this approach was inimical to German interests, as General Johannes Blaskowitz, commander of the German Eighth Army, indicated in his report to the OKW of November 27, 1939: "The lack of newspapers and radio opens the gate wide to all kinds of whispered propaganda and rumors. The most absurd tales — like the bombing of Poznań by English aviators, the advance of the French on Berlin, the flight of the Germans from the Russians, etc. — are far-reaching and widely believed. Under these conditions, the Polish population is very susceptible even to Communist influence, which is no doubt intensively brought to bear in this country by the Russians. It is in the interest of both the Wehrmacht and the civil administration that a reasonable order prevail in Poland."[9]

Not until late 1939 and early 1940 can we discern any change in the attitude toward the press in the GG. That is when high officials of the Third Reich concluded that the economic potential and labor reserves of the GG had to be as fully harnessed as possible. At a meeting on January 19, Frank stated: "Today we see in the territory of the Generalgouvernement a valuable component of the German *Lebensraum.* The [former] policy of total destruction, has been changed to one of treating this territory more carefully to make it more advantageous to the Reich in the current situation. An important consequence of this new approach is the introduction of the Four Year Plan in the GG, to facilitate its integration into German objectives."[10] From then on, the GG was considered a *Nebenland,* a colony of the Third Reich. This is not the place to discuss the economic, political, and social consequences of this new phase of Hans Frank's rule; Polish historians have been tending to this task, and new studies are constantly being published.

The important fact is that the concept of the function of the press in the GG changed in accordance with these new plans. Henceforth, the German authorities regarded the Polish-language press as an important instrument of their policy for the subjugated country.

Above all, they gave up the absurd idea of a press without opinions. Emil Gassner reported how that happened: "In January 1940, when calls for help came from all sides, it was recognized that this line of thinking had to be abandoned. They used editorials to explain the [German] policy to the Polish population."[11] Early in 1940, according to Gassner, the Polish press was reshaped. That, he said, substantially helped ward off the rumors of anticipated inflation.[12] Consequently, it was decided to use the press for the German cause.[13]

There were other reasons for the change, particularly the attitude of the Polish population as expressed in its clandestine publishing activity. From the very first days of the occupation, leaflets, transcribed radio bulletins, and newspapers had passed from hand to hand. Significantly, in Warsaw and Kraków, they appeared even before the *Goniec Krakowski* and the *Nowy Kurier Warszawski* and had the same title in both cities, evidently without prior agreement: *Polska Żyje!* (Poland Lives!). The Kraków newspaper, the first to appear, on September 19, was published by a group of teachers led by T. J. Dobrowolski; the Warsaw paper was published by a commissioned officer, Maj. Bolesław Studzinski, formerly of the headquarters of the border patrol.[14] The first Warsaw issue, signed by Witold Hulewicz, came out on October 10, the day the *Gazeta Wspólna* first ceased publication.[15] The first newspapers of the Polish underground organizations were also circulated very early. The *Związek Powstańców Niepodległosćiowych* (Association of Fighters for Independence) published its *Monitor Informacyjny* on October 10; the military organization Służba Zwycięstwu Polski (Service for the Victory of Poland) began to publish two papers that became very popular: on November 5, the *Biuletyn Informacyjny* and, on December 15, the *Wiadomości Polskie* (Polish News). By the end of 1939, at least forty periodicals had appeared.[16]

They did not elude the occupying force. At a conference for those involved in the propaganda machinery, held in Zakopane in early 1940, and attended by Hans Frank and other officials of the GG, the main concern was the question formulated by du Prel: how to counter the spread of rumors by Poles and prevent unrest.[17] Soon German propaganda was to be observed everywhere. The cities and villages of the GG were immediately inundated with brochures, news sheets, and other materials that appeared in the hundreds of thousands.[18] Especially noteworthy were the numerous journals for individual social and professional groups, as well as for national and religious groups such as Ukrainians and Jews. Loudspeakers were set up for radio broadcasts. The authorities even considered allowing Poles to own radios again; these were to be equipped to handle only one frequency so that receiving foreign or German broadcasts not intended for residents of the Nebenland would be impossible.[19] Moreover, cinemas and theaters, originally to be denied to the Polish population, were now considered additional means of propaganda.[20] The biennial report of Warsaw district chief Fischer sets forth the Germans' goal of winning over Polish public opinion "through press, film, theater, music, writing." The use of these, he wrote, would serve Germany's political objectives "without also contributing to strengthening Polish community life or to sustaining a national Polish tradition."[21]

German propaganda aimed especially at forcing the Polish population to an awareness that the defeat of September 1939 was final, the power of Germany and the Wehrmacht invincible, England and France weak and anti-Polish. Furthermore, the Poles were to be convinced that they were not really in a position to maintain their statehood independently, that only the "new order" brought by the Germans ensured permanence and perfection. Hence it was in the self-interest of the Poles to submit to German leadership.

5

Organizational Scheme

Hans Frank's October 26 proclamation concerning publishing in the Gener-algouvernement gave a name to the office responsible for propaganda — the Department for Public Enlightenment and Propaganda — and the Nazi "scholar" Adolf Dresler regarded the date of the proclamation as marking the beginning of the department's existence.[1] Apart from its name, it already had a permanent manager, a press consultant, and a budget of over 20,000 RM.[2] In the early days of the GG, however, the Reich propaganda offices created during the military administration were still responsible for publishing. In time, these offices were taken over by the new administration of the GG and became the organizational base of the newly established department. In early 1940 the integration process was completed, and only from then on was there an actual propaganda department, commanding an extensive network of offices and branches as well as precisely defined areas of operation and authority. Thus, the change in Nazi policy in the GG and the creation of the Department of Public Enlightenment and Propaganda were closely connected.

A draft dated January 1940 stipulated the following units in the department:[3] administration, propaganda, press, publications, and culture. They were to undergo numerous changes. The publications office, for example, was dissolved at the end of 1940 and its functions transferred to the press office. Responsibility for film and radio was shifted from the propaganda and culture offices, and the two new units were combined into a film and radio department in 1941, when the other offices also became departments.

The press office occupied a special position in the RMVP. Here the most important threads of the daily German propaganda plan came together. According to the organizational chart devised in March 1940 of the office of the governor-general, the press office consisted of the following sections: German press, Polish press, press of the national minorities, internal and official publications, illustrated journals, information service (press agency), correspondents from the Reich and abroad, press archive, and readers' unit.[4]

In August 1940 Frank created an office of press chief. Henceforth, two entities would deal with press issues: the press office (later renamed the press department) and the press chief of the GG. On January 1, 1941, however, the press chief took over the management of the press department.

As press chief, this official was directly subordinate to the governor-general, but as head of the press department he reported to the head of the Department of Public Enlightenment and Propaganda. Frank had simply adopted a model that had long been in effect in the Reich, where questions of the press were handled by two distinct offices: the press department in the Reich Ministry of Public Enlightenment and Propaganda (RMVP) and the office of the press chief. In the Reich, both offices had the same head, Otto Dietrich: as press chief he was directly subordinate to Hitler; as head of the press department he worked for the Ministry of Propaganda, run by Goebbels.

In the Generalgouvernement all questions of press policy, in the broadest sense of that phrase, were under the jurisdiction of the press chief, as was the internal and public information service. His functions included keeping the press in the GG in harmony with the requirements of the press policy of the Reich; examining all periodical publications from officials or institutions throughout the GG; screening and bringing in press publications from the Reich and abroad; and informing the GG leadership on specific as well as confidential political questions.

The office of the press chief was composed of two branches, the department (Dienststelle) of the press chief and the department for associated official enterprises. The former had five divisions and dealt with questions of the press service for the government and administration of the GG, news correspondents, official publications (like the *Amtlicher Anzeiger*), confidential writings like "Information Service for the Wójts" and "Confidential Information," and radio news.

The second branch, which constituted something like a press agency, was divided into two parts: the German press service of the Generalgouvernement and Polskie Wiadomości Prasowe (Polish Press News). After the outbreak of the German-Soviet war and the integration of the District of Galicia into the GG, Polskie Wiadomości Prasowe was renamed Telepress and structured into Polish and Ukrainian sections, then further divided into a daily dispatch and article service, a radio news service, and news sheets for the rural population.[5]

After the establishment of the office of the press chief, the press department in the Department for Public Enlightenment and Propaganda was concerned only with periodical publications and general publication policy. The editorial staffs of newspapers and journals of a political nature were under its control. It primarily granted permission for printing and distribution, and determined the number of copies and the form of sales. An essential function was to track the mood of the Polish population by examining the clandestine Polish press and the journals that appeared abroad among Polish emigrés. The press department also noted all opinions about the GG in the press of the Third Reich and in the foreign press.[6] It was organized into sections for the German press, the Polish press, the press of the national minorities, the Reich press, the foreign press, and the clandestine and emigré press, as well as an archive and a special section for publishing.

Table 5.1 shows the organization and the division of functions of the press department and the office of the press chief.

The Department for Public Enlightenment and Propaganda was one of the largest in the government of the GG. In addition to those employed in the district branches, 70 persons worked in the central office in 1940, 117 in 1941, and 126 in 1943. In 1941, 91 of the 117 staff members were Germans from the Reich, 21 were *Volksdeutsche,* 2 were Ukrainians, and 3 were Poles.[7] The office of the press chief employed 21 persons, but more detailed information is not available.[8]

The first head of the Department for Public Enlightenment and Propaganda was Maximilian du Prel, formerly director of the Nazi party's press department in the Reich. In the GG he was Frank's press chief as well as director of the cultural policy section in the Institut für deutsche Ostarbeit (Institute for German Advancement in the East). Du Prel was generally known as the author of an official publication entitled *Der Generalgouvernement Polen.* (In the second edition, 1942, the word *Polen* was removed from the title.) From the GG du Prel returned to his earlier job in Berlin and, in December 1941, was appointed general secretary of the Union of National Journalists' Associations in Vienna. This union brought together the Association of the German Press and the Italian Nationale Fascista dei Giornalisti, and it included journalists from Germany, Italy, and Spain, as well as from Bulgaria, Romania, Slovakia, Hungary, and Norway.[9] For a brief time (July 18, 1940–January 31, 1941) du Prel's successor in the GG was Erich Schmidt. According to Schmidt's subordinates, under his administration the Department for Public Enlightenment and Propaganda became rife with intrigue and cliquishness. Schmidt, suspected of embezzlement, was relieved of his position in the GG and transferred to Oslo.[10] During Schmidt's tenure, the press chief of the GG from July 27 to December 27, 1940, was Wilhelm Zarske, former editor-in-chief of the party paper *Danziger Vorposten* and also press chief for Albert Forster, the *Gauleiter* of Danzig-West Prussia.

The next and last head of the Department of Public Enlightenment and Propaganda, Wilhelm Ohlenbusch, demands more attention. By the end of August 1939 he had been transferred to the Eighth Army of General Blaskowitz as representative of the Reich Ministry of Public Enlightenment and Propaganda and he came to Poland with the German army. Originally, he

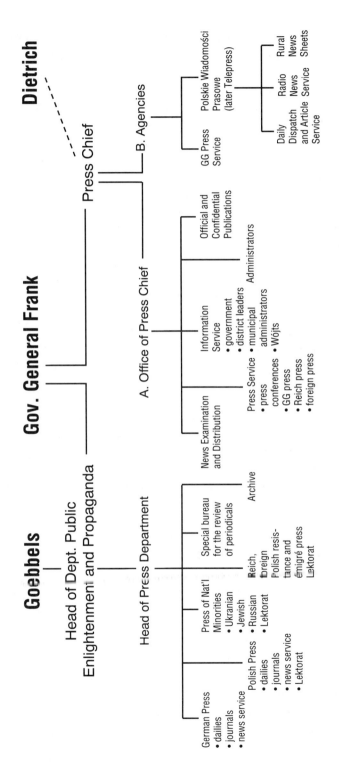

Table 5.1. Press Organization.

was press chief for the Eighth Army. After the surrender of Warsaw he became head of Reich Propaganda Office I and was later director of the propaganda department for the District of Warsaw. On February 1, 1941, Frank appointed him director of the Department for Public Enlightenment and Propaganda, a post Ohlenbusch held until the end of the occupation. During Ohlenbusch's tenure, the press chief and head of the press department was Emil Gasner, about whom we know very little.

The Polish writer and journalist Ferdynand Goetel regarded Ohlenbusch as a limited person with the mentality of an SA man.[11] And Władysław Studnicki later commented about Ohlenbusch, with whom he was personally acquainted: "While in the first German occupation [in World War I] the Press Department was headed by the well-known journalist [Georg] Cleinow, author of the two-volume work *The Future of Poland,* in the second occupation the director of the press department in the District of Warsaw, and later in the whole Generalgouvernement, was a grammar-school teacher who knew no Polish and knew of Poland only what he had taken from propaganda writings."[12]

Ohlenbusch is a typical example of a German whose real life began only after 1933. In the Weimar Republic he had tried many things: he had been a teacher, a representative, and a clerk; he had matriculated twice — at the University of Hamburg and in Frankfurt am Main — without completing a degree. When the Nazis came to power, he had already been in the party for three years, so he was given a responsible position in the Hamburg propaganda department; a year later, he was summoned to Berlin to an administrative position in the RMVP. In Poland, he joined the SA and was awarded the War Cross for special merit.[13]

Like du Prel, his predecessor, Ohlenbusch was directly and exclusively subordinate to Frank, who, specially empowered by Hitler, was careful not to allow any outsider to question his authority as dictator of the GG.[14] The result was endless quarrels and controversies with various central offices in Berlin, including the RMVP, about which Ohlenbusch was to report.

At his first meeting with Goebbels, Frank had already succeeded in enforcing a claim that no department was to be created for the GG in the RMVP. It was also determined that the head of the propaganda department of the GG would be directly under Frank but was to adhere to the general instructions of RMVP.[15] These guidelines were conveyed to Kraków through the so-called proxy of the governer-general in Berlin.[16] Not without irony, K. M. Pospieszalski notes that the creation of a proxy's office was meant to strengthen Frank's notion that the GG was a quasi-state, he himself a chief of state, and his representative in Berlin a quasi-diplomatic representative. Goebbels was opposed; he wanted everything concerning propaganda, wherever German soldiers had set foot, to fall within his purview.[17] His struggle with Ribbentrop for control over foreign propaganda is well known;[18] so too is his fight with Rosenberg for the management of propaganda in the occupied Soviet territories,[19] with Keitel for propaganda in the Wehrmacht,[20] and with Dietrich for the management of the press. These struggles were not primarily about principles, but rather were battles of personalities and authority, common at all levels of the Nazi hierarchy.

These were the issues involved in Goebbels's attitude toward the press in the GG. He expressed himself several times on this subject, but mostly only in terms of his own person and his thwarted ambition. At conferences in his ministry he threatened to put an end to the published German press in the GG if it did not follow his instructions.[21] This threat was also directed at Frank, whom he couldn't bear and whom he wanted to remove.[22] He was much more concerned with Dietrich, however, since after the creation of the Office of Press Chief in the GG, press policy in occupied Poland was directed from that office. Goebbels had in fact opposed the creation of two different press offices.[23] In the GG the fight between Goebbels and Dietrich assumed the form of a conflict between Schmidt, Ohlenbusch, and Gassner for the management of the press, with Frank officially serving as a mediator. Initially, in January 1941, Frank had sided with Goebbels and ordered Gassner to adhere strictly to the instructions of the Department for Public Enlightenment and Propaganda.[24] Later, however, in April 1941, Frank changed his mind and entrusted Gassner with the total press policy in the GG on condition that he cooperate closely with Ohlenbush, as set out in a special agreement.[25] It was a half-measure that in practice only sharpened the conflict. Gassner felt supported by Frank and Dietrich and ignored Ohlenbusch, who sought protection from Goebbels. Both sides were passionately involved, and hence the controversy lasted throughout the entire occupation. Even when the Russians were at the borders of the GG, both sides were still struggling for control of the press. In his diary Frank reported, in the entry of February 6, 1944, that on a visit to Berlin he had had a discussion with Dietrich and had brought up the relationship between Gassner and Ohlenbusch. He had emphasized that Gassner, as press chief of the GG, had to remain the leading authority in dealing with the press. It was agreed that Dietrich and Frank would jointly defend this position against the well-known views of the RMVP.[26] Two months later, Frank sent Gassner to Berlin to consolidate his position, with instructions not to yield under any circumstances to pressure from the Ministry of Propaganda.[27]

6

The Fate of
Polish Periodicals

Between the two world wars, Poland had a strong publishing industry and extensive press institutions. Before the outbreak of World War II, some two thousand publishing enterprises and forty press agencies of various sorts existed. According to official statistics of December 1937, 2,692 press publications appeared in Poland, including 184 daily newspapers, 74 biweekly or monthly periodicals, and 422 weekly journals.[1] The rest were scientific, socio-cultural, literary, religious, economic, and professional journals. The average circulation of the daily press was 2.6 million copies. There were some 1,300 professional journalists in Poland regularly employed by the newspapers and larger journals.[2]

The occupation meant the end of the Polish press. The centuries-long tradition of Polish publishing was resolutely and thoroughly destroyed, as the Nazi authorities had long planned. More than a quarter of the professional journalists fell victim to the war and the terror of the occupation force. In 1944 the *Biuletyn Specjalny* of the Interior Ministry of the Polish government-in-exile in London published a list of fallen Polish journalists, which as of March 14, 1944, contained 81 names. As its publishers noted, the list mainly included members of the Warsaw journalists' association.[3] After the war, Władiysław Dunin-Wąsowicz published statistics on the fates of 350 journalists, based on material he had collected during the occupation and had later supplemented. These showed 22 killed in the September campaign, 6 killed in other battles, 7 murdered at Katyn, 73 shot and killed, 77 killed in prisons and concentration camps, 50 killed in ghettos, 3 killed in accidents and catastrophes, 12 missing, 16 killed in the Warsaw uprising, and 84 who died of wounds, exhaustion, and infirmity.

In the GG, where 55 percent of all the prewar newspapers and journals published in Poland appeared, publishing activity was crippled by orders that the Nazis represented as the "new press laws."[4] The first of these was the order of October 26, 1939, which made the publication and sale of all printed material subject to approval. A few days later, on October 31, Frank signed the first executive order regarding publishing in its entirety, making the continuation, establishment, and supply of publishing enterprises of every kind dependent on permission from the Department of Public Enlightenment and Propaganda.[5] There followed a series of additional implementation regulations specifying more precisely the principles of the "new press laws." For example, the October 26 order resulted in an implementation regulation dated September 5, 1940, which specified that the approval requirement applied to all publications (books, press, leaflets, directories, calendars, news sheets with headlines, games, notes, atlases and globes) regardless of the technique by which they were produced (printing press, mimeograph, typewriter, or by hand).[6] An implementation regulation dated October 24, 1940, for the order of October 31, 1939, forbade authors to publish their own books, brochures, calendars, or music.[7] All these measures simply legalized a situation that had long existed.[8] They lent an appearance of legality, which Frank, an attorney, was especially sensitive to. At the same time, they were designed to discourage illegal publishing activity and were addressed primarily to Polish printers that — especially in the early period of the occupation — accepted orders from clandestine publishers.[9]

Formally, publishing activity in the GG was not banned: the orders spoke only of a requirement of approval.[10] In practice, however, approval was granted only in six very specific cases, allowing the continued publication of *Wiadomości Gospodarcze* (Economic News), *Kielecki Przegląd Diecezjalny* (Review of the Diocese of Kielce), *Kronika Diecezji Sandomierskiej* (Chronicle of the Diocese of Sandomierz), *Posłaniec Serca Jezusowego* (Messenger of the Sacred Heart), *Rycerz Niepokalanej* (Knight of the Immaculate Conception), and *Biuletyn Informacyjny Polskiego Czerwonego Krzyża* (Information Bulletin of the Polish Red Cross).[11]

Wiadomości Gospodarcze

Before the war, *Wiadomości Gospodarcze* had been the monthly bulletin of the Warsaw Chamber of Commerce and Industry, publishing advice on economic and social problems along with official news. After the surrender of Warsaw, the president of the chamber, Minister Czesław Klarner, and its director, Bolesław Rutkowski, endeavored to get from Dr. Alfred Otto, Reich commissar for the city, permission to continue the journal. On October 28 the chamber was informed in writing that the Reich commissar had no objection to the printing of the "News of the Chamber of Commerce in Warsaw."[12] Ten days later, on November 7, the first issue of *Wiadomości Gospodarcze* appeared; the publisher, as before the war, was Andrzej Jeziorański. But the paper had changed; it was now a weekly presenting purely official information, mainly reports of regulations, orders, and instructions of the German authorities on economic and commercial issues, advice to merchants and industrialists on arranging formalities for the opening and continuation of their companies, and updates on the work and plans of the Chamber of Commerce and Industry, including a list of companies and advertisements.

Soon, however, like all other such organizations in the GG, the Warsaw Chamber of Commerce and Industry lost its independence and ceased to be an institution of economic self-administration. In a memorandum of November 20, 1939, the head of the Warsaw district, Dr. Ludwig Fischer, appointed Dr. Friedrich Wilhelm Baron von Gregory provisional director of the chamber and Gerhard Kowal the baron's deputy. Kowal served as Fischer's proxy. At the same time Klarner, the Polish president of the chamber, was dismissed.[13] Subsequently, in late 1940 and early 1941, all Chambers of Commerce and Industry in the GG were coordinated, following the model of the Reich, and placed under the control of the Central Chamber for the Total Economy, in Kraków.[14] Thus, *Wiadomości Gospodarcze* can hardly be considered a Polish journal, and its transition to an organ of the German administration is indicated by the fact that on October 2, 1940, the name of the publisher disappeared from the journal, whose name was changed to *Biuletyn Informacynjy Izby Przemysłowo-Handlowej w Warszawie* (Information Bulletin of the Chamber of Commerce and Industry in Warsaw).[15]

Kielecki Przegląd Diecezjalny and *Kronika Diecezji Sandomierskiej*

Between the two world wars, each of the five Catholic archdioceses and fifteen dioceses in Poland had its own periodical. There was a total of 228 Polish-language religious newspapers and journals.[16] The attitude of the Polish clergy toward the occupation force is generally known. We need only recall that most of the clergymen in the concentration camps were Polish priests.[17] Although the occupying force fought the church and the practice of religion in Poland, it also attempted repeatedly to exploit the priesthood for its specific economic and political purposes. Aware of the authority of the church and its influence on society, German officials endeavored to use it for their own purposes — for example, to recruit forced labor for the Reich, to insure that the obligatory quotas of food were sent to the Reich from the GG, and to assist in the struggle against the resistance movement.

The Nazis' attempt to misuse the pulpit against Polish interests encountered sharp protest from church leaders. As the underground organizations and the government-in-exile in London noted during the occupation,[18] symptoms of a reprehensible loyalty to the orders of the German authorities were discerned only in two dioceses, Kielce and Sandomierz. Both had asked for permission to continue publication of the periodicals.

The first wartime issue of the *Kielecki Przegląd Diecezjalny* (no. 10) appeared in October 1939, put out by its previous editor, the Reverend Jan

Jaroszewski. Not until October 1941 was he replaced by the chancellor of the diocese, the Reverend Leonard Świderski. As before the war, the official section of the *Przegląd* published messages of the Holy Father, orders of the Apostolic See, pastoral letters, and orders and communications from the diocesan curia. There was a spiritual column (which included such articles as "How Do We Form a Conscience?" and "How Can One Train Believers?"); obituaries and discussions of contemporary religious literature were also printed. However, social and political subjects, which had previously appeared under the rubric of unofficial publications, disappeared from the journal. In a pastoral letter printed in the October 1939 *Przegląd*, the bishop of Kielce, Czesław Kaczmarek, appealed to the clergy "to exclude every political element from your addresses and to proclaim only the pure word of God, the Gospels, and their application to life."[19] It is significant, however, that of everything published in the *Przegląd* only the bishop's letter had a serious political tone. The following also appeared in that letter: "I call on you to observe conscientiously all regulations and laws of the administrative as well as the military authorities. We believe in the promise given to us that we will not be ordered to do anything that is contrary to Catholic conscience.[20] Order must reign in society. Hence, we must cooperate loyally with the authorities; for anyone who behaves differently does an injustice to the community and hinders the return to normal life and better days."[21]

In the May–June 1940 issue the *Przegląd* published the third pastoral letter, which was read from the pulpit before the sermon on Sundays and holidays. It, too, called on the clergy to refrain from all comment, an instruction that is understandable in the light of the following: "We must not heed the insinuations of dubious lest they attempt to involve our population, especially the youth, in unpredictable plots. The German authorities have left us freedom in church and religious life, in accordance with their promise. Do not allow this freedom to be taken from us or limited as a result of imprudent steps or some political demonstration."[22]

Similar warnings came from the bishop of Sandomierz, Jan Lorek, who wrote in his pastoral letter of April 2, 1940, published in the *Kronika Diecezji Sandomierskiej:* "As your pastor and the spiritual father of all members of the Diocese, I warn you fervently to maintain great calm and balance in this situation. Heed no rumors and protect yourself against all imprudent acts that expose our country to even greater misery and bring down new misfortune on our tormented people." In the same issue Bishop Lorek ratified a proclamation concerning laborers sent to Germany: "I have received from the Office of the Generalgouvernement for Church Affairs in Kraków a memorandum complaining about clergy who occasionally hinder the recruitment of laborers who want to volunteer for farm work in the Reich. In announcing these warnings, I recommend that the reverend clergy give standard explanations in harmony with the publication of the labor offices, and I request them to maintain contact with members of their flock who have gone off for seasonal labor, urging these members to practice thrift and maintain belief and good morals away from home."[23] The bishop's pronouncements were commented on in a similar spirit appropriately in the July 1, 1940, issue of the *Nowy Kurier Warszawski,* under the rubric "Letters to the Editor": "Bishop Lorek's proclamation . . . is the best example of how the broadest Catholic audience thinks and how, in the face of the terror concocted by the Jews and their Freemason accomplices, they have had to conceal their so-called public opinion."

The *Kronika Diecezji Sandomierskiej,* which printed Bishop Lorek's pastoral letter in its first war edition (9–12), came out in December 1939.[24] Unlike the *Przegląd,* the *Kronika* almost exclusively published official communications and reports of the curia. Eleven issues appeared, each progressively slimmer. In January 1943, by order of the German authorities, publication was ceased — ostensibly to save paper.[25] One month later, the GG authorities also put a stop to the *Przegląd,* after the following incident, which led to considerable confusion among the authorities of the District of Radom and the government of the GG.

On August 18, 1942, the director of the Department for Internal Affairs in the Generalgouvernement, Dr. Ludwig Siebert, sent a memorandum to the Office of the Bishop in Kielce urging that mass on Sundays and holidays not keep the rural population away from their work during the harvest and sowing. The bishop replied that he would order mass held in the early morning hours.[26] The following notice was published in the *Przegląd:* "In view of the catastrophic delay in harvesting and sowing, the government of the GG in Kraków has appealed to the Office of the Bishop to keep the rural population at work in the fields on Sundays and holidays. Out of concern for feeding the population, it is hereby ordered that during this year's harvesting and sowing, mass be read as early as possible on Sundays and holidays so the population can set out for the fields immediately after the fulfillment of their Catholic duty."[27] The phrase "in view of the catastrophic delay in harvesting and sowing" provoked a prompt reaction from the German authorities. This was not surprising since in the German Polish-language press, the precise opposite was to be read. First, the propaganda department in Kielce intervened, demanding that all issues of the *Przegląd* henceforth be submitted to the censor. (Previously, the *Przegląd* had given the propaganda department only oral notification of the planned contents of the issues.)[28] Later, the propaganda department of the District of Radom also intervened. In a memorandum to Bishop Kaczmarek and the editorial staff of the *Przegląd,* the propaganda department sharply demanded the immediate removal of the Reverend Leonard Świderski as editor-in-chief and declared that a suc- cessor would have to be approved by the German authorities. Moreover, the editorial staff of the *Przegląd* was to submit all manuscripts for publication directly to the district propaganda department in Radom, not to the office in Kielce, which was said to lack a person "with an adequate command of Polish."[29] A. Szafrański succeeded Świderski as editor of the *Przegląd* but put out only one issue. In it, alongside items of information from the curia, was the following notice: "By order of the [German] authorities, publication of the *Przegląd* is stopped."[30] That was in January 1943.

Posłaniec Serca Jezusowego

In the early days of the occupation, the Jesuits also resumed publishing, albeit quite modestly. Aside from printing calendars, they were permitted to publish the *Poslaniec Serca Jezusowego,* which had appeared in Poland since 1872. Soon after the appearance of the first war issue (no. 10, October 1939), Gestapo agents came to the Jesuit college at Kraków, where the editorial staff was located, and arrested twenty-six clergymen, including the editor of the *Posłaniec,* Józef Cyrk. He was imprisoned for months, first in the Kraków Montelupie Prison, then in Wiślicz, near Bochnia; he was transferred to Auschwitz and on September 2, 1940, finally succumbed.[31] Nevertheless, until July 1940 nine issues of the *Posłaniec* appeared with exclusively religious contents.[32] The editorial staff had stated its goal in the first war edition: "Despite constant difficulties, we have decided to go on publishing the *Posłaniec,* even in a smaller size and more modest form. In this hard time, as never before, one must stir trust in the protection of God's Heart and in pleas to Him, and also strengthen and reinforce human hearts oppressed by difficult events. The *Posłaniec* would like to carry out this twofold task and remind worshipers of the Heart of God and the great power of prayer."[33] The Germans, however, put an end to the *Posłaniec* as well as to the entire publishing house by plundering the house's well-equipped printing press and book bindery.[34]

Rycerz Niepokalanej

The founder and publisher of the *Rycerz,* the Franciscan monk Maximilian Maria Kolbe,[35] a member of the board of directors of the Polish Association of Newspaper and Journal Publishers, had no illusions about the intentions of the German occupation force when he sought permission to resume his paper in 1940. But he had witnessed and suffered the events of September 19, 1939, when German troops occupied the Franciscan monastery of Niepokalanów. Kolbe and forty-six other monks were sent to the Sachsenhausen concentration camp; the monastery and the publishing enterprise were plundered. Three months later, the monks were freed after the intervention of the pope, the Italian king, the Hungarian Reich regent, and foreign scholars.[36]

On his return from Sachsenhausen, Kolbe wanted to revive the *Rycerz* and applied to the propaganda department of the Warsaw district, submitting all the material in typescript. He received permission to put out one issue, which could be sold only in the Warsaw district.[37] That issue, modeled on the prewar paper, appeared for sale at the end of 1940 (December–January). it consisted of poems and stories devoted to the Virgin Mary, letters of gratitude from people who had been saved by miracles, a description of the salvation of Piotr Ruddler according to the Book of Revelation and the miracle of Lourdes, and so on.

The appearance of the *Rycerz* drew sharp protest from the illegal press. *Barykada Wolności* (Barricade of Freedom), the organ of the Polish socialists, wrote on March 9, 1941: "The Catholic church is under frightening persecution by the Nazi barbarians; all the more amazing is the favor that has befallen the Franciscan fathers of Niepokalanów, whom the German Department for Public Enlightenment and Propaganda has allowed to publish their *Rycerz*. Has the organ of the clerical philistines and obscurantists done something to earn the grace of the occupier, to make the German authorities support everything that debases the Polish population? The activity of the *Rycerz* helps the occupier in his plan to disseminate as much ignorance as possible among the Polish people."[38] The editors of the *Barykada Wolności* evidently did not know that on January 30, 1941, the German authorities had already rejected the publication of the next issue of the *Rycerz*.[39] Three weeks later, Father Kolbe was sent to Auschwitz, where he died a martyr's death, volunteering to take the place of a fellow inmate who had been condemned to death in retaliation for an escape attempt.[40] One year and one week later, the founder and editor of the *Barykada Wolności*, Stanisław Dubois, also perished in Auschwitz. *Ille hodie et ego cras!*

Biuletyn Informacyjny Polskiego Czerwonego Krzyża

There are no extant copies of the *Biuletyn Informacyjny Polskiego Czerwonego Krzyża,* and thus our information comes from secondary sources.[41]

Even its title is in question. One source states that it was called *Komunikat*; according to another, it was *Informator*; and a third claims it was *Biuletyn Informacyjny*.[42] Contradictory information has also emerged about its circulation, and precise data about its contents is lacking.[43] We can only ascertain generally that it was an internal Red Cross staff publication concerned with the work of the central office and the individual departments, as well as with moral and material support for prisoners of war, concentration camp inmates, and evacuated families and other such charitable activities.

The bulletin appeared in Warsaw throughout almost the entire occupation as an information organ of the Polish Red Cross.[44] In some ways it was the continuation of a publication from the Polish-Soviet war of 1920.[45] During the occupation the information office of the Polish Red Cross was a legal institution that the German authorities had to deal with to a certain extent because its activity was based on decisions set forth in paragraphs 77 and 78 of the Geneva Convention of 1929 governing treatment of the sick and wounded and prisoners of war. Thanks to these decisions, agreed on by both Poland and Germany, the occupation force, which had restricted all other Red Cross work, allowed the official activity of the information office to go on. Even though protected by the Geneva Convention, however, the office was not spared the terror of the occupation. In 1942 the publisher of the information bulletin, Emilia Grocholska, perished in Auschwitz; and in October 1942 the director of the office, Maria Bortnowska, was sent to Ravensbrück.[46]

Wiadomości RGO

Wiadomości RGO (News of the Main Welfare Council) was never published, but its history sheds light on German policy with regard to the publications of Polish institutions. It appears to have been initiated at the end of 1939 by Count Adam Ronikier, the president of the so-called Main Welfare Council (RGO), a charitable institution officially recognized by the Germans. Everything seemed to indicate that it would soon appear, and in Polish circles people spoke quite openly of its imminent publication; the *Staatsbibliothek* in Kraków (formerly the *Biblioteka Jagiellonska*) was already waiting for a presentation copy.[47]

According to the publisher's announcement in the draft of the first issue, the paper was to be a "link between those who need help and those who can give help." The publisher's more comprehensive intentions, however, appear in an editorial announcing that, in addition to covering issues of social welfare and charity, the paper intended to carry information concerning the whereabouts of those who were repatriated and evacuated, and to deal with events of significance for the activity of the Main Welfare Council. A letters-to-the-editor section and advertisements were also planned. The paper was to cost fifty groschen in the GG,[48] but the completed first issue, with the blessing of Archbishop Adam S. Sapieha on the title page, was never published.[49] Where and at what stage the decision against publication was made cannot be determined precisely, but the assumption that the highest authorities of the GG were responsible would seem to be borne out by the following summaries from minutes of RGO board meetings and conferences.[50]

> September 6, 1940 — Ronikier announces that the police authorities have withdrawn their objection to the publication of the *Wiadomości* RGO.

> September 29, 1940 — Ronikier states that the highest authority has given permission, in principle; the first issue is with the censor.

> February 10, 1941 — Ronikier presents to the gathering the first issue of the *Komunikat,* published by the Polish Red Cross with permission of the authorities, as proof that further endeavors to obtain permission should be successful and thus should be resumed.

> February 15, 1941 — Dr. Froehl[51] reaches an agreement with the publisher of a *Communiqué of the Main Welfare Council*; the president states that until further notice the Main Welfare Council intends to publish a *Bulletin of the Main Welfare Council* every two weeks in an edition of 1,500 copies. Dr. Froehl accepts the first issue of the *Wiadomości* RGO for inspection. With his approval, it will appear bimonthly as an internal bulletin of the Main Welfare Council.

> March 3, 1941 — The question of the information bulletin is presented by Dr. Froehl for a decision.

> March 28, 1941 — The question of the information bulletin is discussed with Heinrich [probably Froehl's superior].

> March 29, 1941 — Dr. Froehl consents to the publication of the information bulletin and requests submission of an application, which he will confirm before the Easter holiday.

The *Wiadomości* RGO appeared neither before nor after Easter. Specimen copies of the first issue, with various dates (August 15, September 15, October and November 1940) and with several deletions by the censor, are additional proof that this matter was often investigated before permission for publication was finally refused.[52]

The Dissolution of the Polish Association of Newspaper and Journal Publishers

Since the Polish press had ceased to exist, there was a question of whether it made sense to continue the Polish Association of Newspaper and Journal Publishers. *Wiadomości Gospodarcze, Posłaniec Serca Jezusowego,* and *Rycerz Niepokalanej* appeared only sporadically, while the Polish Red Cross's bulletin owed its existence solely to the Geneva Convention. Under the prevailing conditions, the diocesan journals would also have to disappear sooner or later; the only things printed in them were the full texts of papal addresses and messages — in normal circumstances, such a dearth of material would have been inconceivable in a Catholic country like Poland. German hopes for greater cooperation with the church were dashed in both dioceses, Kielce and Sandomierz. From the middle of 1940, there is not a single line in the *Przegląd* or in the *Kronika* that would indicate loyalty to the occupation force. The general resistance of the nation obviously also affected the church in these two dioceses, neither of which had any lack of clergy imprisoned or tortured to death.[53]

All those Polish journals owed their appearance solely to the individual efforts of their publishers; the Polish Association of Newspaper and Journal Publishers was not involved. By November 28, 1939, the executive board of the association decided to recommend to its assembly the dissolution of the association. But even that required official permission from the German authorities. In preparation, the governors decided to cease the activity of the association's agencies for the time being, to break contracts with the staff, and to order the sale or rental of the building. The liquidation committee consisted of Bolesław Biega, Stanisław Kauzik, and Stefan Krzywoszewski.[54]

The legal liquidation of the publishers' association was accelerated by Frank's order of July 23, 1940, requiring the dissolution of Polish associations in the GG.[55] Initially the agencies of the association defended themselves by arguing that their organization had been established according to the Polish law of association, but in 1934 the provisions of the industrial law had been rescinded.[56] The leaders of the association, however, were interested not in continuation — which was hopeless anyway — but in saving the association's property; for paragraph 5 of the order of July 23, 1940, prescribed that the property of dissolved associations was to be awarded to the GG. Kauzik wrote to the commissioner of the district chief for the city of Warsaw,[57] but no German reply is extant. We do know that all the movable property of the association, including the library, was commandeered within forty-eight hours, and the Warsaw building of the association was transferred to a German burial society.[58]

7

The Polish-Language German Press

The press for the Polish population in the Generalgouvernement consisted of three major types: information and propaganda newspapers; propaganda journals of general interest as well as for specific social groups; and professional journals. The daily newspapers were the main organ of German propaganda. The publisher was the Zeitungsverlag Krakau-Warschau GmbH, a typical state enterprise of the GG, with "GmbH" ("Inc.") added only for form. The company used the confiscated property of the *Ilustrowany Kurier Codzienny,* the Warsaw Dom Prasy (Press House), the *Goniec Częstochowski,* the *Kurier Warszawski,* and other Polish publishers. Along with the central office in the Kraków press building, it had branches in Warsaw, Częstochowa, Lublin, Radom, and Kielce,[1] and, after the German attack on the Soviet Union and the annexation of the District of Galicia into the GG, also in Lwów. Throughout the entire occupation the director of the press was Heinz Strozyk.

The number of newspapers for the Polish population in the GG was absurdly small.[2] Including the provincial editions, there were only nine titles (table 7.1).[3] In addition, there were four propaganda journals of general interest and two for specific groups (table 7.2).[4] There were also twenty-two professional journals for individual professional groups, seventeen of them Polish-language and five bilingual (table 7.3).[5] These were published either by German publishers set up especially for this purpose, like Agrarverlag Ost, the publishing house for *Wirtschaft und Handwerk* (Economics and Trade), or by governmental bodies like the Department of Health and the Department of Science and Education. Moreover, German companies (Bayer Pharmaceuticals, for example), and their branches and joint-stock companies under German control, published their own professional journals. Without exception they were granted permission by the Department of Public Enlightenment and Propaganda.

Because there were few titles, the political daily and weekly newspapers and journals in the GG had large circulations, which rose every year despite a constant shortage of paper.[6] The publishers' main concern was the widest possible distribution of their propaganda materials. Hence prices for political newspapers and journals were artificially maintained at prewar levels despite the changed economic conditions.[7] Table 7.4 shows average circulation for the three types of print media — dailies, propaganda journals, and professional journals — in the GG;[8] table 7.5 shows average circulation for a few titles in 1941 and specific figures for October 31, 1942.[9] For large and medium-sized newspapers and journals, prewar circulation levels were fairly well maintained. But gross circulation is not a reliable measure of the size of newspaper and journal production. For a more complete picture, the size and format of individual journals must also be considered; even more instructive is the total paper use of the press as well as the average number of copies per capita annually. It turns out that before the war the annual demand for paper in Poland was over 37,000 tons and in the GG some three thousand tons.[10] The number of newspaper copies per capita before the war came to twenty-two; in the GG the number was only eight.

The Composition of Press Staff

The management and editorial staff of every newspaper and journal for Poland were in the hands of *Reichsdeutsche* and *Volksdeutsche*. Hans Frank commented in his diary that the GG was the only occupied territory where newspapers for foreigners were written by Germans.[11] The *Volksdeutche* were especially active. Most of them had been editors and journalists for the German papers that had come out in Poland from 1918 to 1939: Kurt Seidel of Łódź, editor-in-chief of the *Nowy Kurier Warszawski,* had been in charge of the *Freie Presse*; Leopold Reischer, editor of the *Goniec Krakowski,* was a former journalist and publisher from Bielitz; Karl Fenske, the head of Telepress, came from Bydgoszcz and had been a correspondent for the German press in Łódz and Poznań. Journalists of German origin who had worked with the Polish press before the war now went over to the occupation force. Alexander Schedlin-Czarliński, who became the editor of the occupation newspaper *Gazeta Lwowska,* was the prewar editor of the Polish telegraph agency in Poznań as well as a member of the Poznań department of the Polish Writers' Association; Józef Mazur, on the editorial staff of the *Nowy Kurier Warszawski,* had been a journalist for the *Kurier Poranny* before the war; Eugeniusz Riedel, the manager of the Warsaw department of the newspaper publisher "Warsaw-Kraków," had been the head editor of the Press House in Warsaw before 1939. Among the most important of the other *Volksdeutche* who were employed in the press for the Polish population were Felix Rufenach, editor of the *Nowy Kurier Warszawski* and the *Gazeta Lwowska*; Baron Felix Dangel, the director of the anti-Soviet department of Telepress; Zenziger, a representative of Fenske; and Felix Sandor, a member of the editorial staff of the *Nowy Kurier Warszawski.*

The number of *Reichsdeutsche* employed by the press for Poles was not

Table 7.1. Polish-language newspapers.

Title	Place of Publication	Dates of Publication	Ed'ns per Week	Pages	Format (cm.)	Distribution	Time of Day	Remarks
Nowy Kurier Warszawski	Warsaw, then Łódź	11/23/39–1/45	6	6–20	37.5×56	Warsaw city and district, other large GG cities	afternoon	
Goniec Krakowski	Kraków	10/27/39–1/45	6	4–8	31.5×47	throughout GG	afternoon	
Kurier Częstochowski	Częstochowa	11/4/39–1/45	6	4–8	31.5×47	Częstochowa, Radom district, Piotrków, other large GG cities	afternoon	
Nowy Czas	Kraków, occasionally Kielce and Jędrzejów	End of 1939–?	3	4–6	31.5×47	Jędrzejów, Radom district	afternoon	local ed. of *Goniec Krakowski*
Nowy Głos Lubelski	Lublin, occasionally Warsaw	1/20/40–7/44	3, later 6	4–8	31.5×47	Lublin city and district	afternoon	

Title	Place	Dates			Size	Localities	Time	Notes
Kurier Kielecki	Kraków, then Kielce	3/1/40–1/45	6	4–6	31.5–47	Kielce, Stopnica, Pińców, Włoszczowa	morning	local ed. of *Goniec Krakowski*
Dziennik Radomski	Kraków, after 12.2/41 Radom	3/1/40–1/45	6	4–6	31.5×47	Radom, smaller cities	morning	to 12/2/41 local ed. of *Goniec Krakowski*
Gazeta Lwowska	Lwów	8/9/41–6/44	6	4–8	32×41	Lwów, Galicia district	afternoon, after 8/28/41 morning	
Dziennik Por-anny	Kraków	3/1/40–7/42	6	4–6	31.5×47	Będzin, Bielsko, Sosnowice, Chrzanów, Olkusz, Blachownia, Zawiercie	morning	local ed. of *Goniec Krakowski*

Table 7.2. Polish-language journals.

Title	Publisher	Place	First Issue	Last Issue	Frequency	Format (cm)	Circ.	Remarks
Co Miesiąc Powieść	newspaper publisher	Warsaw	9/1/40	to 12/43	monthly	18×26.5	10,000	
Fala	newspaper publisher	Warsaw	5/1/40	to 12/43	weekly	17×23.8	10,000	illustrated tabloid
Ilustrowany Kurier Polski	newspaper publisher	Kraków	10/13/39	to 1/45	weekly	25×33.5	50,000	illustrated magazine
Kolejowiec	gen. admin. Ostbahn	Kraków	1/43	to 1944	monthly	24×31.7	130,000	prof. and propaganda journal
7 Dni	newspaper publisher	Warsaw	5/1/40	7/44	weekly	28×37.5	40,000	illustrated magazine
Siew	Agra-Verlag	Kraków	9/1/40	to 1/45	weekly	24.5×33	50,000	prof. and propaganda journal for agricultural workers

very large. A leading role was played by men like Georg Aurel Machura, editor-in-chief of the *Kurier Częstochowski*; Gustav Becker-Endemann, editor-in-chief of *Fala* and *7 dni*; Albert Georg Lehmann, editor-in-chief of *Siew* and *Gazeta Lwowska*; and Hans Apfel, editor of the *Ilustrowany Kurier Polski*.

The names of these *Reichsdeutche* and *Volksdeutsche* editors were not listed on the mastheads of the newspapers, and in the professional journals they were polonized. Thus, for example, on the editorial staff of the Agrar-Verlag. Franz Peter Lerz appeared as the agronomical engineer Franciszek Łorzyński, Hans Huppelsberg as Janusz Górski, and Heinrich Kwilitsch as Henryk Kwilecki.[12]

Approximately one hundred Poles were on the staffs of various papers and journals, including the editors of Telepress.[13] Who were these Poles and why did they choose to work in the reptile press? Many well-known Polish journalists, like Witold Giełżyński, Marian Grzegorczyk, Kazimierz Pollack, and Wanda Rostworowska firmly opposed cooperating with the press published by the occupiers despite receiving attractive offers of employment. Władysław Studnicki did not want to have anything to do with the reptile press either. In his memoirs he writes: "The director of the propaganda department asked me to write for the *Goniec Krakowski,* an organ of the occupation force. I refused since that was a German newspaper. 'But you have written for German papers.' 'A German paper for Germans is quite different from a German paper for Poles,' I replied. 'You offend us quite uselessly by printing your articles denouncing the Polish government. We were dissatisfied with it and we could curse it — but that was not an offense to our own people.' "[14]

The clandestine organization of journalists took a clear position when Frank issued the "Order on Cultural Activity in the Generalgouvernement"[15] on March 8, 1940, requiring all professional and nonprofessional publishers, booksellers, photographers, art dealers, journalists, writers, artists, painters, and musicians to register at the appropriate propaganda office and apply for permission to practice their professions.[16] This was an attempt to make writers, journalists, and artists serve German aims and to organize cultural life on the German model.

Registration itself did not mean a willingness to collaborate. Nevertheless, in private conversations with representatives of other professions, the journalists supported a total boycott of the order. Their scheme hardly had a chance of success under the conditions of terror, and the boycott was not as complete as the journalists demanded. In any case, even together with writers and publishers, the journalists were a minority among those professional groups who had to register. Since registration figures are, unfortu-

Table 7.3. Professional journals.

Gospodarka Wyżywienia. Wiadomości Centralnej Izby dla Ogólnej Gospodarki GG. / Die Ernährungswirtschaft. Mitteilungsblatt der Zentralkammer für die Gesamtwirtschaft im GG. Polish and German. Agrar-Verlag. Kraków. 10/20/41–1944. Biweekly. Quarto. Circ. 6,000–20,000.

Informator dla Spółdzielni Spożywców [?]. Polish Związek Spółdzielni Spożywców "Społem." Warsaw 7/20/40–1941. Biweekly. Octavo.

Las i Drzewo. Organ Oficjalny GG dla Spraw Leśnych, Drzewnych i Łowieckich. / Wald und Holz. Offizielles Organ des GG für Forst-, Holz- und Jagdwesen. Polish and German. Verlag Wald und Holz. Kraków. 10/1/40–1944. Weekly, then biweekly. Quarto. Circ. 5,500.

Mały Inwentarz. Organ Związku Hodowców Drobnego Inwentarza w Generalnym Gubernatorstwie. Polish. Agrar-Verlag. Kraków. 3/10/43–1944. Monthly. Quarto. Circ. 6,000.

Mały Ster. Ilustrowane Czasopismo dla Najmłodszych. Polish. Published by the Department of Science and Education, for use in elementary schools, grades 2–4. Warsaw. 2/1/42–1944. Monthly. Octavo.

Medycyna Współczesna. Miesięcznik Referatowy. Polish. Published by the Serological Institute. Warsaw. 5/40–1942. Monthly. Octavo. Circ. 3,000–7,500. (Before 9/39 published by *Towarzystwa Przemysłu Chem. Farm.*)

Miesięcznik Teatru Miasta Warszawy. Czasopismo Teatralne. Polish. Published by the Warsaw City Theater. Warsaw. 5/40–1942. Monthly. Octavo.

Ogrodnictwo. Organ Związków Ogrodniczych Generalnego Gubernatorstwa. / Der Gartenbau. Organ der Gartenbauverbánde des Generalgouvernements. Polish and German. Agrar-Verlag. Kraków. 9/1/42–1943. Monthly. Quarto. Circ. 6,000.

Pszczelarz Kielecki, after no. 9 (9/41) *Pszczelarz. Miesięcznik pszczelarski.* Published by Kielecki Związek Pszczelarzy, then Naczelny Związek Pszczelarzy GG; Agrar-Verlag. Kielce, after 1/41 Radom, after 9/41 Kraków. 6/1/40–1944. Monthly. Octavo, then quarto. Circ. 8,000, then 50,000.

Rolnik. Ilustrowane Pismo Rolnicze. Polish. Agrar-Verlag. Kraków. 5/4/41–1944. Weekly. Quarto. Circ. 50,000.

Rzemiosło. Czasopismo Grupy Głównej Gospodarka Przemysłowa przy Izbie Centralnej dla Gospodarki Ogólnej w Generalnym Gubernatorstwie. Polish. Verlag für Wirtschaft und Handwerk. Kraków. 6/1/42–1944. Biweekly. Quarto. Circ. 50,000.

Ster. Ilustrowane Czasopismo dla Młodzieý. Polish. Published by the Department of Science and Education. Warsaw. 10/1/40–1942. Monthly. Octavo. Circ. 100,000–600,000. Reader for grades 5–7.

Spółdzielca. Organ dla Spółdzielni w GG, later *Organ Państwowej Rady Spółdzielczej w GG.* Polish. Agrar-Verlag. Kraków. 10/20/41–1944. Biweekly.

Table 7.3. *(continued)*

Quarto. Circ. 12,000–19,000. Continuation of *Wiadomości Międzyzwiązkowej Spółdzielni Wydawniczej*. Polish and German. Published by Wirtschat und Handel. Kraków. 8/15/42–1944. Monthly. Quarto.

Weterynaryjne Wiadomości Terapeutyczne. Polish. Published by Bayer-Pharma. Warsaw. 1/41–1942. Quarterly. Octavo.

Wiadomości Aptekarskie. Organ Urzędowy Izby Aptekarskiej w Izbie Zdrowia dla Generalnego Gubernatorstwa. Polish. Published by Izba Aptekarska. Kraków. 6/15/40–1944. Biweekly. Quarto. Circ. 300,000.

Wiadomości Międzyzwiązkowej Spółdzielni Powierniczej. Organ Związku Spółdzielni Rolniczych i Zarobkowo-Gospodarczych. Polish. Warsaw. 8/1/40–1941. Biweekly. Quarto. Title taken over from a journal of 1938–39.

Wiadomości Terapeutyczne. Published by Bayer-Pharma. Warsaw. 1/40–1943. Monthly. Octavo. Before 9/39 published by Remedia.

Wzorowa Gospodarka. / Der Musterbetrieb. Polish and German. Agrar-Verlag. Kraków. 5/15/40–1944. Biweekly. Quarto. Circ. 12,000.

Zawód i Życie. Czasopismo Poświęcone Wiedzy Rzemieślniczej, Handloweji i Rolniczej. Polish. Published by the Department of Science and Education. Kraków. 3/41–1944. Monthly. Quarto. Circ. 40,000.

Zawód i Życie. Czasopismo Poświęcone Wiedzy Handlowej i Zawodom Kobiecym. Polish. Published by the Department of Science and Education. Kraków. 10/41–1944. Monthly. Quarto.

Zdrowie i Życie. Dziennik Urzędowy Izby Zdrowia w Generalnym Gubernatorstwie. Polish. Published by Izba Zdrowia / Gesundheitskammer. Kraków. 10/1/40–1944. Weekly. Quarto. Circ. 9,000.

---

nately, unavailable for the GG as a whole, we cite data for the District of Warsaw as illustration. The German statistics show the professions of the 4,801 persons who submitted registration cards to the propaganda department of the District of Warsaw. booksellers, 681; journalists, writers, and publishers, 165;[17] photographers, 582; actors, 1,356; musicians, composers, and singers, 1,412; painters, art dealers, and graphic artists, 605.[18] The low figure for journalists, writers, and publishers indicates that the representatives of these professions felt their work especially threatened by registration. A bookseller, photographer, musician, painter, or even an actor, not to mention an art dealer, who registered with the propaganda department did not necessarily have to act against his or her personal and national dignity. But that was hardly the case with journalists and writers, whose cooperation in publishing propaganda for the occupation force had to be unambiguous.

Table 7.4. Average circulation, 1939–1945

YEAR	1939	1940	1941	1942	1943	1944
Daily Newspapers	80,000	275,500	392,420	363,800	400,000	700,000
Propaganda Journals	—	62,750	228,280	319,000	—	620,000
Professional Journals	—	12,600	727,320	771,650	—	—

This was the view that was held a that time by Polish public opinion and by underground organizations.[19]

But every rule has an exception: among the numerous journalists and writers there were some who not only registered but also began working in the reptile press for various papers or the press agency. The composition of this group of about twenty persons was quite heterogeneous. Stanisław Wasylewski, for example, was a well-known novelist and essayist; he began collaborating with the *Gazeta Lwowska*; Tadeusz Starostecki, formerly a member of the peasant party (Wici) and the editor of two leftist papers advocating a united front, *Front Ludowy* (Popular Front) and *Głos Ludu Miast i Wsi* (Voice of the People of Cities and Country), worked on the *Kurier Częstochowski*; Zygmunt Kawecki, the prewar editor of the Katowice *Polonia,* and Józef Sierzputowski, a writer and broadcast journalist, worked for the *Nowy Kurier Warszwaski*; one of those employed at Telepress was Witold Horain, a renowned tennis player and sports reporter of the *Ilustrowany Kurier Częstochowski* in the prewar period. A few second- and third-rate journalists also worked in the reptile press, like H. Wielgomasowa, previously with the *Dziennik Łódzki,* H. Bukowska and Z. Stanisz, who had been with the *Kurier Poranny,* and L. Ziemkiewicz, formerly with the daily *5 Groszy.*

Most of the personnel in the reptile press, however, had had no previous connection with the press or journalism. These brand-new journalists — primarily young people — came from diverse circles. The editorial staffs of the occupation press generally recruited their personnel by themselves, either through advertisements — the Germans didn't force anyone to do *Pressearbeit,* even if it was extremely difficult to give up the work once undertaken — or through direct offers to many people at random. An illustration of this is a memorandum of November 12, 1940, from the editor of the *Kurier Częstochowski,* G. A. Machura, to the owner of a newspaper stand in Wloszczowo, one P. L., announcing that for business reasons a local chroni-

Table 7.5. Circulation of specific titles, 1941–1942

TITLE	1941	10/31/42
Nowy Kurier Warszawski	200,000	132,753
Goniec Krakowski	60,000	100,000
Kurier Częstochowski	30,000	27,831
Dziennik Radomski	30,000	13,143
Kurier Kielecki	20,000	1,764
Nowy Głos Lubelski	20,000	10,971
Gazeta Lwowska	—	65,103
Nowy Czas	—	2,915
Ilustrowany Kurier Pol-ski	50,000	80,729
Siew	50,000	14,980
7 Dni	40,000	30,000
Co Miesiąc Powieść	10,000	30,000
Fala	10,000	30,000

cle was being started. P. L. was asked if he would undertake the local reporting or would designate someone else for the task; naturally the work would be paid. The reporter would have to work closely with the municipality and other authorities. P. L. was further asked to give the names of the local Polish and German mayors.[20] The result of such solicitations was that among the Polish staff of the occupation press there were, for example, a former bookseller, a chauffeur, a student, a civil servant, and a teacher.

Various reasons and motives prompted these people to work for occupation publishers. Whatever one may think of the staffs of the occupation press, one thing seems certain: this collaboration was based neither on firm conviction nor on ideological motives. We can speak of collaboration in the true sense of the word only with regard to Emil Skiwski, Feliks Burdecki, and Jerzy de Nisau. (They are discussed in more detail later.) For many people, working on an occupation paper or journal was quite simply a well-paid job offering relative security and a sense of stability in difficult times. Aside from their own salaries, workers for the occupation press also got special bonuses; and the press card (red for Germans, white for Poles) was protection from street roundups and from deportation to Germany for forced labor or to the concentration camps. Others saw this work as an opportunity for social or career advancement. Among the workers of the reptile press there was no lack of credulous people[21] or of those who had accepted the reality of the occupation as a necessary and final evil. Frequently, those working on behalf of German propaganda claimed that they had been so assigned by Polish underground organizations, supposedly for espionage.[22] But at present there are no credible documents to confirm this explanation.[23] On the other hand, there were Poles who ceased working for the occupation press because of their experiences or under various other influences.[24] And it is known that a few journalists employed in the reptile press were engaged in sabotaging the editorial staffs, either in cooperation with secret organizations or on their own. This is proved by the arrest of many Polish staff members, for example, the arrest of five Telepress journalists in the summer of 1942 by the Gestapo.[25]

Poles also worked on professional journals. Aside from the regularly employed staff members, a small group of doctors, agronomists, and technicians undertook assignments to write articles on medicine, agriculture, and trade.[26]

8

The Press System in
the Third Reich and the
Generalgouvernement

Historians and sociologists have continued to be interested in how Nazism brought the press into line.[1] Any examination must necessarily deal with the most fundamental underlying questions: How did the author of *Mein Kampf* become the ruler of minds in such a highly civilized country as Germany, and how did he succeed in harnessing almost the entire nation to the realization of the goals and ideals elaborated in his book?

Most scholars agree that Hitler's success was achieved largely through terror and propaganda. These two dovetailed with each other, although as Franciszek Ryszka aptly comments, "Especially in the Anglo-Saxon countries, there is a whole literature on the history of Nazism and the Third Reich in which propaganda is described as a second instrument of rule, equivalent to terror. This view is correct only if we conceive of 'propaganda' very broadly, far beyond the generally accepted scope of the concept."[2]

When it came to propaganda — both in the narrow and in the broad sense of the word — the Nazis proceeded from the conviction, confirmed by their understanding of mass psychology, that with the right technique the average person can be made to believe in anything. They did not care, especially after their rise to power, whether the public was composed of persons of low intellectual development or of academics. All propaganda, declared Hitler, must be generally comprehensible; its level had to be calibrated to the powers of perception of the most limited among the target audience. According to Goebbels, the correct propaganda method was to pound something into the readers' heads until reason finally gave up.

The press, the best print medium for propaganda, was the optimal instrument in the pursuit of these goals, reaching almost all levels of society every day. And the press had at its disposal very simple methods of creating and shaping information to systematically influence readers in a precisely determined direction. All that was required was the appropriate technique and the machinery of terror, and the rulers of the Third Reich possessed both.

Hitler dealt with the politically differentiated German popular press with unusual haste and brutality. When he took power in Germany, there were 4,700 press titles. In 1944, toward the end of his rule, there were only 970, including those in the occupied territories, over 80 percent of which were publications of the Nazi party and its organizations.[3] The rest, mostly professional journals, had to conform strictly to the party line.

Like all other liberal professions in Germany, journalism was tightly controlled. After the Press Leadership Law (*Schriftleitergesetz*) was proclaimed on October 4, 1933, only German citizens of Aryan origin, married only to Aryans, could be staff members of the press; moreover, they had to possess the requisite characteristics for ideologically influencing public opinion. Among other things, paragraph 14 of this law required that journalists exclude from their newspapers whatever could weaken the Third Reich, the popular will, German military power, culture and economics, or anything considered harmful to the German people.[4]

The 1933 law obviously meant the end of freedom of the press. Hitler had never made any secret that freedom of the press was the greatest danger to the state. What was involved was not mere opposition to expression; internal foes required more drastic measures, and there were other means for that. As chief of propaganda for the Reich, Goebbels was concerned not with "dissidents" but with fellow Nazis. Thus, it was his conviction that legally determining who could be a publisher or a journalist and which goals the press staff had to serve were not sufficient guarantees that there would be uniformity throughout the press. Journalists, including the more than 15,000 members of the Reich's Association of the German Press, were only human and could err.[5] But they were not permitted to: their goodwill as Nazis was a lot, but not enough to insure the correct line. To achieve the desired effect, a proper system of information and control had to be created. Only thus could the Nazis achieve total control of the press; indeed, no undesirable news could escape these rules.

For a state with the motto *ein Volk, ein Reich, ein Führer,* there could be only one source of information; hence the German News Agency. The average citizen in the Reich and abroad knew the abbreviation DNB (Deutsche Nachrichtenbüro) mainly from the stylized press and radio reports. Before these reports reached readers and listeners, however, they had to go through the appropriate authorities of the control system. The most important function of the DNB was hardly editing news or gathering information, but rather selecting information, determining its level of secrecy, and distributing it to editorial staffs and others according to a predetermined list. The agency issued more than a dozen special bulletins, each in a different color to indicate the level of importance of the contents and the place of the recipients in the hierarchy of the state and party. According to Bernard Ferou, the unrestrained proliferation of secret bulletins led directly to police terror, but in Nazism it was precisely the reverse.

Publications of the DNB included the so-called blue service (*blauer Dienst*), a "glossary" for journalists providing correct commentary on news and information; the yellow service (*gelber Dienst*) for editors, which contained materials about specific recurring subjects (antisemitism, anti-bolshevism); a red bulletin (*DNB-rot*), for a very small group of senior editors, containing secret news; and a top-secret white bulletin (*DNB-weis*) restricted to ministers, higher state and party functionaries, and a few select journalists.[6] Of course, all the information in the two secret bulletins could be read in every newspaper abroad. Aside from private, secret, and top-secret publications, there were also the so-called daily and weekly catch phrases of the Reich's press chief (Dr. Otto Dietrich), distributed by telephone or telegraph to the local propaganda departments and the press.

The final, but most important, branch in the Nazi press system was the so-called press conferences in the Reich's Propaganda Ministry, in which the individual ministers, sometimes Goebbels himself or his deputy, participated. These took place daily—sometimes twice a day during the war. At these conferences, the press slogans were commented on for the benefit of representatives of almost all the newspapers of the Reich and the districts, as well as the political journals. Here the journalists learned firsthand, and with painstaking precision, what and how the press was to write, and what it was to keep silent about. These instructions mainly determined which news was to be published in the Berlin press and which in the provinces, as well as the contents of the editorials—which propaganda campaigns were to be accepted and which were to be stopped. The wording, size, and color of the headlines, and the selection and layout of illustrations, were also determined.

The press slogans and the interpretations given at the press conferences extended to all phenomena of public life—the problems of high politics as well as day-to-day life. Here are a few illustrations:

(October 10, 1935) On Sunday, an international dog show took place in Berlin. The dog of Fräulein Hess, sister of Rudolf Hess, is not to be given special mention [so as not to show that the dogs of people in high positions were better fed than working people]. (Directive No. 1774)

(February 13, 1936) Publicity in any form for Charlie Chaplin is absolutely undesirable. (Directive No. 166)

(January 26, 1937) A west German newspaper has engaged in polemics with Thomas Mann. This is absolutely undesirable. Thomas Mann is to be obliterated from the memory of every German since he is not worthy of being called German. (Directive No. 135)

(May 13, 1938) The problem of "whether Christ was a Jew" is often discussed in the journals. The entire German press is instructed not to deal with this question anymore. After 2,000 years this problem is no longer to be decided, and detailed treatment will only reinforce religious tension. (Directive No. 606)

(February 20, 1939) No more attacks are to be made on the late Pope Pius XI. [Previously, Pius XI had been heavily attacked in the Nazi press for his anti-Nazi encyclical *Mit brennender Sorge*.] (Directive No. 192)

(October 7, 1940) Prop. Min. Orders: the wearing of trousers by women is not subject to public criticism. We are not Puritans, and if it now becomes colder, women can safely wear trousers, even if the party has rebelled against it here and there. (Directive No. 138)[7]

After the attack on Poland, the Reich's Propaganda Ministry introduced a new type of press conference chaired by Goebbels, which took place from October 1939 until the end of the war and to which higher state and party functionaries and press liaisons of other key ministries were invited. These then conveyed the directives to the lower officials.[8] Since in such a system as this censorship as a special institution is superfluous, none was ever established.

The Mechanism and Structure of the Press in the Generalgouvernement

The press system in the Generalgouvernement bore only limited resemblance to the system in the Reich. The press in Germany had different tasks to fulfill than in the GG, as well as a completely different readership, a different subject matter, and a different sphere of activity.

In comparison with the Reich press, the structure of the occupation press was extremely simple. The main source of press information in the GG until July 1941 was the Telepress agency, Polskie Wiadomości Prasowe (Polish Press News), a counterpart — or more precisely a substitute — of the DNB. Telepress put out articles on various subjects following the guidelines of the GG press chief. Basic sources were teletype and cable from Berlin, which went into the office of the Kraków press building, as well as the general DNB bulletin (the "green service," *grüne Dienst*) and the Reich press. Telepress also had its own correspondents, who gathered material in government offices, bureaus, and other institutions of the GG. The selection of subjects, final editing, and control were in the hands of the German editors of Telepress, under whose supervision Polish journalists worked. Their main function was to translate articles and reports from German into Polish. When Ohlenbusch accused Gassner of a lack of vigilance over the Polish staff of Telepress, the latter explained that it was impossible to "have translations made by Germans into Polish, for it would be clear to every Pole who read such translations that the article was badly translated into Polish, and by a German to boot."[9]

The material processed at Telepress then went to individual editorial staffs as dispatches or bulletins. The press chief transmitted precise instructions as to how this material was to be processed and distributed to publishers through offices subordinate to him (Press Bureau, Telepress, newspaper Publishers). For example, in a long-distance telephone call on April 6, 1940, the newspaper publishers instructed the editorial staffs of individual papers to increase circulation by 10 percent the next day because certain documents of the Polish Foreign Ministry, found by the Germans in October 1939, were to be published. All street vendors were to shout the identical headlines for all publications: "This Is How Poland Was Deceived."[10]

The daily press presented the news and the articles of Telepress on the first two or three pages. There were abridged versions of events on the battlefield or military analyses from the Reich press, foreign news, and news from occupied Poland, reviews of the newspapers in the satellite and neutral countries, speeches of leading figures in the Third Reich and the GG, commentaries, editorials, notices, and so on. Practically identical articles appeared in all the newspapers, but they might appear on different dates and on different pages or columns, and the number of lines, the syntax, the headlines, and the signature might differ. Compare, for example, items run on the same day by the GG newspapers *Goniec Krakowski* and *Kurier Częstochowski* on August 8 and September 2 and 5, 1940:

Goniec Krakowski, August 8, 1940, p. 1:
　　Imposing Survey. Five Million Tons Sunk
　　Reconnaissance Flights over Malta
　　Southern England's Ports in Rubble
　　Vatican State Citizenship for Diplomats
Kurier Częstochowski, August 8, 1940, p. 1:
　　Almost Five Million Tons on the Bottom of the Sea
　　Italian News Front
　　Southern England's Ports in Rubble

Goniec Krakowski, August 8, 1940, p. 2:
　　English Confiscate Japanese Mail
　　Sensational Arrest in Canada
　　Japan's Decisive Position on English Provocation
　　Arrest of Salvation Army Officers in Japan
Kurier Częstochowski, August 8, 1940, p. 2:
　　Vatican State Citizenship for Diplomats
　　English Steal (Japanese) Mail for South America

Sensational Arrest in Canada
Japan's Decisive Position on English Provocation
Arrest of Salvation Army Officers in Japan

Goniec Krakowski, August 8, p. 3:
Dismissal of Reservists in Sweden
"American Legion" Against Intervention in the War
Kurier Częstochowski, August 8, p. 3:
Dismissal of Reservists in Sweden
Protests Against Introduction of Military Service in the U.S.
Article, August 8, 1940

Goniec Krakowski, August 8, 1940, p. 2:
We Speak Out!
England's Retreat in the Far East
Kurier Częstochowski, August 8, 1940, p. 1:
Slow but Systematic
England's Retreat in the Far East

Goniec Krakowski, September 2, 1940, p. 2:
From the Black to the White Sea [on the success
of the German military]
Berlin, September 1
Kurier Częstochowski, September 2, 1940, p. 1:
From the Black to the White Sea
Kraków in September
September 5, 1941
Goniec Krakowski, September 5, 1941, p. 2:
Finns on the Attack
Berlin, September 4
Kurier Częstochowski, Septermber 5, 1941, p. 1:
Finns on the Attack
Kraków in September

The following identical or nearly identical headlines appeared in the *Goniec Krakowski* and *Nowy Kurier Warszawski:*

Goniec Krakowski, October 9, 1940:
Reinforcement of Japan's Internal Front
Japanese Air Force Controls the Situation
Nowy Kurier Warszawski, October 8, 1940:
Japan Will Not Tolerate Foreign Intervention
Japanese Air Force in Indochina Controls Roads from Burma to China

Goniec Krakowski, October 16, 1940:
  Largest Bombing Attacks in World History
Nowy Kurier Warszawski, October 17, 1940:
  Largest Bombing Attacks in World History

Goniec Krakowski, October 24, 1940:
  Former Foreign Minister Beck Arrested in Bucharest
Nowy Kurier Warszawski, October 23, 1940:
  Józef Beck Arrested in Bucharest

Goniec Krakowski, October 26, 1940:
  Reichschancellor Hitler Receives Marshall Pétain
Nowy Kurier Warszawski, October 25, 1940:
  Hitler-Pétain Conference

Goniec Krakowski, October 29, 1940:
  Unsuccessful Flight [of Józef Beck, the Polish foreign minister]
Nowy Kurier Warszawski, October 29, 1940:
  Beck's Unsuccessful Flight

Goniec Krakowski, October 8, 1940:
  Polish Building Service [*Polnische Baudienst*] Works on the Recon-
  struction of Streets and Bridges
Nowy Kurier Warszawski, October 10, 1940
  Polish Building Service Works on the Reconstruction of Streets and
  Bridges

Goniec Krakowski, July 9, 1941:
  Bolshevism — The Work of Satan
Nowy Kurier Warszawski, July 9, 1941
  Blood Runs Everywhere . . .

Goniec Krakowski, September 12, 1941:
  A Steel Ring Around Leningrad. From a War Correspondent
Nowy Kurier Warszawski, September 12, 1941:
  Wanderings of the Russian Captives. Macabre Procession of the Rem-
  nants of the Bolshevik Army [Report of a War Correspondent]

It would be superfluous to compare the *Goniec Krakowski* with the *Kurier
Kielecki, Dziennik Radomski,* or *Nowy Czas.* These were essentially faithful
copies of the big-city newspaper — except for the name and the fourth (last)
page, which printed local news and announcements followed by exact
reprints from the *Goniec Krakowski,* the so-called "leading organ of the
Polish press for the entire Generalgouvernement." [11] The other newspapers

of the GG, for example *Głos Lubelski* and *Gazeta Lwowska,* reprinted material from Telepress.

The news service of Telepress was reprinted in the newspapers anonymously, and the articles were not signed. Foreign news was supplied with local information to give the impression that it came directly from the major cities of the world, and was dated arbitrarily. Similar battle reports from the Pacific appeared under the dateline "Tokyo, December 14, 1941" in one newspaper, and "Tokyo, December 17, 1941" in another.[12] Extracts and articles from the Reich German press and from the foreign press often appeared only when they were long outdated, and without specific information about their origin. For example, some seven days after the beginning of the massive Russian counteroffensive northwest of Moscow and two days after the breakthrough, the *Nowy Kurier Warszawski* reprinted an article that said: "The battle in Moscow . . . has taken a definitely favorable course for the Germans in recent days. . . . German circles state that the progress of the German attack on the Bolshevik capital has assumed such dimensions that with a good pair of binoculars you can observe the city of Moscow clearly.[13]

All publications in the GG press — war reports, agency items, announcements and newspaper reviews, articles, feuilletons, and illustrations — would be aligned on a certain subject or issue. In the first phase of the war this most often was England, but after June 22, 1941, it was the Soviet Union. The reader who bought the ten pages of the *Nowy Kurier Warszawski* on November 25, 1939 — six pages were filled with announcements — found the following headlines on the first page:

New British Cruiser Sunk by Torpedo
Clear Inflation Tendency [in England]
English Explanations . . . of Catastrophes Caused by Mines
England Saves Foreign Currency
Export Blockade Contradicts International Law. The American Press on
the Announcement of English Reprisals
Asocial England [headline over illustration]. "Liberal" England Treats
People with Other Views with Unheard-of Brutality. Our Picture
Shows the Imprisonment of People for "Disturbance of Public Order."

And on the third page:

England Asks — Germany Answers. Search for the War Aim in England
Goes On
"Revelations" of British News Services
Overwhelming Superiority [of the Luftwaffe over the RAF]

On page 4:

The Neutral Press on Britain's Difficulties

Without Payment or Support. Legal Proceedings Reveal Frightening
  Conditions in England

Pacifist Demonstrations in the House of Commons

He Who Goes to England Trembles for His Life

Churchill's War Trophies [political feuilleton]

A Neutral Look at the Food Market in England

The *Kurier Częstochowski* of July 9, 1941, devoted the entire front page
and most of the second to the Soviet Union. The headlines on page 1 ran:

Progress of the German-Romanian Assault in Bessarabia
The Stalin Line Breached in a Few Places
An American on the Bloodbath in Lwów
The Theory of Bolshevism Must Be Defeated

Second page:

Bolshevism — the Work of the Devil
Beastly Massacre of 1500 Prisoners in Łuck
How the Bolsheviks Are Preparing for an Attack on Europe
The Meaning of the War Against Russia
Catholic Circles in the U.S. Against Help for Moscow
French Legion of Volunteers Against Russia

The Jews were the target of a systematic propaganda campaign from the
first day of the occupation to the last. For example, in one week selected at
random (August 25–31, 1941), the *Gazeta Lwowska* published, along with
their own articles, eleven agency items:

Riots in Baghdad. Death Sentences for Antisemites
Bulgaria Seizes Two Billion Contributions from Jews
Jewish Locusts in Syria and Lebanon. Deceit Infuriates the Population
The Judeo-Communists at Work. Abuse of the Right of Asylum [by
  Jewish immigrants in the U.S.]
Jews in England Protected [by the government]
Jewish Airplanes — and the Crews? Goyim
Forced Labor for Jews in Romania
"The Jew in France" (Paris Exhibit on the Pernicious Role of the Jews
  and the Synagogue)
France Liberates Itself from the Judeo-Communists
New Law Against Jews in France
What Is Going On in the Country? Modern Balagulys [rickshaw drivers]
  in [the ghetto of] Warsaw

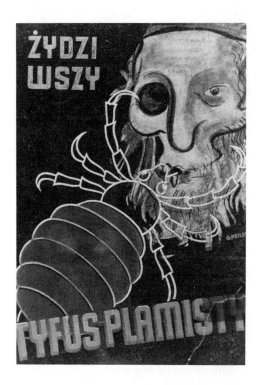

Fig. 2. "Jews, Lice, Spotted Fever," a Nazi propaganda poster put up throughout Warsaw to justify the establishment of the ghetto.

Telepress material comprised some 50 to 60 percent of all newspapers, not including announcements and advertisements. The editorial staff filled out the rest of the space with its own material, but even here a standard pattern was obligatory for all newspapers in the GG.

Despite so much directed uniformity in subject matter, each of these papers also had its own special character. Thus, the *Kurier Częstochowski* published a supplement primarily for Catholics with contributions on the "defense" of religion and Christianity;[14] the *Nowy Kurier Warszawski* published more agency news, an expanded theater and entertainment section, and a letters-to-the-editor column; the *Nowy Głos Lubelski* printed numerous articles on agriculture; the *Gazeta Lwowska* was distinguished for especially intensive anti-Soviet propaganda; and the *Goniec Krakowski* was known for its editorials and for its detailed section for official announcements and orders.

All editorial work in the individual papers was in German hands, and Germans also served as censors. In cases of argument or doubt, the manuscript was sent to the Press Department for confirmation before printing. The head censor was the press chief of the administration of the General-gouvernement.[15]

About a dozen Polish journalists were employed on every editorial staff. They were under double supervision — by the German journalists and by the Gestapo.[16] They had no influence over the direction and character of the press in the GG, even though they wrote most of the articles that did not come from Telepress. Polish journalists had to fulfill the tasks they were assigned and handle the subjects ordered as best they could, and be helpful to the German editors with ideas and advice. The Germans entrusted certain political columns of their paper to especially zealous journalists, for example, "Light and Shadows," "Magic Lantern," "With the Broom"; others were allowed to run ostensibly neutral sections like "The Week in Theater," the style section, the woman's section, and "Housewife's Corner." Polish journalists signed their articles with their own name, a pseudonym, initials, or a pen name.

9

The Content

The press of the Generalgouvernement generally covered three subjects: the war and international events; Polish affairs; and issues of the GG. This arrangement was, in a certain sense, both natural and logical. However, the criteria applied by the press to the choice of material on the war and foreign affairs differed from those used for the treatment of Polish affairs and issues of the GG; hence the two groups of subjects need be analyzed separately.

War and Foreign Events

Publications in these two areas were to serve as proof of and testimony to the invincible might of the Third Reich. That was the main theme of Nazi propaganda. It was proclaimed *per fas et nefas* during the whole occupation in Poland, at the time when no one questioned the victory of the Wehrmacht but also later, when the Wehrmacht suffered serious defeats on all fronts. Even on January 14, 1945, one could read in a Polish-language German newspaper: "For all Poles who dream of a German collapse, it is high time to wake up. The German Reich is still a great power and it will create the New Europe."[1]

That a fundamental trait and function of the German press was propaganda is abundantly clear. Indeed, people have grown accustomed to the notion that the occupation press contained no information that conveyed an idea of the real course of events in the world and on the war fronts. But that was only partially true. Certainly, the value of the occupation press as a source of information was extremely limited. For five years it systematically and consciously kept silent about or trivialized failures of the Third Reich through information lifted out of context or falsified; and it lied or made up "facts" out of whole cloth. Nevertheless, the regular reader of the occupation press did have adequate information to form a clear idea — at least very generally — about events in the world and about the real situation of the war. Readers of this press got information about these two most important concerns not only from what they found between the lines but also from specific publications about England, the Soviet Union, the United States, and France; all they had to do was disregard the propagandistic judgments and commentary.

Specific publications and the press in general were integral parts of Nazi propaganda but were noteworthy for the shrill tone of their content. In the first phase of the war, the Polish readers were especially interested in the attitude of the United States toward the war in Europe and the Middle East. The underground press and clandestine radio broadcasts presented detailed information on this subject. However, not everyone could or would use these sources, although they were numerous and well organized in the GG. But the average readers of the *Goniec Krakowski* or *Nowy Kurier Warszawski* could also determine rather easily that Roosevelt ("Freemason, Jew-lover, and dogged enemy of Germany") had been elected to a third term as president with an overwhelming majority.[2] From an article entitled "Astronomical Numbers of the American National Budget" (January 7, 1941) one could learn that the United States allotted $10.8 billion (17 percent more than in the previous year) to arms production — 62 percent of the budget.[3] The occupation press also announced (January 10, July 23, October 20, 1941) that a special weapons bureau had been established in the United States, that the draft had been extended, and that the Congress had passed an amendment to the Neutrality Act by a vote of 259 to 138.[4] A month before, during a discussion on the introduction of this amendment in the Senate, readers had learned correctly that this was the "last step of the U.S. on the road to war."[5] The daily press in the GG also conveyed concrete notions of the extent of the aid the United States gave England and Russia ("Alliance of Capitalism with Bolshevism"). On January 7, 1941, the newspapers announced that the personal representative of the American president, Harry Hopkins, would set out for London, where he did indeed arrive on January 10.[6] On January 12, detailed reports on the American Lend Lease Act appeared in the press; and on October 13, the *Nowy Kurier Warszawski* reported: "Congress has decided on $6 billion for Roosevelt. Roosevelt's new financial proposal of a sum of $5.985 billion for the support of England was accepted by the House of Representatives. The bill now goes to the Senate. The attempts to reduce the sum demanded and to eliminate the Bolsheviks from receiving aid in the framework of the law for England were thwarted."[7]

Thus, readers could infer the emergence of the antifascist coalition even from the occupation press. Interestingly, the GG press presented the news of the agreement between Great Britain and the Soviet Union[8] after the House of Commons, led by Winston Churchill, declared that England would come to Russia's aid, even if it added the propagandistic fillip that this was evidence "of a long-standing conspiracy." Additional reports about the coalition concerned the release of Soviet funds in the United States,[9] the signing of the British-Soviet alliance by Sir Stafford Cripps and Vyacheslav Molotov,[10] and the statement by Hopkins that the United States was providing assistance to Russia and was ready to send war matériel immediately and to continue supplying it for the duration of the war.[11] In the daily press, there were several reports of the Atlantic Charter, the Moscow Conference, and similar meetings of the Big Three.[12]

Items about Free France are also noteworthy. Rare at first, they became much more frequent, especially about Charles de Gaulle ("who set out under Churchill's command"). Thus, for example, one read on February 13 that de Gaulle was in command of armed forces in Cyrenaica; on May 5 that Eva Curie had been deprived of French citizenship because "she supported de Gaulle's resistance movement"; on May 8 of the death sentence against de Gaulle's followers in France.[13]

The occupation press devoted a lot of space to the Axis powers and the satellite states, naturally with an extremely positive tone and great benevolence. But from time to time readers could deduce that things were not at their best there, from mention of raids against rebels in Sofia, a purge of Bulgarian officials, or Croatian conspirators.[14] More important news about Germany, like Rudolf Hess's flight or the assassination attempt of July 20, 1944, also found their way into the press of the GG.

Not least, readers of the GG press could find out about the course and result of some battles and campaigns. That this information was not objective did not present much of an obstacle, since people understand that in war each side tends to enhance its successes and minimize its defeats. As long as the Germans were winning, the press had no problems. Along with military news, precise maps and sketches of troop movements were published; voices from the world press complemented the news from the front; the conquest of big cities and the most important points of resistance were announced in special editions.[15] But how were the front pages of the newspapers to be padded out during the collapse of the German offensive before Moscow, the defeat of El-Alamein, or the catastrophe of Stalingrad?

German propaganda had prepared, if in vain, for the case of Moscow. On July 14, 1941, the expert Rohowsky had composed a detailed program for the celebrations in the GG of the impending German victory. This plan, entitled "Moscow Conquered," foresaw the following:

1. Posters "Moscow Conquered." Today, the . . . at . . . o'clock, great rally at Adolf Hitler Square [the Kraków market square]. Herr Generalgouverneur Reichsleiter Dr. Frank will speak (similar rallies in the districts).
2. Appeal on the radio and in the press: Germans! Hang flags on your houses! Moscow Conquered!
3. Special edition of the Kraków newspaper in German and Polish: Moscow Conquered!
4. Fireworks in Błonie or on the Weichsel [Vistula] across from the Wawel [seat of the Generalgouverneur].

5. Free performances in the German cinema for Wehrmacht, SS, and police, as well as for the *Sonderdienst* of the GG.

6. Military concerts on squares and streets.

7. Concerts in the bigger German pubs.

8. Extension of the police hours:

In German pubs until 2 a.m.

For the Polish population in Kraków until 24:00

In other places according to special announcement

For the Jewish population — curfew!

9. Dignified decoration of the rally squares.[16]

According to the press report, the moment for such celebrations was at hand. It was repeatedly published that the Russian campaign was drawing to a close, that the enemy in the East was completely knocked out. After the Germans took Orel on October 8, 1941, on Hitler's order Otto Dietrich, the press chief of the Reich, announced in Berlin: "For all military purposes, Soviet Russia is finished. The British dream of a two-front war is dead." The cities and settlements already conquered on the way to the final goal were eagerly listed. On December 4, 1941, on the front page of the *Kurier Częstochowski,* the latest news was trumpeted in boldface: German troops had achieved a deep breach in the defense line outside Moscow. The next day Soviet troops on three fronts mounted a counteroffensive and the word "Moscow" disappeared from the military reports. Henceforth, reports were always, vaguely, "on the eastern front." On December 8, for the first time, the *Goniec Krakowski* mentioned the enemy attack "which was nipped in the bud." But by December 9, readers could ascertain that things were exactly the opposite. First the press admitted that Soviet attacks had taken place on many sectors of the eastern front; then, that these attacks were to be taken seriously, that they were violent and strong; and still later, that the Germans conducted dogged defensive actions and that, here and there, "tactical alignment maneuvers of the front lines" had been carried out.[17] Finally the truth was told. The *Nowy Kurier Warszawski* led the way for other GG newspapers in publishing Hitler's speech of December 30, 1941, in which he stated clearly that the enemy had succeeded in advancing in a few places and that the attack had turned into a defensive war. Besides, said Hitler, the Germans were forced not by the Russians but by the cold.[18] At El-Alamein it was the heat; but otherwise everything was going according to plan.

Reporting on the events of the African theater took the following course. On September 11, 1942, the *Nowy Kurier Warszawski* stated in headlines that the only thing left of the British Eighth Army was its name. On October 23, this army, under General Bernard Montgomery, took the offensive. Two days later, the first report appeared in the press of the GG that the British offensive had completely collapsed.[19] Over the following days, the truth leaked out: they admitted that a great battle was in progress at El-Alamein and that, after strong artillery preparations, the enemy was incessantly attacking Italian and German positions with tanks and infantry.[20] On November 3, it was no longer a secret for the readers that Italians and Germans were in retreat. An article entitled "Desert Caravans in the Sand" said: "Of course, in this enormous desert, it was always possible for the foe to penetrate the Italian territory over the invisible borders."[21] On November 6, it was clear that the German-Italian units had retreated to new positions in the west, and on November 8 it was said that these positions were in Fuka and Mersa-Matruk.[22] Readers could then follow the retreat of more than two hundred kilometers on the maps published by the *Nowy Kurier Warszawski* in the first phase of the battle at El-Alamein.

If a certain level of intelligence and some practice was required to understand the war reports on Moscow and El-Alamein correctly, the catastrophe of Stalingrad was evident from reading the press reports.[23] The first, somewhat belated report from the Stalingrad front (November 25, 1942) was relatively enigmatic, stating that grim battles were in progress south of Stalingrad and at the great bend of the Don River.[24] Three days later, the riddle was cleared up, for now it was said outright that "the Bolsheviks had succeeded in achieving a breach in the German-Romanian defense front on both sides of Stalingrad." In subsequent reports it was completely clear that the front had collapsed, shifting to the west and south, and that now the German troops were also attacked from behind.

On December 16, German troops at the lower reaches of the Don River went on the offensive. A week later, the *Nowy Kurier Warszawski* reported that in that area of the Don the enemy had been attacking for days with very heavy tank units and had been able to breach the defense front.[25] In January 1943, a German military report mentioned attacking Soviet troops between the Don and the Donets and the shift of the fighting (according to "a planned abridgment of the front") to the Kuban (in the foothills of the Caucasus), "where heavy downpours hindered German operations."[26] In January, the press also began talking about the fate of the German Sixth Army, which had been surrounded in Stalingrad for some time. At first indirectly, then conspicuously, it was said that the troops of General Field Marshall Friedrich von Paulus had conducted a defensive struggle for weeks against an "enemy attacking from all sides."[27] In early February 1943, one no longer needed to read the reports; now the headlines were enough: "The Last Battle of General Field Marshall Paulus's Infantry"; "Assault on the Last Bastion in Stalingrad"; "True to Their Oath of Allegiance, They Fought to the Last

Cartridge on the Ruins"; "The Sacrifice of the Heroes of Stalingrad Was Not in Vain"; " 'We Have Done Our Duty' — General Strecker's Final Radio Address."[28]

The foregoing press reports must be explained further. First, there is the question of why the German publishers of the press for Poles allowed them to be published at all. Ultimately, it was no secret to the occupation authorities in the GG that the newspapers they published provided the Poles with unfavorable reports and material for speculation. This problem was discussed in leading circles of the German administration; for example, during a press discussion with Frank on April 14 there was criticism that, despite the principle of telling the Poles only what was absolutely necessary, items now appeared in the Polish-language newspapers that were in sharp contradiction to the general press policy.[29] Later in the discussion, the department of press and Telepress were called on to tighten control over the publication and work of the Polish writers, who, it was emphasized, colored news in the Polish spirit.[30]

Through such tightened control, the German authorities could naturally keep all undesirable world news in the GG press to a minimum or exclude it altogether. But they could not silence the facts, for example, that the juggernaut of war was rolling steadily over the borders of the Reich, or that the Russians were at the borders of the GG and the Allies were on the Rhine. In local and purely political matters, the press offices of the GG followed their own journalistic information program. Here, absurd and mendacious news was published without any embarrassment or any concern for how the readers would accept it. Under the same principle, the press remained silent about important events and phenomena in the GG, limiting the lies and suppression to a certain extent to the GG and its population, which played no role in the German calculation. On the other hand, world news, and especially information about the situation at the front, had to be treated differently. Those were fundamental problems which concerned everyone in the territories under German rule. The source of news was the same: the DNB and reports of the OKW. The latter appeared daily from September 1, 1939, to May 9, 1945, with the same text[31] in all the newspapers of Germany and the occupied territories on the first or second page, never in a less prominent place. Although these reports hardly corresponded to the truth, from 1941 on,[32] the degree of truth hardly varies from what is usual in other countries that find themselves on the defensive.[33] Even if occasionally late by a week or more, the OKW reports did reveal all the losses of territory and gave information about all the heavy air raids in Germany or the occupied territories.[34] And through the publication of the military reports, the German press, including the Polish-language newspapers, was in a certain sense a continuous daily chronicle, first of the victories and later of the defeats. "The victory march of the Germans has turned into an obituary," wrote the Polish underground press with perfect accuracy.[35]

Polish Issues and Problems of the Generalgouvernement

Here the press coverage dealt with quite different issues. Depending on the momentary or constant needs of German propaganda, individual issues of politics, economics, administration, or "culture" either found their way into the press or did not. For a better understanding, it is necessary to isolate those themes which were characteristic of the press. The following selected items, which kept coming up in the GG press, are to be examined: the Polish government- and army-in-exile; Poland and its population; and the GG and the position of the Polish population in the German system of government.

"In the long run, the fate of Poland . . . will be decided by peace." "A new period is beginning which, in the future, will build a bridge between the German and the Polish peoples." Those were perhaps the only expressions of German propaganda that could occasionally make people believe that the occupation of Polish territory by German troops in September 1939 did not mean the complete annihilation of the Polish state.[36] Such theses came from the period of the military administration and appeared at that time in the *Dziennik Krakowski* (*Ilustrowany Kurier Codzienny*) and the *Goniec Częstochowski*.[37]

Soon after the establishment of the GG, however, the guidelines of propaganda changed, leaving no doubt that the Germans were expecting the final solution of the Polish question after the victory in September. Henceforth, one of their fundamental theses was that the Polish population had to be persuaded to accept indefinite occupation as a *fait accompli* to be respected unconditionally. Hence, the Germans publicly regarded the defeat as the national debilitation of Poland, even though the Polish state continued to fight, even though the troops of its allies — even if at first in the so-called *Sitzkrieg* — fought for the liberation of the country, and even though Poland possessed a government-in-exile recognized by many countries.[38]

Moreover, according to the original plans of the German press policy, the Polish population was not to be informed at all of the existence of this Polish government and army. In the first two years of the war, in the occupation press, there was practically total silence about both of them, except for sporadic and general invectives against those described only as "émigrés."

Not until September 1941 did Gassner reach the conclusion that there was a magnificent opportunity for a frontal assault on the London Polish government, about which, as he stated, the population was already adequately informed by underground radio broadcasts and resistance journalism. At the same time, anti-Soviet propaganda, which had been the main subject of the occupation press since June 22, 1941, could thus be given new ammunition. Gassner took as a pretext the crisis of the Polish government-in-exile after the resignation of ministers K. Sosnkowski, M. Seyda, and A. Zaleski in protest against the Sikorski-Majski accord.[39]

On September 1, the *Nowy Kurier Warszawski* published a news item with the headline "Split among the Polish Emigrés"; the next day, all the other newspapers of the GG presented the identical article with the same headline.[40] This was a report of the DNB which had reached Telepress a month before. The news item paraphrased the Polish-Soviet pact and stated that Premier Sikorski was not authorized to conclude it. Moreover, after a sharp exchange of words in which General Sikorski was attacked in an insulting and violent way, the former minister Seyda as well as General Sosnkowski tendered their resignations from the offices they had held in the Polish government-in-exile.[41] This was the first news report in which the word "government" had been used; previously, there had only been nebulous talk of "among the émigrés."

The first report was followed by others — all of them, however, only concerning Sikorski's accord. For example, on September 14 an article entitled "Sikorski's Red Toga" appeared;[42] on November 6, "Polish Political Thought on the Wrong Track: The Tragedy of the Polish Army in Soviet Russia";[43] on December 31, "Will a 300,000-Man Polish Army Be Raised among the Bolsheviks?"[44] Finally, on February 17 and 18 all newspapers of the GG published an identical article explaining the "reproaches" against the Sikorski government (this time called by its right name).

This article is especially noteworthy because of the repercussions it provoked in leading circles of the German administration, and also because of the propagandistic tricks used in it. Its title was in the form of a question, "Do Sad Experiences Justify Hope?"[45] and it attacked Russia, England, and the Polish government-in-exile about the Polish-Soviet discussions during Sikorski's visit to Moscow in December 1941. That in itself would not have been especially new or interesting if the tenor of the article had not given the appearance that the occupation press henceforth wanted to use a new language in discussing certain questions. The author (anonymous as always) took special pains to report his remarks in an objective and unbiased tone. In discussing General Sikorski he was quite evenhanded. "General Sikorski," he wrote, was "too well-known and popular before the war to need to be described. A good soldier and a man of integrity who would devote himself to a chosen mission without hesitation or reservation." In another place, the author also granted that Sikorski, "who is an honest man," acted "to serve his people best." Only after this statement came reproaches: "For large segments of the Polish population, however, it was no secret that Sikorski, who occupied a high office even before [Piłsudski's May 1926 coup d'état], was not very talented politically . . . nevertheless he lacked the capacities and instincts of a great politician." Therefore, it went on, Sikorski obediently did everything London ordered him to do, as the just-concluded pact of friendship with Moscow demonstrated. "The tragedy of General Sikorski's government-in-exile," concluded the author, was that he was "misused for the game between the hypocritical London cabinet and the perfidious diplomats of the Kremlin."

German propaganda promulgated the position that England (specifically Anthony Eden) had handed over all of eastern Europe to Russia. To present new arguments for this thesis, the author of this article launched the false report that during Sikorski's stay in Moscow the Soviet government had committed itself to recognizing and guaranteeing the borders of the former republic of Poland. "Thus, the Polish-Soviet pact," concluded the author, "is taken seriously neither by Russia nor by England."

After this article, Sikorski suddenly disappeared from the GG press, even though since September 1941 he had been appearing increasingly on the front pages of the German and foreign newspapers. The reason for this abrupt turnabout is revealed in the generalgouverneur's diary. Hans Frank was vehemently opposed to any mention of the Polish government-in-exile in the press for Poles, and was especially furious about the tone and substance of the February 17–18 article, about General Sikorski. Frank viewed it not as a simple blunder but as a serious political error, as he stated at the press discussion of April 14, 1942, which included State Secretary Dr. Ernst Boepple, Ministerial Counselor Dr. Ludwig Siebert, Ohlenbusch, Gassner, Strozyk, and Fenske.[46] Frank's press secretary went to great lengths to explain how these publications had materialized. Gassner explained that the news had been presented in the papers because one could not keep secrets from the Poles in any event, particularly since at the same time the German press in the GG had written in detail about the Polish army in Russia. Ohlenbusch replied that it was absurd to assume that listening to enemy radio broadcasts could be curtailed by publishing such information. And Frank asserted, in long harangues, that giving the Poles such news encouraged its legal propagation. If a Pole learned of something from an underground flier he could be arrested for it, but not if he could plead that he had read the news in the *Goniec Krakowski*. Finally, Frank prohibited the German-run Polish press from ever again running a story about General Sikorski. Henceforth if papers from the Reich printed any news about the

Polish émigrés, they could not be sold in the GG. By April 15, 1942, the weekly *Das Reich* was in the newsstands and bookstores of the GG, available only on presentation of a German identity card. This information comes from the underground journal *Głos Polski i Komunikat Informacyjny Pobudki,* no. 201, April 22, 1942, which says that the object of this order was intended "to limit the circulation of Goebbels's counterpropaganda in occupied Poland" aimed at stemming the flow of unpleasant news to the Poles.

This ban on writing about the government-in-exile was observed from February 1942 to April 1943. At the same time, however, the *Nowy Kurier Warszawski* mentioned Sikorski's name twice, in passing, in articles on quite different problems. Alleged letters to the editor leveled the accusation that "there are people among us who are enthusiastic about Messrs. Sikorski, Anders, etc., who have forgotten that Poland is called upon to be the frontline of Christian resistance and who, instead of that, are in the service of the Jewish Freemasons and the most determined enemies of the Cross. . . . Sikorski will not succeed in creating a second Jew-Poland."

Not until the Katyn massacre and General Sikorski's death did the Polish government reemerge as a leitmotif of propaganda.[47] Nevertheless, even during this period the Polish population learned from the occupation press that a Polish government existed. On January 21, 1943, the Polish-language *Ilustrowany Kurier Polski,* under German management, published a poem that supposedly was a satire of kitsch verse but in fact was an acrostic in which the first letters of every line, read from top to bottom, announced: "Poles, Sikorski Doing Well!" The author was Eugeniusz Kolanko, a staff member of several underground journals (including *Na ucho,* a satirical weekly, as well as the youth journal *Watra: Pismo Polskiej Młodzieży*).[48]

Poland and Its Population as a Topic in the Occupation Press

The judgments and opinions of the Nazis about non-German peoples, especially the Slavs, are well known and hardly stir any interest anymore. More important here are the ways and means they purveyed their views to readers, and their objectives in doing so.

We must begin by citing a few "maxims" of the occupation press: Poland is the most squalid country in Europe; the Polish state was an instigator of unrest in Europe; Poland was a toy in the hands of the Jews and foreign powers; the Poles are a people without common wishes and ideals, without even a common language; Poland was a country of anarchy and corruption; the Polish government and the people behind it are responsible for the war; the vast majority of the population feels that the Polish state was a foreign body.

These and other similar judgments, often contradicting one another, were represented only rarely as the opinion of the Germans.[49] To be more effective, they were published in the press for Poles as comments of "unaffiliated" observers, as emanating from "prominent" Polish and foreign sources or as the voice of "enlightened Poles" who could render a critical judgment on their own history and recognize their national errors. The Polish-language press also quoted negative expressions of various statesmen, diplomats, and philosophers of the past and present (for example, David Hume, Sir Peter Carew, Napoleon, Talleyrand, Carlo Sforza). From time to time, the newspapers published secret documents of the Polish and French foreign ministries, which were supposed to demonstrate that the Poles had provoked the war. The internal situation in "former Poland," meanwhile, was also illustrated by material that had previously been top-secret.[50] Most often, however, the GG press used counterfeit letters to the editor when it wanted to express negative opinions about the Poles. This tactic was employed especially by the *Nowy Kurier Warszawski,* which claimed — as its publisher formulated it, in any case — to be an unaffiliated information paper and a faithful barometer of the mood of the population.[51] It published letters in a regular column, "The Readers Have the Floor," with a caveat: "The editorial staff takes no responsibility for the contents of this column. Anonymous letters are not published."

In the early months of the occupation, these letters usually consisted of complaints against the injustice done to their authors by fellow citizens (for example, an inhumane landlord, a shopowner who demanded black-market prices)[52] or reports about deplorable customs (for example, ladies who fed their dogs delicacies while children went hungry).[53] In some the former Polish government and the Jews are cursed in a vulgar manner (for example, "The Former Polish Rulers in the Mirror of Rhymes from Częstochowa," "An Open Letter to Former Marshall Śmigły-Rydz," "The Jews in [Piłsudski's] Legion and Why They Joined It").[54] Even now we can hardly ascertain reliably which of these letters, some of which bear the full name and address of their authors, are real and which were ordered or simply faked by the editorial staff,[55] but there is no doubt that some of the published letters were authentic. A few original letters to the weekly *Siew* (Seed) have been preserved in envelopes bearing postmarked stamps, indicating that they are authentic. Among other things, these letters contain praise of *Siew.*

Naturally, the editorial staff also used commissioned material. This is proved indirectly by certain sources as well as by the so-called great discussion in the *Nowy Kurier Warszawski,* in which many well-known persons participated. The subject was the judgment of the government and the "real" situation in prewar Poland. The discussion was begun in a letter to the editor from a reader who did not initially disclose a name but who later signed the pseudonym Henryk Zrąb. In fact, it was Stanisław Brochwicz-Kozłowski, a former fellow of the National Culture Fund and a journalist before the war. When it was discovered that he had worked for the German Secret Service, he was tried and convicted of espionage and imprisoned in Brześć.[56] Released by the Germans in 1939, he went to work for the Warsaw Department of Propaganda and, on their orders, wrote the anti-Polish brochure "Hero or Traitor? Memoirs of a Political Prisoner," which was published in Warsaw in 1940 by Wydawnictwo Nowoczesne.[57]

Brochwicz-Kozłowski's article in the *Nowy Kurier Warszawski* appeared at the same time as it published a series of articles entitled "Causes of the Defeat of September 1939."[58] In the issue November 26, 1940, next to the eighth in the series, "President and Government," appeared the first detailed letter from Brochwicz: "They governed us. The paterfamilias and the trio of worthies. The ladies in the [Warsaw] castle and their friends." This letter was followed by more, all in the same vein; for example, "Ambassador Michaś, the lost son of President Mościcki"; "Rivals for the president's chair"; "Kazimierz Sosnkowski — a leader who was never a soldier"; "The rule of Sławoj-Składkowski — the achievement of the temperamental Frau Żermina"; "The evil love of General Kasprzycki — Casanova in the seat of the war minister," and others. Brochwicz-Kozłowski's libelous letters were a strange mixture of truth and half-truth, lies, and sinister hints in the form of a scandalous chronicle, as Wacław Borowy rightly noted.[59]

A great deal had already been written about the Polish prewar government. It was a common topic: hardly had one story ended than another was begun. The discussion about the campaign of September 1939 and the scurrilous articles by Zrąb/Brochwicz were in effect the continuation of a series of stories entitled "A Year Ago." Somewhat earlier, all newspapers had printed Rudolf Stach's report "The Flight of the Bankrupt Rulers." This time, however, it was more than just another infusion of the old subject. Even during the publication of the Brochwicz letters, the *Nowy Kurier Warszawski* printed letters to the editor that either confirmed Zrąb's disclosures or corrected a few facts and judgments. To give the appearance that the discussion of Zrąb's article was absolutely free, letters were also published by persons whom Zrąb and others had attacked by name and who were now trying to defend themselves and explain the motives for their behavior.[60] In some letters the authors indeed did not question Zrąb's general conclusions but condemned the publishing of material during the war which disparaged the Polish state and its government.[61] In short, in an occupation newspaper a grim struggle was conducted between the followers of Zrąb — who, naturally, were in the majority — and his opponents.[62] Zrąb replied to these opponents immediately, or rather, he cursed them; but other readers also came to his aid. Among the contributors who supported his remarks were Jan Pękosławski and a certain Pachlewski, who during the twenties had been the mainstays of the fascist secret "Squad of Polish Patriots." Adam Pragier, who had then been a member of the Sejm's committee investigating secret organizations, later wrote of the effects and program of the Squad:

> Pękosławski, the founder and head of the Squad, was an engineer by profession, a dedicated nationalist and advocate of government by a strong man. He was not very smart, but was very energetic, as is often the case with paranoids. He was able to create an organization that was not large but functioned well. It can best be compared with the early Russian "Black Hundreds," which it also resembled in phraseology. . . . Pękosławski was seriously prepared to take power. He had established an impressive list of ministers and was determined to repeal the constitution and proclaim himself dictator. He had chosen a path that was not so much worthy of a Mussolini as of a Machiavelli: he was determined to use a few unwitting ministers as a springboard for his takeover.[63]

In his letter to the editor, Pękosławski attacked persons who had deemed this discussion inappropriate to the times: "It is precisely now that we have the possibility and opportunity, that we must not only reveal these sins and sloppiness but must brand all those who once governed us with a red-hot iron. . . . In the end, Poland had to fall because it was not yet ripe for independence."[64] Pachlewski, on the other hand, regretted that the Polish people had not then spoken out for the Squad of Polish Patriots. "Perhaps," he added, "we wouldn't have to suffer so much today, and the history of the years 1920–1939 would not have been so gloomy."[65]

The discussion in the *Nowy Kurier Warszawski,* whose spicier parts were also reprinted in the *Kurier Częstochowski* and the *Goniec Krakowski,* lasted not quite two months, from November 26, 1940, to January 16, 1941. The newspaper printed thirty-three comments, twenty-five of which supported Henryk Ząb; eight judged the discussion more or less harshly as unsuitable; in five letters, details were simply corrected. Nineteen contributors gave their name; one claimed to be a Legionnaire of Piłsudski's II Brigade, two introduced themselves as Master of Arts and three as doctors.

In the summary of the discussion, the editorial staff expressed its full satisfaction that the debate had filled its mission, as the "real rage" and the "fury of the readers" proved. But it was a mistake to accuse only bad leaders. The people had also been guilty because "after 150 years of foreign rule [it] was not capable of kicking out the government clique"; and the editors regretted that there had been little discussion of that. The editors concluded: "The leaders would never have dared such a risky policy if they had not known that the people, the whole people, stood behind them. That is unfortunately the truth."[66]

This discussion in the Warsaw "reptile press" was no doubt one of the most perfidious anti-Polish propaganda campaigns. Nevertheless, the method of referring to the "man in the street," the attempts to enlist former opponents of the Polish regime to do propaganda work but then to publish corrections, represented something new in the practice of the occupation press. Wacław Borowy writes that these articles "had nothing to do with an honest critical analysis; nevertheless, you could not dismiss them en bloc as 100 percent false either. They were dangerous, for they were one-sided and contained half-truths, and it was just this dangerous influence on the Polish people which was no doubt their purpose."[67]

Aside from its racist ideological goals, the anti-Polish propaganda in the *Nowy Kurier Warszawski,* as in the other GG newspapers, was also intended to meet current needs of German policy in the GG. This mainly meant inculcating an inferiority complex and a guilt feeling in the Polish population in order to weaken the will to fight and resist, and to sharpen the antagonism between the Polish ruling class and the rest of the population.

The "discussion" in the *Nowy Kurier Warszawski* was typical for another reason, too. Both sides — Zrąb and the letter writers — attacked for the first time a person whom the occupation press had thus far discussed in extremely positive terms. This was Józef Piłsudski, who was spoken of in superlatives and with great respect in the newspapers published during the military administration, as well as later. Thus, on September 29, 1939, the *Gazeta Łódzka* had written: "Stone on stone, the Marshall tediously built Poland; but he was not permitted to complete his work — he died." On October 15 of the same year, the *Kurier Radomski* reprinted a report of the correspondent of the *Schlesischer Zeitung* on the Warsaw Belvedere Palace, Piłsudski's residence, which "was not destroyed as a living monument, which testifies to the greatness of this man." Even when he was little, wrote the correspondent, his mother had roused in Józef ("Ziuk") a love of fatherland and a sense of responsibility. And on the fifth anniversary of Piłsudski's death, the *Nowy Kurier Warszawski* wrote that "his work lies in rubble, destroyed by his adoptive sons."[68] On the first anniversary of the outbreak of the war, the *Goniec Krakowski* wrote that there was only one man in Poland who had wanted an agreement with Germany. On November 11, 1940, the *Nowy Kurier Warszawski* commented that if the marshall were still alive, Poland would no doubt have joined the Axis.[69] That all these remarks appeared at anniversaries is evidence that these publications were planned. The articles by Zrąb and the discussions about them introduced new elements into the anti-Polish propaganda. Now it said that things had gone just as badly in Poland under Piłsudski as under Rydz-Śmigły. This turnabout was not accidental and was expressed not only in press propaganda. The underground press called this change "the end of German clowning around." In an article of that title, the *Biuletyn Informacyjny* wrote: "After the occupation of Poland, for propagandistic reasons and to create confusion among the Polish population, the German rulers demonstrated their reverence for the memory of Marshall Piłsudski as the representative of a realistic foreign policy. The smear sheets wrote respectfully about the Marshall; honor guards marched at his tomb on the Wawel, portraits of him remained hanging. . . . Now by order of the Generalgouverneur all tablets and pictures of the Marshall in schools and public buildings must be removed."[70] This order, signed by Bühler, said that all objects that keep the memory of Józef Piłsudski alive and could thus influence the national feeling of the Poles were to be taken down.[71] The occupation press preserved the memory of Marshall Piłsudski again during the Soviet-German war, when it paid tribute to his merits in the struggle with the danger from the east. But now Pilsudski was celebrated as a farsighted politician, a great statesman, and an advocate of neighborly relations with Germany and the Third Reich.

Another striking series of articles about Poland and its population appeared in September 1941 in the *Nowy Kurier Warszawski* under the general title "The Causes of the Fourth Partition of Poland."[72] Its author signed it with the initials "Z. M." and used phrases common thus far only in the German press, such as in the *Krakauer und Warschauer Zeitung*.[73] It began by stating that the Poles were not a nation, "there were simply unconnected social classes on Polish soil who had no common language." The Polish state, it went on, emerged as the result not of the common strivings of the people but rather of the dictate of Versailles, and the majority of the population had considered it as something completely foreign. Since Poland had not in fact been an independent country ("Judeo-Poland"), it had collapsed from the inside in 1939; German troops had only given the mortally ill creature the coup de grace. As in the three previous partitions, the Poles had been incapable of conducting an independent national existence in the Western European sense of the term.

That I have concentrated in this chapter on the *Nowy Kurier Warszawski* does not mean that the other newspapers represented a different view of Poland and its people. But in the *Nowy Kurier Warszawski,* the largest Polish-language newspaper, which came out in Warsaw and was sold throughout the GG, the anti-Polish propaganda was most continuous, most systematic, and most ruthless.

The Position and Significance of the Polish Population in the Governance of the Generalgouvernement

Along with negative or destructive propaganda against the Polish republic and government-in-exile, there was also in the press for Poles a propaganda that was positive or constructive in tone. Indeed, the former was designed to create a favorable climate for the latter. Since the Polish state had been an artificial monstrosity and the incapacity of the Poles for an independent existence had been proven, the only reasonable and worthwhile solution of the Polish question consisted of the subjection of Poland to German order. For now, all positive propaganda proclaimed, German rule would establish order, peace, and justice on the former Polish soil. The press repeated such assurances and explanations daily, in contradiction of the facts and common sense.

What the occupation press had to say about the place and the significance of the Polish population in the system of the GG can be summed up in a few of Frank's expressions that appeared in all newspapers: the Germans did not want to strip the Polish people of their ancestral rights; instead, Hitler had designated the GG as a homeland for the Polish people; the management and administration of this homeland had devolved upon the Germans who would erect a model administration and an orderly economy for the welfare of the population; anyone who fulfilled his duty loyally would be treated well; Anyone who declared his attitude unambiguously through willingness to work could count on being taken care of with an appropriate position. The slogan was strict rule, but it was also the will of the German leadership to impose justice. In terms of the decision of Reichschancellor Adolf Hitler, the GG today and in the future formed the habitat of the Polish people. Naturally, the Germans did not intend to de Polonize the area and Germanize it. The Poles could develop according to their own customs and character traits, as long as they simply acknowledged the new order and grasped once and for all that any playing with independence or sovereignty belonged to the past. The mountains might crumble, but the Germans would never again leave this country.[74] The press commentary added nothing substantially new to these and similar expressions, although the roles and tasks of the Polish population in the framework of the New Order was always being written about. At best, the occupation papers explained in a few words what was meant by the concept of loyal cooperation or how work

for the benefit of the common good was to be seen.[75] Only sporadically —
primarily before July 27, 1940, when the name was changed to the Generalgouvernement—did the press mention in quite general and mysterious
formulations the possibility that Poland (not only the Poles) might participate in the foundation of Adolf Hitler's "New Europe."[76] For understandable reasons, the press did not utter a word about the real intentions of the
Germans with regard to the GG and the Polish population. In any case, that
emerges clearly enough from Bühler's cynical comment on a meeting of the
government in January 1943. He said that the major task consisted of
concealing German intentions from the Poles, or else the current war aims
would be unattainable; if the Poles knew what the Germans planned for
them, they would not offer any help.[77]

On the other hand, the press wrote in great detail about the development
and flourishing of the GG and the beneficial consequences of German rule.
Thus, only the Germans had produced a healthy currency.[78] The country
developed through the *Baudienst,* and the standard of living of its population rose;[79] the Vistula was regulated for flood control, "which no one had
previously bothered about";[80] the condition of the health services had never
been so good as in the GG;[81] the Warsaw neighborhood of Wola, "previously
forgotten and neglected, is continually cleaned up";[82] livestock production,
"neglected by the responsible authorities between the wars," was on the
rise;[83] the marketplace in Kraków was paved, "which had previously not
occurred to anyone";[84] and the special courts worked for the protection of
the Polish population.[85]

Literally not a day passed when the press did not discuss new and
splendid achievements under German rule. As for the Polish population, the
overwhelming majority, according to the press, performed their duty loyally
and intelligently because "the hope for bread, work, and a better future this
time has an undoubted prospect of being fulfilled."[86] The mendacity of these
and other assertions was obvious, for despite all propagandistic efforts, the
daily life of the population in the GG was miserable. It also emerges from the
reptile press. One need only glance at the advertisements, the announcements and official orders, the information about rationing cards and the
conditions of life of the population, the official population statistics (more
deaths than births), or a few reports about the municipal economy. The
attentive reader can also gain a general idea from the news of the struggle
against the "gangsters," and from the information given under "Legal
Advice" (what was allowed and what was forbidden). From some (even if
rare) publications one can also learn that "not all Poles cooperated loyally
with the Germans, nor did they acknowledge all German orders." Thus, for
example, the *Goniec Krakowski* of July 27, 1940, divided the Poles into

three groups: (1) those who openly declared that they had been led astray by the prewar authorities and now wanted to accept the reality of German rule; (2) those with similar views about the former government and military leadership, who however rejected German leadership and longed for their independence; and (3) those who had not learned anything and advocated that everything should remain as it was. But in general the occupation press did not allow such reflections: the *Goniec Krakowski* article is a reprint of excerpts from an article by Wilhelm Zarske that had been carried in the *Krakauer und Warschauer Zeitung*.[87]

But such details about daily life always describe a drop of truth in the flood of great lies. No doubt Ludwik Landau was right when he kept noting in his "Chronicle" sentences like, "As usual in the official press, there was no trace of reality."[88] Wacław Jastrzębowski noted the same thing in his study *Gospodarka niemiecka w Polsce* (The German economy in Poland), which was written during the war.[89] Kazimierz Wyka put it more incisively: "The reptile press written for the Polish population was composed on the moon. It had as much to do with real life as moonlight has to do with growing plants."[90]

The GG press distorted the real picture of daily life by falsifying facts or lending them false dimensions: with empty words and misinformation, but primarily by concealing and evading the most important events. Naturally, in the contemporary press there was no indication of the extermination of the Jews, nothing about the resistance movement, the terror, or the mood of the people. The persecutions, street roundups, and waves of arrest, or even the great campaigns like the so-called Aktion AB (Extraordinary Pacification Campaign) and the public executions, were never mentioned in this press. Nor was there a word about the concentration and extermination camps. The press was so careful that, even in reports of people caught "in the act," it avoided words like "shot," "killed," or "hanged." An indication of this is a memorandum, dated March 7, 1941, from the editorial staff of the *Kurier Częstochowski* to the mayor of the town of Tomaszów saying that people took no notice of the train robber Wojdara because the phrase "caught and shot during the theft of coal" had been unclear. "The Polish reader could have inferred that the German barbarians had once again committed a murder."[91] Three weeks earlier, the Gestapo in the city where the *Kurier Częstochowski* was published had arrested 131 Poles within two days. A list of the names of these Polish victims is in Jan Pietrzykowski's *Hitlerowcy w Częstochowie* (The Nazis in Częstochowa). The German authorities also publicized the names, usually on posters and through street loudspeakers. Meanwhile in the press, so as not to disturb the deceitful impression of calm or to give anyone proof of the crimes, such lists were rarely printed. A copy of a legal newspaper in which the number of those shot was officially announced is obviously an incriminating document that can easily be preserved without any danger for the possessor. Much more dangerous is a poster with the same content torn off a wall or photographed. One of the first death sentences in Warsaw, for example, was carried out against the student Elżbieta Zahorska for tearing down the German poster "England — this is your work."[92]

Along with praise of the new order went the publicity campaign to attract labor for the Reich and the GG. Frank told the German heads of the press for Poles, "We cannot settle the struggle by shooting sixteen million Poles and thus solving the Polish problem. As long as the Poles are alive, they must work for us and be introduced into this work process by us."[93] This sentiment appeared frequently in many papers and over a wide span of time. The only and best way before us is work, active participation in the building of a new future, the creation of new values and ideals;[94] "Pray and work" (ora at labora) is the motto; work, farmer, and God will bless you; he who does not work shall not eat, writes Saint Paul; the Third Reich — land of labor for the population of the GG; and so on.[95] These importunate slogans and appeals were complemented by accompanying remarks that the GG would be the real homeland of the Poles only when they mastered the new kind of work and developed a real sense of duty.[96]

The occupation press also entertained. Crime reports, travel accounts, sensational and genre novels occupied a lot of space in the newspapers.[97] The policy of the *Goniec Krakowski* was that these novels were not to deal with any sad subjects, which everyone knew well enough, but were to avoid political questions as well, because people wanted to relax from politics. A crime novel should tell of people and things as they are not — no war, no food ration coupons, no lines in front of shops, etc.[98]

Another constant feature was reviews of films, plays, concerts, and performances in cafés or circuses, along with coverage of horse races and other events. Without getting into an evaluation of the contents of these events produced by the German Propaganda Department, or judging the attitude of the Polish artists, musicians, and performers who cooperated in them, one must observe that the occupation press conveyed an accurate picture of public cultural life in the GG. In this area, the Polish-language press can serve as a reliable, often even the only source for research on these issues.[99]

The cultural features were written more liberally than other parts of the occupation press. This is apparent not only in treatment of subjects but also in the choice of certain publications from the life and work of representatives of Polish culture. Indeed, there were not many such articles or items.

Among the fifteen or twenty subjects covered in the period 1939–1942 were the "modern poetry" of Adolf Dygasiński, "the poet and friend of animals," and the fortieth anniversary of his death; "In the Hometown of Reymont and Chełmoński/Prazki — the Village where W. S. Reymont Lived"; a visit to "the place where the great writer [Reymont] lived and drew the material for his great rural epic"; the fiftieth anniversary of the death of Karol Szymanowski; an obituary, in 1941, for Ignacy Paderewski, including "a biography of the artist up to 1922"; and an obituary for the composer Wacław Berent — "Thinker, Scholar, and Artist." Excerpts from Polish and foreign literature appeared (including excerpts from Reymont's "Peasants"); works by Mikhail Zoshchenko, for example, were published before and after June 22, 1941.[100] There were probably two reasons for this: the German authorities liked to organize a substitute for real cultural life in the GG,[101] and the cultural section in the occupation newspapers was written almost exclusively by Polish staff members.

10

German Professional Journals in the Polish Language

Aside from the daily newspapers, propaganda and professional journals also appeared in the GG. The propaganda journals followed approximately the same course as the dailies. The *Ilustrowany Kurier Polski,*[1] *Siedem Dni, Fala, Co Miesiąc Powieść, Siew,* and *Kolejowiec* treated only weekly or monthly the problems dealt with in the daily newspapers. There was even a journal with the word *Polski,* "Polish," in the title, which began publication during the military administration. The title did not change even after July 24, 1940, when the concept of the Generalgouvernement replaced the previous term, "occupied Polish territory," and the words "Poles" and "Polish" were removed from the names of all offices and institutions, except for the Polish Red Cross and the Bank of Issue in Poland. The *Ilustrowany Kurier Polski* was the only newspaper allowed to keep the word "Polski" in its title, probably for export. A document in the government files of the GG signed by Johann von Wühlisch, deputy of the Foreign Office of the Generalgouverneur, says that "in the early discussions with the press chief of the government of the GG, it was considered that the well-equipped Polish weekly *Ilustrowany Kurier Polski* . . . is to be used for the purpose of foreign propaganda.[2]

The professional journals were different from the reptile press. These journals were directly subordinate neither to the press chief nor to the propaganda department. Their publishers, the determination of their editors and their contents were exclusively within the jurisdiction of the individual departments of the government of the GG.

With the publication of the professional journals, the occupation authorities pursued the same goal as with the reopening of primary and vocational schools in the GG, for the economy of an industrial state can hardly function without a constant influx of skilled labor. True, Himmler did say once that for the non-German population of the East, a four-grade grammar school was sufficient, that children had only to learn to count to five hundred, write their name, and accept as a divine commandment to be obedient, reverent, diligent, and courteous to the Germans.[3] But the Reichsführer SS could think only in the categories of the concentration camp. On the other hand, as soon as the decision was made to exploit the economic potential and manpower reserves of the Generalgouvernement for the military needs of the Third Reich, the development of skilled labor became an important problem for Frank. It was solved according to the principle that a Pole should know and be able to do only as much as the current interest of the Third Reich demanded. Therefore, Frank upheld the previous decisions about the liquidation of Polish universities and high schools but ordered that elementary school instruction be resumed (except for geography, Polish, and general history), and the vocational schools be reopened. In September 1941, aside from grammar and vocational schools, so-called institutes were created to develop agriculturalists, health-care workers, veterinarians, pharmacists, and, later, physicians. These institutes were initially intended for the privileged Ukrainian population, but eventually they also accepted Poles. At the same time as the elementary and vocational schools were reopened, the first professional journals appeared.

A precise analysis of the content of the professional journals is beyond the scope of this study; it would take experts in the various fields to judge the level and substantive value of the publications on beekeeping, livestock breeding, agriculture, trade, forestry and hunting, medicine, and veterinary medicine. So far no one has yet investigated the professional journals that appeared in the GG, and the only comments on this subject in the underground press or in the documents of the underground movement, as well as in postwar publications, are too general, sometimes even misleading. Thus, for example, a report of the Delegacy of the government-in-exile states: "Naturally it is not the function of the agrarian press to be concerned or take pains about Polish agriculture, to enlighten our farmers or train them professionally, but rather solely to make propaganda for the delivery of quotas. Indeed, in the publications of these undertakings . . . all political propaganda is carefully avoided, they all wear the masks of professional technicality as far as possible, but there's a fly in the ointment, and this fly is always and everywhere the food quota."[4]

The reference to the introduction of food quotas was certainly correct, and it was discussed directly only in the professional journals. Even a cursory reading of such journals as *Pszczelarz* (Beekeeper), *Rolnik* (Farmer), and *Mały Inwentarz* (Small Livestock) shows that they almost exclusively contain articles, information, and professional advice for agriculture and for organizing work in field and backyard. Interesting statistical information that can be helpful for professional investigations is also in these journals, especially the valuable reports in the journals about problems of cooperatives.

The character of the youth journals *Ster* and *Mały Ster* is also ambiguous,

• KRAKÓW • LISTOPAD • 1940 • NR. • 3 •

STER

• ILUSTROWANE CZASOPISMO DLA MŁODZIEŻY •

Fig. 3. *Ster,* Fall 1940. This illustrated youth magazine was often accused of being collaborationist, but its articles were more clearly anti-Soviet than pro-German.

even though they were dismissed in postwar Polish publications as pure propaganda mouthpieces. Both journals substituted for textbooks in grammar schools. One issue of *Ster* (5–5, 1943/1944) was completely devoted to the geography of the GG. Moreover, the content of this journal consisted mainly of works of Polish literature, from classics like Jan Kochanowski to modern writers like Maria Dąbrowska, who are part of the curricula of Polish schools to this day. Yet the works of living authors were reproduced without their knowledge or agreement.[5] Aside from these works, stories, novels, and poems also appeared by authors who cooperated with the German school department, primarily works by Feliks Burdecki, the editor in chief of *Ster* and *Mały Ster,* as well as Edward Chodak, who had also written for children before the war. All in all, both journals are on a very low level, and can bear absolutely no comparison with the textbooks and youth journals of the prewar period, which were proscribed and withdrawn from the bookstores. In addition, representatives of the German school authorities kept popping up for surprise visits in the schools to check whether banned schoolbooks were being used. One report of such a visit says, "At the examination of a Polish elementary school I ascertained that, aside from *Ster* and the allowed reading material, the children had undesirable and un-authorized books. I request that attention be paid at school examinations to what is read by Polish students aside from *Ster*."[6]

But the professional journals were not directly concerned with propaganda that was political or hostile to the Poles. And the comment of T. Kułakowski in his book *Gdyby Hitler zwyciężył* (If Hitler Had Won; Warsaw, 1959, p. 104) that *Ster* spread the cult of Germanism, demoralized the youth, and trained them in antisemitism is supported only by a single article ("What Is Typhus?," no. 8, p. 29) and by the statement of the publisher: "Authors are asked to send their contributions. . . . The first letter should contain a declaration of the Aryan origin of the author."

On the other hand, the inserts and supplements to individual issues of *Ster* (including nos. 1 and 15, 1942/1943, which had anti-Soviet contents or concerned food quotas) were pure propaganda. In instruction in Polish, the publisher used the principle of "rationing knowledge," as K. Pospieszalski described it. Readings from Polish literature were selected from very narrow subject areas, mainly labor, natural beauty, prayer, and adventure. Anything suitable for influencing the mentality of the younger generation more comprehensively was not published.

The character of the other professional journals was diverse. Some were concerned exclusively with special problems — *Medycyna Współczesna, Weterynaryjne Wiadomości Terapeutyczne, Wiadomości Terapeutyczne, Zawód i Życie, Informator dla Spółdzielni Spożywców*. Others contained propaganda articles and reports along with professional material and information. Two journals were particularly distinguished in this area, *Zdrowie i Życie* and *Wiadomości Aptekarskie*, the official organs of the physicians' and pharmacists' boards during the occupation. In the view of an underground medical journal, *Zdrowie i Życie* energetically strove to detract from the Polish achievement in public health service and make it ridiculous, to disparage the Polish medical profession, and to incite doctors and assistants against one another; it sang hymns to the sanitary methods of the Nazis, to every individual order, and to the most trivial work supposedly achieved by the Germans; it promised medical care to the Polish population in a naïve and deceitful way, care whose real purpose was the protection of the German population and the health of the soldiers; and it published articles and reviews that incorporated Nazi principles of medical science based on pseudo-scientific foundations.[7] The same is true for *Wiadomości Aptekarskie*.

The journals *Wzorowa Gospodarka (Die Musterwirtschaft), Twórczość Gospodarcza, Las i Drewno (Wald und Holz),* and *Spółdzielca* also served as propaganda, although not in such a sharp and distorted form as in the cases mentioned above. They were indeed written objectively and were specially designed to train and advise professionals and workers. From time to time they also contained articles on the economic achievements of the "New Order" and the benefits German rule brought for the GG. Such articles were unfounded and mendacious, like the claim of the *Kurier Częstochowski* that the level of the professional journals in the GG was far beyond that of the prewar period.[8]

11

The Press and
Its Readers

Thus far, we have observed the press in the GG from the publisher's perspective, primarily to determine how it was written and what it contained. But other, equally important questions also arise: Who was the reader of the German press published in the Polish language? How was it read? No doubt this is one of the most difficult problems, and it is doubtful that it can be solved on the basis of the few extant sources. It is impossible to determine the readership precisely, for there is no statistical material on the number of copies sold in the city or in the countryside, per week, month, or year. Nor can it be stated with certainty what influence the press exercised on its readers. In this area, too, no research has been done either during the occupation or after the war. Thus, any attempt to illuminate the perception and effect of this press must be on the basis of fragmentary sources.

Fighting Poland, that is, all underground parties and organizations as well as the entire clandestine press without exception, was openly hostile to German publications. This hostility was expressed in armed attacks and acts of sabotage against the institutions and staff of the occupation press, in the struggle against Nazi propaganda, and in the stigmatization of the Polish journalists employed on the editorial staffs of the occupation newspapers. The underground movement also called for a boycott of the Polish-language German press, but the groups and press organs of the underground movement were not in complete agreement over the form and scale of these schemes. *Barykada Wolności,* for example, the organ of the Polish socialists, advocated the complete boycott of the reptile press.[1] Other underground newspapers, including almost the entire press of the Home Army (Armia Krajowa) and the Delegacy of the government-in-exile, exhorted the population not to buy pure propaganda papers like *7 Dni, Fala, Co Miesiąc Powieść,* and *Ilustrowany Kurier Polski.* The demand for a total boycott of the occupation press, however, seemed unrealistic to them. Instead, a limited boycott was to be in force against the dailies; the Polish population was encouraged not to buy newspapers on certain days: "Every Friday, the entire edition of the reptile press must remain unsold, untouched, boycotted!"[2] The boycott was also called for annually on September 1 (the anniversary of the German attack on Poland), as well as May 3 (Constitution Day) and

November 11 (Independence Day). This was meant to be a realistic and achievable request.

It is impossible to say whether the call for a boycott on Fridays and national holidays was successful. One may assume, however, that this exhortation did not have the desired effect. Most people bought their newspapers at a specific kiosk near their home or workplace, so anyone who did not buy on Friday might call attention to himself — a dangerous thing under the conditions of the occupation. The circulation of 275,000, 392,000, 363,000, 400,000, or even 700,000 copies a day — the average daily circulation in the years 1940–1944 — caused no difficulties. Moreover, materials of the resistance movement and documents of the occupation period agree that the daily press of the GG generally sold well and very quickly, even if in certain circles it was not touched.[3] Finally, it was the only legal source of information. A black market in newspapers was even carried on; for a time, two to five złoty were paid for a copy, at a sales price of twenty groszy.[4] To understand this ostensible contradiction, it must be remembered that there were three times fewer copies of the newspaper per capita than before the outbreak of the war, and from 1939 on, the Polish population was deprived of radios.

The resistance movement also opposed all contact with the editorial staffs of the reptile press. Nevertheless, part of the population of the GG came to regard this press as a means of communication, as indicated by thriving classified advertising sections in the *Nowy Kurier Warszawski, Goniec Krakowski,* and *Goniec Częstochowski:* want ads for goods and services, offers of foreign language instruction, lost and found, change of address, wedding announcements, etc. Advertisements in these newspapers took up took up 20–50 percent of every issue.[5] Obituaries announcing the place and time of the funeral came from almost all social and professional classes, including the aristocracy, the intelligentsia, the military, the clergy, craftsmen, tradesmen, and clerks.[6]

People bought the reptile press because there was nothing else in the kiosks. In civilized countries, in peacetime, buying the daily newspaper is a pleasant custom, but under wartime conditions reading the press becomes a necessity. An underground press, however — even one as variegated and well-organized as the Polish press was — cannot replace the legal press. Among the some 1400 titles of resistance newspapers, relatively few were daily papers; and barely one hundred radio bulletins and informational papers appeared more often than once a week. Moreover, they were not published regularly, the overwhelming majority were short-lived, and their circulation varied each time between fifty and five hundred copies. "Thus," correctly wrote the organ of the Home Army headquarters, *Biuletyn Infor-*

macyjny, "for many readers, the German or 'reptile press' is the only place where people can learn news of international politics and the theater of war."[7]

How was this press read? People undoubtedly sought news of German defeats and failures in the official press, as indicated by contemporary memoirs and written records, reports of the underground press, and the general popularity of jokes and phrases about "planned front curtailments," "retreat to a previously planned position," "moving into a position on a curtailed line," "the elasticity of the front" — designations and expressions from the communiqués of the OKW and other press publications. At the time of the Soviet counteroffensive before Moscow, Aurelia Wyleżyńska noted in her diary: "We learn to speak with agreed-upon word signs, you catch them in flight. Behind the words, you sense the hidden meaning. This is in official announcements as well as in personal conversations. The last communiqué no longer hides the hopelessness. It was whining and full of undisguised worry. What was said there about the courage of the German soldier, who will overcome and remove all obstacles, must be seen as a disclosure of the conditions existing in cold of -50° C." (*Dziennik,* January 29, 1942, p. 29).

Ludwik Landau had an especially admirable talent for commenting on the German press, discovering internal contradictions in it and "scraping out" the truth. The precision was enhanced since Landau, the author of a three-volume chronicle of the war and occupation, was not limited to the Polish-language press but primarily consulted newspapers and journals published in the Reich.

The underground press often called attention to the so-called confessions of the reptile press. Thus, for example, *Barykada Wolnosci* (no. 34, February 16, 1941) wrote under the headline "Dlaczego przegrywają" (Why they are losing): "At last the *Nowy Kurier Warszawski* has disclosed the secret of why the Italians in Africa are getting a proper thrashing. An article from a German military journal says it: there is too much sand in the desert, seawater is too transparent, the English tanks are too big and the Italian ones too small, the English fleet (which had already been sunk) is too strong, etc. Il Duce would certainly have won if England had not had any airplanes or cannons, ships or tanks. But what to do — Albion is once again perfidious."

A few underground newspapers even introduced special sections in which selected quotations from the press about German failures were provided with brief commentaries. For example, the underground newspapers *Znak* (Sign) and *Jutro* (Morning) had sections called "How the German Press Must Be Read" and "In the Mirror of German Propaganda." The *Głos Polski i Komunikat Informacyjny Pobudki: Organ Walki z Propaganda,*

Wroga (The Voice of Poland and Information Report of the Reveille: Organ of the Struggle against Enemy Propaganda) made a typical comment in the section "What Is Allowed — What Is Not Allowed": "It is allowed," said the *Głos* ironically, "to read German newspapers. From them we learn that the Germans who, yesterday, still wanted to rule the world, today are fighting for their survival" (no. 202, May 11, 1942).

The mood that really prevailed in Polish society was also clear from German secret documents. One of them, the weekly account of the Main Department of Propaganda to Berlin headquarters, drawn up by Ohlenbusch or his deputy, Arnold, merits special attention. The following excerpts come from reports composed during the battles of Moscow, El-Alamein, and Stalingrad:

(December 22, 1941) In Warsaw, the bulletin boards we put up with sketches of the course of the front in Soviet Russia were provided last night with black labels referring to 1812. The boards were cleaned immediately. The Polish police were ordered to place a permanent guard at every board for eight days.[8]

(January 12, 1942) The development on the eastern front, to which the Polish resistance movement has recently devoted great attention, did not lead to the formation of a homogeneous point of view among the Poles. In the District of Kraków, the situation looks like this: In the western part of the district, the Poles like to talk of the possibility that 1812 will still be repeated this winter. In the eastern part, the repeat of 1812 is only a wish whose fulfillment is doubted.[9]

(November 9, 1942) Since yesterday, the Poles have been whispering among themselves. Every rumor about the situation in North Africa is passed on by them. They give ear to all possible combinations according to which the situation of the Axis powers can be seen as ominous. Thus, this morning it was circulated among them that Algeria was in the hands of the Americans.[10]

(November 28, 1942) The Polish population sees in the recklessness with which the present campaign [the collection of food quotas] is carried out a further sign of the growing difficulties of the German conduct of the war. The calls coming from Warsaw out of the resistance movement persuade them, moreover, that Stalingrad is a generally visible symptom of the bleeding of the German front in the East.[11]

(February 3, 1943) The Polish population again believes in the final defeat of Germany, especially now because of the events on the eastern front, the skirmishes in Casablanca and also as a result of the development of the situation on the Libyan front.[12]

All the available sources, both German and Polish, lead to the conclusion that German propaganda in Poland did not achieve its goal.

There was no point of contact between the reality of the occupation and the news of the press. Hardly anyone believed in Germany's final triumph, and certainly the number of Poles who wanted it was not great. The occupation regime and the proclaimed "New Order" were generally hated. The prospect of eternal German rule ("Even if the world collapses we will never leave this land") or the notion of a people condemned to forced labor ("The GG becomes a genuine homeland of the Poles only when they are capable of a new way of working and have got a distinct sense of duty") could only reinforce the conviction in the necessity of the struggle against the occupier. Despite calls in the press for calm, docility, and obedience, the resistance of almost the entire society grew stronger and stronger, turning the GG into a powderkeg—to use an expression from Hans Frank's diary. On another occasion, Frank admitted that there could be no talk of exercising political rule over the Poles, and he also spoke of the minuscule influence of German propaganda on the Polish population.[13]

In Germany, writes Franciszek Ryszka, "Nazism wanted to win over the broad masses of the population and was sure that fear was not enough, that they had to let the people feel the advantages of the new system, that they had to comply with explicit material and spiritual needs."[14] But the Germans did not want to offer the Poles anything; nor did they have anything to offer them. Therefore, Nazi propaganda, which was attractive in its own country and was well received by German society, turned out to be completely unsuitable for a subjugated people.[15] In Germany, propaganda and terror complemented each other excellently; in Poland, they got in each other's way at every turn.

That German propaganda did not achieve its goal does not mean, however, that it had no effect. Even during the war and shortly after its end, people considered whether Nazi propaganda, with all its cynicism and the obvious crimes of the regime, had any hope of success with the Poles. The question was generally answered in the affirmative. "It is not true that one can completely withdraw from the influence of the printed word," wrote the illegal *Barykada Wolności*. "You can know every one of the Nazis' lies precisely; you can believe not a single word of the reports—a vestige of the force of conviction remains even in the lies and hatred. The Germans are sure that, aside from imbeciles, no one in Poland takes the idiocy of their propaganda seriously. Yet they invest enormous sums in this propaganda; for they know that even the critical listener or reader cannot completely escape the influence of the constantly repeated lies."[16] Stanisław Płoski, former director of the Instytut Pamięci Narodowej in Warsaw, who was an expert witness in the trials against the staff of the reptile press, stated: "The propaganda of the German press, although it was sometimes dumb and boorish, did have a certain success. Two elements contributed to this: the length and the exclusivity, i.e., that for five years there was nothing else to buy at the kiosks except the German press."[17] Bolesław Dudziński, the first after the war to try to analyze the success of the reptile press, wrote in the *Kuźnica* (Forge), which appeared in Łódź: "Its printed word naturally struck readers of various intellectual and moral powers of resistance. That's why not everything the reptile press wrote was written in vain; that's why throughout all the years, terms were taken from it which the propaganda had pressed into a cliché, particularly maliciously simplified political facts and ideas, which even now are a burden and a trauma for us."[18]

In his extremely interesting article on the politics of the German occupation forces in the Generalgouvernement, which appeared in 1946 in *Strażnica Zachodnia* (Westward), Antoni Szymanowski remarked: "We must not overlook the fact that despite all the mendacity of this policy and its simultaneous imbecility, some extraordinarily poisonous residues remain in society, especially in the petit bourgeois class at which it was primarily aimed."[19] And Kazimierz Wyka wrote in *Życie na niby* (Warsaw, 1957): "This German propaganda did not have a positive effect, i.e., it did not bring anyone to the side of the occupation power. But it very certainly did have a negative effect, because it destroyed the proportions of the world horizon, because it mystified, lied, and kept silent, it created an atmosphere of magical uncertainty" (p. 96).

The damage done by the Polish-language German press is hard to estimate. But there were also propaganda campaigns that did have a limited success from the German point of view, especially the call for Poles to go and work in the Reich. This was probably the only time that the propaganda and terror of the Germans complemented each other. In an entry in her interesting wartime diary, Aurelia Wyleżynska writes a propos of this: "(February 16, 1942) Another summons to work in the Reich with the promise of being able to chose the place of work and other amenities. In spring, when this encouragement doesn't help, is a new conscription awaiting us?"

In fact, about 1.5 million people went to work in Germany, but mainly — as almost all sources state — as a result of constant pressure and compulsion. Nonetheless, the work of recruitment officials was no doubt eased by persuasion and promises (such as pledges to Poles that they could send part of their salary to their families, that they might return home on leave, and their families [among peasants] would be exempt from the food quota), as well as by the threat of force and the increasingly difficult conditions of life in the Generalgouvernement. To illustrate, here are excerpts from the diary of a young worker, Kazimierz Szymczak:

(March 22, 1940) A "new idea" is taking shape in German heads to get Poles to Germany for work. . . . Because they need a labor force, they organize an enormous propaganda campaign. In the city and in all offices they have hung pictures of their factories and farms [to show] how clean it is in their country, how well and comfortable it is for a Pole who works for them, how good he is paid, and what riches he can buy for marks. A lot of people are out of work and are taken in by Nazi propaganda and have signed on and gone away. I don't have any work either, but I am not going. I will eat only once a day and accept any work I can get, but I am not going!

(April 4, 1940) "Separation." Stasiek is no longer here. We have separated. He signed on and has gone. It happened like this: two co-workers and I have similar names: Stasiek Szymanowski, Felek Szymań-ski, and me. When I found out they wanted to go, I decided to go with them. They went because of the hard living conditions, I [wanted to go along] for company and also from the wish to see a new country for nothing; it has always been my dream to travel, to see and learn as much as possible. So, the three of us went to the labor office, there was a crowd of people there. We were pushed up to the counter.

(July 16, 1940) "Letter." Got a letter and a photograph from Stasiek from Germany. In the photo he looks good, and he writes that he is well, for he has food and a warm and clean place to sleep and he didn't have that at home. But he writes that I shouldn't come, for the work is hard and is miserably paid; and it doesn't make any sense. But I wouldn't go now anyway, for I have gotten it out of my head, and in the organization they said we may not help the occupation. Anyone who goes to Germany to work extends the war and is not a good Pole. It matters whether you go by force or voluntarily.[20]

The consequences of Nazi propaganda against the Jews are a special problem. Here the effect of the propaganda was especially sweeping because it was supported by the underground press of all Polish parties from the center to the right, including the fascist organizations and the political and military organizations. All these groups published about three hundred clandestine papers (not counting brochures and fliers), in which a bitter propaganda campaign against the Jews was conducted from the beginning of the German occupation to the end. In form and content, these articles are no different from those of the Nazi reptile press. Some clandestine papers considered the extermination of the Jews as a happy and favorable circum-

Fig. 4. "We are going to Germany!" This Nazi propaganda poster sought to encourage Poles to register voluntarily for work in the Third Reich.

stance for the final solution of the Jewish problem in Poland. Among them were *Walka* (Struggle), the central organ of the rightist Stronnictwo Narodowe, edited by the well-known Catholic writer Jan Dobraczyński; the newspapers of the Konfederacja Narodu (Confederation of the Nation), published by Bolesław Piasecki's organization; and *Szaniec: Narodowe Siły Zbrojne* (Earthwork: National Armed Forces), known before the war as *ONR-ABC*. (The latter and the so-called Falanga, which during the war became the Konfederacja Narodu, were the two most radical fascist organizations in prewar Poland).[21]

German propaganda against the Soviet Union also had some success, as did the press campaign against the policy of the Polish state from 1918 to 1939. On this question the occupation press undoubtedly contributed to the deepening of resentment that had formed independently of German propaganda, both before and during the war, which was reflected in the clandestine press.

When the Third Reich was at the height of its power, German propaganda had unfavorable consequences which are not to be underestimated. The rapid spread of news about the victories of the Wehrmacht, the absolute lack of understanding for the most elementary needs of society all had a devastating effect on the mood of the populace, which in any case is likely to be fickle in wartime. There are countless examples of that gloom in the diary entries and memoirs from the war period. On October 15, 1939, Karol Irzykowski wrote: "This [*Nowy Kurier Warszawski*] poisons my life; it advises us to accept this reality as an irrevocable fate and we don't even know if it is really worth it to get used to it."[22] On July 28 and August 5, 1940, Ludwig Landau noted:

> We are constantly depressed, everyone seeks only a tiny glimmer of hope, but it is hard to find a basis for such hope. The city is constantly full of soldiers, especially police, i.e., units of the Waffen-SS with death's heads. . . . Nothing interrupts the silence. Although the events — even if nothing happens — have recently been constantly unfavorable for us, you nevertheless feel the silence as hard, so much hopelessness is in it. It calls forth various reactions: in one person blatant pessimism, in another even less reasonable optimism based on English air raids and on hope in a revolt against the Nazi regime and the collapse of Germany.[23]

And Halina Krahelska, on March 24, 1942, wrote:

> In the third year of an occupation like the German one, after a hard winter and in view of an extraordinarily gloomy economic perspective, it is no wonder that many people lack patience, that they are depressed, reluctant, defeated, which very often leads to strange expressions like: Nothing is happening; Everything is treading water; German power is just as strong as at the beginning of the war, unlimited, yes, invincible; The German population in the Reich has not changed their attitude, they are excited about war production, etc.[24]

In this light, the role and significance of the underground press become even more understandable. It was a mighty weapon in the hands of the Polish resistance, and almost every step of the occupier was exposed to its criticism. The underground press revealed the lies of the Nazis and roused in the population the will to resist and the belief in the certain end of the Third Reich. The underground press, as well as the political parties and organizations of the resistance movement, conveyed the general attitude of the majority of Polish society and were unanimous in their opposition to the Nazi occupiers.

Part 3
The "New" Nazi
Press Policy, Spring
1943–January 1945

12

The "New Polish
Policy" of the
Occupation Force

At the end of 1942 and the beginning of 1943, Germany's military and political situation underwent a fundamental change. The retreat of Rommel's army in North Africa and the defeat of the Wehrmacht in Stalingrad frustrated the hopes of the Third Reich for a quick and triumphant conclusion to the war. The idea of pacifying the occupied territories was just as deceptive, for terrorizing the subjugated population turned out to be a completely unsuitable means of eliminating the constantly shifting centers of resistance. A classic example was the resistance movement in Poland, which succeeded in taking the law out of the hands of the occupation force. In the GG the situation became so critical that Hans Frank could state — even if with some exaggeration — that the soldier on the front was in less danger than an official in the German administration.[1]

In view of the defeats on all fronts and the growing uncertainty in the GG, German authorities took pains to create a different attitude toward the Polish population. The first signs of such a change of line appeared early in 1943, as the underground *Biuletyn Informacyjny* noted in an editorial on May 20: "Since the end of January this year, German policy in Poland has taken a new line. Two factors contributed to this change: the defeats in the winter war in the Soviet Union as well as the complete failure of the method of terror in Poland. . . . It is the goal of the new line to calm the hinterland of the eastern front and to win over Polish society for economic and, eventually, military cooperation against the Soviets."[2] In the Generalgouvernement it was Hans Frank who came out with the idea that the policy toward the Poles should be changed. His recent noncommittal comments (December 1942–January 1943) about the necessity of using somewhat more moderate and elastic forms and methods of government led to the development of a program between February and June 1943.[3] The views of the usually cautious Generalgouverneur were influenced by information and hints that discussions about a change of the so-called policy vis-à-vis the people in the East were being held in party and government circles of the Reich.[4] Goebbels's circular of February 15, 1943, with new stipulations about the treatment of the people under German rule completely convinced Frank that the time had come to subscribe openly to "his own" standpoint, which

Redakcja „Biuletynu Informacyjnego" składa wszystkim współpracowni-
kom, czytelnikom, kolporterom i przyjaciołom pisma gorące życzenia Nowego
Roku 1944 — z wiarą, że będzie on ostatnim rokiem wojny i niewoli.

BIULETYN
informacyjny

| Rok V | Warszawa, 30 grudnia 1943 r. | Nr. 52 (207) |

DO SPOŁECZEŃSTWA POLSKIEGO

Mija już dwa miesiące od momentu, gdy okupant rozpoczął stosowanie nie
tylko wzmożonego, ale i jawnego terroru, gdy w stolicy i na terenie całego Kraju
plutony niemieckich katów publicznie mordują dziesiątki i setki Polaków. Jest to
ze strony wroga cyniczne wyprowadzanie na światło dzienne planowej akcji

Fig. 5. *Biuletyn Informacyjny,* Warsaw (December 30, 1943), the main clandestine
weekly published by the Home Army.

he did in a conference he called on February 23. In the course of the
discussion, Frank commented: "This circular is an almost revolutionary
announcement. A new epoch has begun. The previous system of extermination, exploitation, and discrimination is broken. Finally, they see in the
Reich that a system of force cannot last, for force is merely the use of a
momentary technical advantage of weapons."[5]

Frank's intentions were a bit too clear. Moreover, he did not conceal, as
emerges from almost all of his later expressions, that the change in line was
only a tactical maneuver; that the renunciation of the Nazi solution of the
Polish question must be seen simply as the postponement of implementing a
decision made long ago; and that it finally concerned only how the economic
and human potential of the Generalgouvernement could be exploited for the
German victory.[6]

However, Frank understood clearly that every significant change of policy or tactics in the Generalgouvernement required the official confirmation
of a superior. Above all, he knew that Friederich-Wilhelm Krüger, as SS
lieutenant general and undersecretary for security issues in the GG, did not
share his opinion in the least. On the day after the above-mentioned conference, two of Frank's deputies, the undersecretary Dr. Ernst Boepple and
the department head Dr. Ludwig Losacker, of the Office of the Generalgouverneur, conducted exploratory conversations about a change of Polish
policy in the Reich Chancellery in Berlin. They called attention primarily to

The "New"
Nazi Press
Policy
126

the harmful consequences of the brutal resettlement campaigns in the territory of Zamość and the policy of intimidation, terror, and annihilation of the Polish intelligentsia,[7] which had failed to yield any practical result. In this situation, Frank decided to appeal directly to Hitler. On June 19, 1943, he addressed to him personally an extensive memorandum in which he explained the urgency to revise German policy in the GG.[8]

In this memorandum, Frank admits that German rule in the GG had recently come up against the increasingly active resistance of broad masses of the Polish people. This was the result, he concluded, of a policy of starvation, resettlement, exploitation, mass arrests and mass shootings, and persecution of the church, as well as a well-advanced paralysis of cultural life. In this situation, the Germans lost the possibility of drawing Polish society into the struggle against Bolshevism which Frank considered imperative and saw as a realistic goal, especially after the circulation of the DNB report on the murder of a few thousand Polish officers by the Russians at Katyn, near Smolensk.[9] If the Poles were to be used in the struggle against Russia and in support of the German war economy, a change in attitude toward the population of the GG was necessary. It was imperative, thought Frank, to improve the material situation of the population, to expand the area of cultural activity and school training, to guarantee privacy, to give up the Germanization campaigns, to refrain from acts of force and terror, and not to hinder church activity or encroach on church assets. Frank also found it necessary to express himself on the "future fate of the Polish people in the new European space." He reinforced a few points of the memorandum with various reservations to assure Hitler that he did not consider the settlement of German-Polish relations a "matter of heart and feelings, but rather an act of sober reason"[10] and that his remarks did not refer to the long-term goals German leadership would and should attain when the life-and-death conflicts in the East were finally settled successfully.

The generalgouverneur's memorandum did not meet with a welcoming response in the summer of 1943. Neither Hitler nor Himmler wanted to hear of fundamental concessions to the Poles, even if they were only temporary and tactical.[11] Only after some time, as the economic situation in the Reich increasingly worsened and security in the GG kept diminishing as the Soviet army menaced the borders, Frank succeeded in assuring Hitler's support for at least a few points of the so-called new line. That happened during Frank's stay at the Führer's headquarters in February 1944.[12]

In fact, in the last two years of the GG, from January 1943 to January 1945, occupation policy consisted of two contradictory phenomena. On the one hand, the German administration made certain concessions which could have indicated a renunciation of the draconian methods of governing. On the other hand, orders and decrees were issued that formed the "legal" basis for new acts of terror and violence. Thus, for example, on January 22, 1943, street roundups and mass arrests were officially forbidden; but, on the other hand, German settlement in the area of Zamość was continued. In mid-July, expulsions and resettlement in this area were stopped; at the same time, the exceptional status of "protection of the seizure of the harvest" was announced in the entire GG territory.[13] Between May and July, there were new street roundups and arrests based on prepared lists; but on July 7, the *Teatr Rozmaitości* in Warsaw was reopened. They were permitted to perform *Krakowiacy i Górale* (Krakowians and Highlanders), by Wojciech Bogusławski, the father of Polish theater, but in a version that had been cut by the German censor and retitled *Sen nocy lipcowej* (July Night Dream).[14] In September and October, food rations were raised a little, and the ceremonial opening of the Chopin Museum in Kraków took place;[15] but on October 2, 1943, an "Order to Combat Attacks against German Reconstruction" was issued, giving the police unlimited power to use the principle of collective responsibility and carry out mass shootings of hostages.[16]

The two-track German procedure was typical in 1943 and continued the following year; only the proportions changed. The government of the GG, henceforth with Hitler's support, enlarged the area of concessions somewhat, especially in the cultural sector and elementary and professional schools, and increased the percentage of Poles in the lower ranks of the administration. However, as Martin Broszat noted, those were still only simplified measures to strengthen German rule in Poland.[17] Characteristic of 1944 were such far-reaching promises as the opening of high schools and even universities; the expansion of the jurisdiction of the Polish Main Welfare Council and its reorganization into a Polish National Committee; the introduction of advisory committees and representatives of the population at the district, regional, and government levels;[18] and the opening of a Polish sports federation. The promises, which were not followed by any concrete action, were accompanied by conciliatory words and gestures, by probing, and by persuasion to take the outstretched hand — the same hand that as in previous years had signed thousands of death sentences, strangled Poland as soon as it stirred, and, at the end of 1944, condemned Warsaw and its inhabitants to annihilation.

With the so-called new line of 1943 and 1944, the oppression was loosened somewhat, but the basic principles of German policy vis-à-vis the Polish population remained the same. Through deceitful tactical concessions, the Germans now made an effort to win the favor and goodwill of the Poles. As we will see, changes in the German press policy were designed to serve the same aim.

13

Change of Press Policy: Planning and Failure

Goebbels's circular of February 15, 1943, addressed to higher functionaries of the NSDAP, contained the following central points and demands:

1. All forces of the European continent, but especially the people in the East, must be used against Bolshevism.
2. The people must be imbued with the conviction that the victory of Germany is in their own interest.
3. In this context, the degradation or offense, directly or indirectly, of individuals is not allowed.
4. Similarly, the impression may not be given that the Reich intends to create long-lasting subjugation.
5. Every expression on the subject of the German policy of colonization, and colonization in the East, is to cease.
6. Similarly, new or large German settlement, the distribution of lands, or any Germanization may not be mentioned. Nor may the deportations of the population be spoken about.
7. Anything that may damage the necessary cooperation of the people in the East and thus impede the German victory is to be avoided.[1]

Goebbels's circular arrived in the GG on February 22. That same day, Undersecretary Bühler told about it briefly at a meeting of district governors. Declaring that he wanted "to be able to state explicitly that this edict also applied to the treatment of the Poles,"[2] Frank diverted the discussion onto other tracks. To judge from the minutes of the meeting, nothing more was said on this subject. On the other hand, it is known that Undersecretary Boepple and Department Head Losacker, who went to Berlin on the same day to participate in a conference to prepare for the proclamation of total war, were to have clarified whether Goebbels's circular also applied to the GG.[3]

The next day, February 23, Frank made a puzzling decision. At a conference on press policy in the GG, without waiting for the results of the Berlin conversations and despite his own doubt, which he had expressed at the governors' meeting on February 22, he described the questionable circular as an order whose validity for the GG was incontrovertible. What led Frank to change his mind on this matter, indeed within only a few hours, is not known. The governors' meeting ended in the late afternoon of February 22, and the conference on press policy began on February 23 at 10:35. The Generalgouverneur's diary gives no indication that any event or conversation took place between the conferences which could have influenced his decision. But we may assume that Frank, to whom Goebbels's edict seemed like a panacea for all the inadequacy and wretched state of affairs in the policy of the Generalgouvernement, wanted to create *faits accomplis* in an accelerated procedure. And it seemed appropriate to inform this audience, who were to proclaim the new propaganda formula, of his far-reaching administrative decision.

The following persons took part in the conference: Ohlenbusch, Gassner, Fenske, Strozyk, Coblitz (director of the Institute for German Advancement in the East in Kraków), as well as almost all the editors in chief of the Polish-language newspapers and journals. The presence of SS Lieutenant Colonel Heim, head of Department III in the office of the Chief of the Security Police in the GG, was to result later in difficulties for Frank. Heim, however, performed great service for future investigators, even if unintentionally; thanks to him, we now have two reports at our disposal which partly complement and partly contradict each other.[4] One was made by Frank's official recorder, the other by the representative of the police. The following account of the conference proceedings relies on both texts.

The very first pronouncements of Gassner and Fenske clearly indicate that the objective of the conference was to find new methods of propaganda to influence the Polish population. Nor was there any doubt that both speakers were informed of Frank's views and were familiar with the Goebbels circular. Gassner, who detected a "change in mood in the GG," spoke against continuing the press policy that had prevailed since the time of Dr. Maximilian du Prel, that is, since October 26, 1939. He thought the situation in the GG had resulted from the bad treatment of the Poles by the Reich: "That is why our opponents possess all possibilities of winning Polish sentiment. The English promise them freedom, justice, prosperity, sufficient food, the punishment of all those who assaulted the Polish people. We Germans could deal with them propagandistically only with the empty concept of the new Europe, which is meaningless to Poles."[5]

Frank was the third to speak.[6] He began by reading Goebbels's circular; then he stated that this was a document that changed the relation to the "foreign peoples" by 180 degrees and that, in this way, the objectives he had pursued for so long would be crowned with success. One also had to keep in mind, he added, that Goebbels and the chief of the party chancellery (Martin

Bormann) had cloaked these views in the form of a decree. Thus, he directed the assembled group to take note of the appropriate points of the edict and consider them obligatory for the GG.[7]

According to Frank's remarks, all participants in the conference unanimously condemned the previous press policy and made practical suggestions for the future. These included increasing the number of publications concerning Polish cultural life and expanding their subject area in an attempt to win over the Polish intelligentsia; lifting the long-standing ban against writing about the Polish government-in-exile; permitting polemics with an "English report bias"; continuing to publish anti-Bolshevik material, which had been begun by the Poles in 1919; allowing, instead of *Fala,* publication of a political journal for the Poles; improving the material and social situations of Polish journalists employed on the editorial staffs and extending their influence on the formation of the Polish-language press, even delegating a Polish journalist to the headquarters of the deputy of the Generalgouverneur in Berlin.[8]

The request of Widera, editor in chief of *Nowy Głos Lubelski,* merits special attention. According to him, two kinds of Polish-language newspapers should be created in the GG: those run by Poles as well as one newspaper run by Germans (whose editors would be the previous editors in chief of the press for the Poles). The former should certainly submit to the censorship of a German supervisory authority, but they should be allowed to comment on edicts of the GG administration and enter into debate with the Polish underground press. The newspaper run by the Germans was to explain the official German point of view to the Poles and carry on a controversy with the Polish journalists, "thus rousing them from possible hesitation to deal with problems."[9]

Frank accepted all suggestions amiably, even the one to send a Polish journalist to Berlin. When he summarized the results of the conference, he announced that he wanted to publish them as a service manual to be sent to the editors in chief of the newspapers in the Polish language.[10] All district chiefs and authorities were to be told of the content of the Goebbels circular letter.

The next day, February 24, Frank confirmed the draft of an order for the new propaganda lines proposed to him by Ohlenbusch and Gassner. However, he did not yet sign this document, but gave instructions not to deal with the issue until Ohlenbusch and Gassner along with Bühler and the Security Service had conducted another substantive investigation.[11] What happened further with this order is, amazingly, not known. That it was even published is quite doubtful, for the police in the GG were strongly opposed to the interpretation Frank had given to Goebbels's circular. Moreover, the report of SS Lieutenant Colonel Heim became one of Krüger's most important trumps in his quarrel with the Generalgouverneur. Krüger attached Heim's note to the extensive report to Himmler on the situation in the subordinated territory; he observed that, in his opinion, the circular letter did not refer to the GG. In addition, the conference on the new press policy resulted in Polish circles learning of the secret circular before the German executive authorities. This assertion in no way dispensed with the principle: in the report of the underground Delegacy of the government-in-exile on the situation in the Polish territories under German occupation for the period May 22–June 19, 1943, there is news "about a meeting of the highest officials of the German administration of the Warsaw district [*sic*] in the spring, at which an edict from Minister Goebbels to the Propaganda Department was read, discussing the need for restraint vis-à-vis the Poles."[12] Reliable news about this occasion was also presented by the *Informacja Bieżąca* (no. 22/95, June 9, 1943): "This edict is commented on by the Germans in the following way: The change in line has propaganda and internal significance. The terror of the police and the SS will continue, for moderation of the line and security are two completely incompatible things." Finally, Krüger still expressed the fear that the circular could not make up for political damage, since the Poles would view it as proof of the greatest weakness of Germany since the GG had come into existence, and the Polish resistance movement would be even more encouraged by it.[13]

In short, the quarrel over the interpretation of the questionable edict was superfluous. First, it was established that the population of the GG was not to be counted among the "people of the East," and second — what is most amusing — that the orders of the propaganda minister were also not obligatory for the territory for which they were intended, that is, for the occupied part of the Soviet Union, where they were subject to the vociferous objections of Alfred Rosenberg, Reich Minister for the Eastern Occupied Territories.[14]

On March 18, 1943, the Reich propaganda ministry addressed a memorandum to Ohlenbusch containing guidelines exclusively for the GG.[15] This time they were very moderate proposals, which indicate that the issue was not a change in policy but rather trivial modifications and essentially insignificant concessions directed primarily toward the propaganda effect. At the beginning, the Main Department of Propaganda in Kraków was informed that, in view of the tense situation in the GG, the central office had investigated how Polish matters were to be handled and had determined that certain steps vis-à-vis the Poles would have to be taken; the conclusion was that "the right to existence and life" was not to be taken from them. In this context, Goebbels approved the following suggestions:

1. Not to use offensive phrasing in public statements, such as "The Pole is like the Jew."

2. To use all means of propaganda to move the Poles to accept working in the Reich.

3. To take pains to win over the working masses. For this purpose, the cabarets have had to be closed and workers' pubs and restaurants opened instead. Persons who indicate special eagerness to work should occasionally receive higher food rations. These changes are to be prepared accordingly and used propagandistically.

4. In principle, already concluded resettlement campaigns are to be represented as necessary: the *Volksdeutsche* had to leave their previous area of settlement because of the Bolshevik menace. Such an adaptation of propaganda, however, demands coordination with the Reichskommisar [Heinrich Himmler] for the consolidation of German race and culture.[16]

Barely a month later, on the night of April 12/13, 1943, the DNB published its report on the Katyń massacre. German authorities both in the Reich and in the GG attached great and far-reaching hopes to that publication: "The propaganda effort will be well supplied for a few weeks," Goebbels noted in his diary.[17] His subordinate in Kraków, Ohlenbusch, planned to exploit the events in Katyń throughout the whole year.[18] Ohlenbusch thought that new possibilities had opened for propaganda in the GG, where the Germans had not previously been able to secure political leadership in Polish society.[19]

In two subsequent government meetings, on April 15 and 20, 1943, Ohlenbusch presented his detailed plans. He wanted to make use of all types of mass media — movies, radio, newsreels, journalism, brochures and posters — to order a national day of mourning, to erect memorials in Lublin, Warsaw, and Kraków, and to have religious ceremonies carried out with the participation of the Polish clergy. According to these plans, German authorities were to keep out of this whole campaign as much as possible and leave its execution to the Polish Red Cross, the Main Welfare Council (RGO), and a not yet summoned Polish commission. Ohlenbusch also thought that the "chauvinistic and Bolshevik circles of the population" must now be deliberately played off against one another even if that should lead to an increase in the activity of the former. However, as long as the new policy in the GG was not specified in Berlin, results could hardly be expected. He personally "represented the point of view that the mass murder of Katyń offers a perfect opportunity to induce a change in Polish policy without shaking the prestige of the Greater German Reich."[20]

Frank certainly shared Ohlenbusch's opinion but was less optimistic, since he remembered too well the recent defeats. Nevertheless, he promised to undertake energetic efforts to break the resistance of the position of the Reich, which — as he put it — believed "that the sharp, hard fist is the only correct method."[21]

Berlin remained deaf this time, too, and did not listen to the "reasonable" Frank. Thus, in the planned reform of the press for Poland, the deadlock could not be overcome. Without the fundamental support of the central office even in issues of propaganda, the administration of the GG could execute only minor changes, if any: among others, the ban on writing about the Polish government-in-exile was lifted;[22] in the press, sarcastic and malicious expressions about Poland and the "national character of the Poles" were avoided and, at the same time, the willingness of the German occupation power to maintain "good, even friendly relations" with the loyal population of the GG was emphasized. The first indications of this were reports and articles in the press on the occasion of a new transport of Polish workers to the Reich; according to German accounts, one of those in this transport was the "millionth volunteer." The Generalgouverneur, who personally appeared at the Kraków railroad station, gave him a gold watch. In his address to the assembled workers, Frank then said: "We are all fighting for a new Europe, where peoples can develop in peace. The population of the Generalgouvernement, which will be able to develop peacefully under the protection of the great triumphant Reich of Adolf Hitler, is also part of it." All the daily newspapers printed the last sentence in boldface. The next day, the *Goniec Krakowski* presented its own report of this event, emphasizing that the Generalgouverneur did not leave the railroad station after the conclusion of the departure ceremonies but "went through all the cars, looking into the compartments to exchange a few more words with the valiant travelers."

Reports and descriptions of this kind of "warm and friendly meetings with the population" were henceforth the favorite subject of the reptile press. These meetings were attended by district chiefs and heads of departments of the GG, but most often by the Generalgouverneur himself. He received a delegation of Polish farmers at the Wawel Castle and told them he "regarded the presence of a representation of Polish farmers at the castle as a symbol of friendship." A few days later, Frank met with Polish workers who were employed in restoration work at the Wawel. At this opportunity he declared: "It would be a fortunate symbol if the building of the castle, constructed by Poles and Germans in common, was a sign for a happy future life of the two societies in a Europe freed from Bolshevism." Here the correspondent of the *Goniec Krakowski* added on his own that the Generalgouverneur shook hands with every worker and accompanied the handshake with kind words, that he sat at the same table as the workers and talked and laughed warmly with them.[23] In a word, the wolf spoke in the voice of the lamb, as Olgierd Budrewicz wrote of it years later.[24]

The organization and structure of the German press in the Polish language, however, remained unchanged. All newspapers were henceforth managed by German editors in chief, the old subject catalog was retained, and new newspapers and periodicals did not appear.[25]

14

Nazi Press Policy
at the End of the
Occupation

More than a year after the discussion of Goebbels's letter, the press policy of the occupation force underwent a fundamental change, indicating that the authorities of the GG had begun to enact the proposals raised at the conference of February 23, 1943. Thanks to the general support Frank now received from Hitler, he was able to realize his old plan of press "reform"; this resulted in greater independence for the Generalgouverneur as well as a free hand in dealing with his old adversaries, who could have torpedoed his views both in the Reich and in the GG. Paradoxically, as Czesław Madajczyk notes, the renaissance of the power of the civilian administration in the GG coincided with the beginning of the defeat of the Third Reich.[1]

From spring to autumn 1944, nine new journals were founded: *Przełom* (Breakthrough), *Straż nad Bugiem* (Watch on the Bug), *Strażnica* (Watchtower), *Nowa Polska* (New Poland), *Głos Polski* (Voice of Poland), *Gazeta Narodowa* (National Newspaper), *Nowy Czas* (New Time), *Informator,* and *Wola Ludu* (People's Will). The journal *Signal,* which had been banned in 1940, was now sold again in the GG as a common edition of the Reich propaganda ministry, the German Foreign Office, and the Wehrmacht. Interestingly, toward the end of 1944 the Wehrmacht wanted to buy up the *Nowy Kurier Warszawski* to run its own propaganda among the Polish population, but nothing came of it. Gassner, the press chief in the GG, who reported to Frank on this matter, noted that even during the phase of the military administration, in September and October 1939, the Wehrmacht had not published a newspaper in the Polish language.[2] None of these nine journals was edited according to the model of the reptile press, which moreover appeared continuously and unchanged until the final days of the occupation. The nine journals in the GG can be divided into three main groups: (1) purely political journals, edited by a Polish staff which openly admitted its collaboration with the German occupation power (*Przełom*); (2) German journals, which formally emphasized their Polishness (*Straż nad Bugiem, Strażnica*); and (3) journals which claimed to be put out by independent Polish organizations (*Nowa Polska, Głos Polski, Gazeta Narodowa, Nowy Czas, Informator, Wola Ludu,* as well as the pseudo-conspiratorial *Goniec Krakowski*).

Przełom

Right after the first issue of the political biweekly *Przełom* appeared in May 1944,[3] the delegate of the government-in-exile in Poland, the engineer Jan Jankowski, sent the following telegram to Prime Minister Stanisław Miko-łajczyk in London:

Press
Policy
at the
End
of the
Occupation
137

1. German efforts to find new forms of Polish-German cooperation are still clearly aimed at creating a Polish Quisling regime. Professor Leon Kozłowski [former member of the Sejm and prime minister in 1934–35] was recently mentioned as premier and, under pressure, he declared himself willing to undertake efforts in that direction. Kozłowski, who had remained in Berlin, was not cognizant of the situation in the GG. His family then explained it to him and thus diverted him from his plan. The death of Professor Kozłowski has forced the Germans to seek other persons who are willing to cooperate with them.

2. The publication of the "political" biweekly *Przełom,* published by the propaganda department in Kraków, must be regarded as a propagandistic concomitant to this campaign. The first issue is dated April 17; in early May, it was sent as a wrapped package to a few persons, and not until May 17 did it appear for general sale. The issue contained an appeal by Dr. Feliks Burdecki for cooperation with the Germans as well as an article by Jan Emil Skiwski, who condemns the Polish policy of resistance and German reprisals as wrong. The article urged making an end to reprisals and, in view of the Bolshevik threat, cooperating with the Germans.

3. *Przełom* was to give the impression that Polish society itself was resisting the policy of the Polish government and wanted a new political leadership.

4. Skiwski's article in *Przełom* exposed the essential goal as well as the weak position of the Germans in Poland. They wanted to appease the GG at any cost. This was covered by the demand they addressed to Ronikier at the beginning of the year: "An end to reprisals."[4]

Jankowski's assumption in point 1 was quite unfounded, judging from documents available to us today. Just as imprecise is the characterization of *Przełom* as a publication of the Reich Ministry for Public Enlightenment and Propaganda (RMVP), although the journal undoubtedly came into being at the instigation and with the financial support of the German authorities. In fact, *Przełom* was the organ of a Polish group which was ideologically close to the Nazi movement. Thus, in the history of the GG it was the first and only "reptile" newspaper in the real sense of the word. The publisher and editor in chief of *Przełom* was Dr. Feliks Stefan Burdecki, a former member of the *Stronnictwo Narodowe* and the author of several popular books on technol-

Fig. 6. *Przełom* (Breakthrough), a political biweekly issued by a group of Poles in collaboration with the Germans. In the August 1944 issue an analogy was drawn between the Bolshevik campaign against Poland, in 1920, and the Jewish uprising in the ghetto.

ogy, chemistry, natural science, and astronomy. He published works not only in Polish periodicals but also in foreign newspapers and journals, including *Kurier Poranny, Polska Zbrojna, Tygodnik Ilustrowany, Naokoło świata* (Around the World), *Państwo Pracy* (State of Work), *Przegląd Techniczny* (Technical Review), and the *Revue de Synthèse*. Burdecki was also the author of the historical-philosophical tract *Podstawy energetyki dziejowej* (Elementary Forces of History), in which he expressed his totalitarian views. Since the beginning of the occupation, Burdecki had maintained increasingly close contacts with the Germans and had showed his willingness to cooperate with them in the "re-education" of the Poles. In a memorandum for the German school authorities, he wrote on January 6, 1940: "It must be the goal of instruction to educate the youth in sober, rational, economic thinking, and to evoke the consciousness that only a firm cooperation with the National Socialist People's State (*nationalsozialistischen Volkstaat*), only common work in economics, technology, and culture, can be advantageous for the Polish ethnic group."[5] It is not known if the Germans replied and, if so, what answer they gave; there is no trace in the Polish archives. The occupation force, however, probably reacted negatively to this proposal. Even if the Germans did not need Burdecki as an ideologue at that time, they did make good use of his willingness to collaborate and turned over to him the administration of several school and professional journals (*Ster, Mały Ster, Zawód i Życie*).

The next person on the editorial staff of *Przełom,* after Burdecki, was Jan Emil Skiwski, a political commentator and literary critic before the war and former deputy chairman of the Federation of Polish Professional Authors (the Polish PEN Club). Skiwski had first been connected with the national-democratic *Myśl Narodowa* (National Thought), later with the liberal *Wiadomości Literackie* (Literary News), from which he switched to *Pion* (Plumbline), a journal that had been close to the prewar circles of *Sanacja*. In the last years before the war, Skiwski got close to the national radical camp (ONR), and during the occupation he openly acknowledged his sympathy for the Nazis, which is often discussed in the contemporary diaries and memoirs of Aurelia Wyleżyńska, Halina Krahelska, and Zuzanna Rabska. In April 1943, Skiwski was invited by the Germans on a trip to Katyń and gave an interview to the reptile press after his return, thus putting himself at the disposal of the broadly constructed campaign of the Reich propaganda ministry.[6] Skiwski also took part in the Nazi party–organized inspection of the officers' camps to show that Polish officers in German prisoner-of-war camps — unlike Russian ones — were treated humanely. In autumn 1944, after a few issues of *Przełom* had appeared, Skiwski gave Joseph Bühler, the undersecretary of the GG, an extensive memorandum expounding his and Burdecki's views on German-Polish relations. Along with a general change of Third Reich policy toward Poles and other Aryan peoples under German occupation, they advocated a change of the current day-to-day propaganda. The comments and demands in this memorandum largely coincided with what Burdecki and Skiwski regularly proclaimed in *Przełom,* but the confidential nature of the document allowed them to take up certain issues they either would not have wanted to deal with publicly or could not have because of the censor. This was particularly true of the appraisal of German Polish policy as well as the anti-German attitude in Polish society.[7]

Burdecki and Skiwski's biweekly (the two of them alone contributed half of all articles) was joined by Jerzy de Nisau, formerly a political commentator of the socialist press and, since 1923, of the National Camp.[8] There is not much that can be said definitively about the other staff members of *Przełom;* they were persons of whom nothing had previously been heard (for example, Stanisław Kościelski and Jan Kaczmarek) or who remained anonymous, signing themselves as "e.w.," "r," or "Obserwatero." The twenty-some letters which supposedly came from sympathizers and readers of *Przełom* were also signed with pseudonyms.

On the other hand, some persons, who had wanted to play the role of Quislings in the early period of the occupation or who had only sympathized with Nazism, refused all offers to work on *Przełom*. Władysław Studnicki must be mentioned especially here; he had repeatedly appealed to the German authorities both in the Reich and in the GG with definite proposals, always unsuccessfully. Now, in the fifth year of the war, the roles were reversed: this time the Germans were courting Studnicki. In his memoirs, Studnicki describes his conversation with Ohlenbusch in early 1944:

> Ohlenbusch: Frank is now very friendly to Poland and the Poles. He asked me to ask you what he can do for the Poles at this moment.
> Studnicki: He should pack his bags and leave Poland.
> Ohlenbusch: What!? Generalgouverneur Frank has come to know Poland and the Poles; he has dropped his prejudices and gained a certain sympathy.
> Studnicki: Someone who has carried out a policy of extermination for years, deported our farmers, brought in Germans from other countries and wanted to create colonial relations, even when he wants to pursue other policies, no longer finds any trust and even the friendliest statements will encounter disbelief and leave a bad taste.[9]

That is indeed a one-sided description, but it can be regarded as relatively credible since the style and character of the author are known from two memoranda addressed to the Germans. In any case, Studnicki did not write for *Przełom,* although the Germans had planned on his becoming editor in chief, as underground sources confirm.[10] Other potential proponents of Polish-German rapprochement also stayed away from *Przełom* — for example, Ferdynand Goetel and Stanisław Wasylewski, who had received explicit offers. Wasylewski, who had previously been associated with the *Gazeta Lwowska,* was indeed the only real representative of the literary world. That such men turned *Przełom* down means a good deal and testifies to the isolation of the obviously small and hardly representative group around Burdecki and Skiwski. Thus, Burdecki and Skiwski were in practice the only authors of *Przełom.* Their political line was embodied in countless articles which can be boiled down to one central statement: that it was simply necessary to cooperate with the occupation force and submit to Nazi Germany, at present as well as after the end of the war.[11]

The arguments justifying this necessity were presented by the publishers of *Przełom* in an ostensibly logical but essentially abstract train of thought. The starting thesis was that in the present world the sovereignty of individual small- and medium-sized states is obsolete and no longer corresponds to the course of events. The only state that can be completely independent is one with access to a potential to guarantee the protection of the nation and its cultural and material value in case of war. Poland by itself could not and would not be such a country. This recognition did indeed offend Polish national pride, but — as Burdecki asked in one of his articles — what value is there to independence if "within barely twenty years, it must lead inevitably to a war in which the national substance will be annihilated, the nation indescribably impoverished, and even the Polish name will slowly be wiped out?"[12] To counter this, a policy that holds onto the idea of national sovereignty must be renounced once and for all; instead, one must entrust oneself to those in a position to guarantee the best possibilities of development for Poland, as for the other small- and medium-sized nations of Europe. According to *Przełom,* the power capable of this sort of honorable mission cannot be England, for many reasons. England has shown by its previous behavior that "it does not possess the trace of a moral right to lead the European people."[13] Nor does it possess any such capacities, although it is a state with a powerful military and economic potential. In peace, as in war, the Britons demonstrate a lack of leadership capacity and a frighteningly low ethical level. Their tactic has always consisted of letting themselves be represented by weaklings — here the old thesis of the "continental dagger" of England arose again — and extracting their own advantage out of the efforts of foreign people.

Further, according to the authors of *Przełom,* the main victim of English policy had been Poland, which had entrusted its own fate after promises and guarantees given in 1939 and, after 1943, had been surrendered, along with much of Europe, to Russian influence. The Polish nation bore part of the blame, especially the prewar government and the current Polish emigré government. In this context, Burdecki wrote: "Ever since Minister Józef Beck — no doubt with the consent of a large part of Polish society — decided to conduct Polish policy in accord with the English, the Polish nation has fallen out of its life path and into catastrophe and defeat."[14] Somewhat earlier, Skiwski had expressed this very graphically:

> From 1939 to the present day, the street makes policy in Poland. General Sikorski of blessed memory was an upright patriot and a man with the best will, but he was no statesman on the European model. Even less can be said of the current premier of the emigré government [Stanisław Mikołajczyk]. For one, the efforts of these two men were and are aimed at obtaining the favor of the Anglo-Saxons; for another, they wavered between the various streams of public opinion in Poland so as not to wound anyone and to make everything right. It was not they who led and do lead the nation, but rather it is the moods in certain classes of society, which feed on political agitation, which lead it. In this way, a mountain of often contradictory demands was amassed, but they promised to satisfy all of them at the same time. We are not going with the Bolsheviks, but we are not going with the Germans either.[15]

Meanwhile — and this is the essential programmatic point of *Przełom* — reality demanded making a choice, since from time immemorial, in order to exist, Poles had to be supported either by Germany or by Russia. Not only did the idea of independence based on the guarantee of a distant alliance turn out to be unrealistic, but it also facilitated the disastrous idea that one could build national sovereignty on the base of German-Russian antagonism. As a thousand years of history shows, because of the abyss between the mentality of easterners and westerners, joining Russia—in particular Communist Russia—was unacceptable for Poland. As Skiwki wrote:

> The word *racism* is not popular in Poland; but it must be said openly: it has a profound meaning. We don't need to foster any hostile feeling toward other peoples and races; but that hardly leads to the conclusion that without protest we let a whole civilization perish, which is a fruit of the race we belong to and among whose creators we definitely are. The advance of the Soviets deep into Europe is not the advance of a new order with new political and social concepts and institutions. This is the advance of a foreign people which has long been hostile to us. This is the advance of a new Attila and Genghis Khan with modern methods of subjugation assisted by tanks and airplanes.[16]

The answer to the question of with whom and against whom the Polish people must go was declared in almost every article in *Przełom*: with Germany against Russia. One must join the Germans — whether they win or lose. In the first case, they would protect the Poles and other civilized nations against the fatal danger from the East; in the second, they would be the only support in the impending struggle against the Russian yoke. However, the *Przełom* group was profoundly convinced of a German victory in this war, even though many Poles, as Skiwski admitted, regarded their defeat as certain. The result of this victory would be a free, strong, and unified Europe directed by the Germans, with their undoubted capacity for leadership. They who had destroyed the make-believe order of Versailles had proved that they were prepared to take on the burden of responsibility for a new and better organization of the European international community. As Burdecki wrote: "We can obviously have doubts or concerns about whether the Germans are capable of properly filling their significant role; but in the current critical situation, in which the cultural independence of Europe is threatened, we do not have the right to refuse our support and our energy because of this concern when it is a matter of continuing European society." In another place, *Przełom* stated that it was indeed regrettable that the Poles had suffered under the Germans and had been humiliated by them, but now is not the time "to debate old pains and still-bloody wounds."[17]

In Burdecki's view, the solution was simple: Leave the underground! To him, everyone who raised weapons against a German soldier fighting in defense of Europe against Russia betrayed the Polish cause. Moreover, terror against the Germans led merely to the weakening of the biological strength of the Polish people. Today's Germany, declared Skiwski, was not the old czarist Russia. A state that conducts a titanic struggle with the greatest world powers is certainly not afraid of a group of terrorists, even if they could take credit for several successful attacks. A state that uses radical methods of government on its own people certainly does not flinch from the harshest reprisals against the Polish people.

Press
Policy
at the
End
of the
Occupation
143

As always, it is essential to evaluate this thesis independently of the persons who formulated it; but it must be stated that *Przełom* was very cleverly edited, something that cannot be said of the rest of the press in the GG. This time, the new propaganda policy of the occupation force was enunciated by men who had considerable intellectual capacities, who knew their society better than the Germans did, and who commanded a much richer arsenal of arguments to affect public opinion. Hence *Przełom*'s ostensibly scientific discussions — obviously with an answer in advance — for example, over the place of Poland in the European geopolitical system; the facility with which they found appropriate analogies from the most ancient and most recent history of the country; and, finally, the constant recourse to the authority of great and famous Poles, Batory, Sobieski, Żółkiewski and Zamoyski, Kościuszko and Mickiewicz. Those are only a few of the historical figures named and conscripted to support the political program launched by Skiwski and Burdecki in the columns of *Przełom*. The national mantle, in which the publishers of *Przełom* cloaked themselves, was coarsely stitched, however. For everyone who knew how to read the journal, it was only the "Polish" version of Goebbels's propaganda. This truth could not be concealed by Burdecki's and Skiwski's assurances and vows that *Przełom* was independent from the Germans; nor could all the verbosity explain the blank spaces in a few issues attributable to the supposed or actual censor.[18]

Burdecki, Skiwski, and de Nisau left Poland along with Hans Frank. On February 12, 1945, Frank wrote in his diary: "Arrival of the Polish High Committee in Neuhaus. Professor [?] Burdecki, Professor [?] Skiffski [!], Herr de Nisau. The gentlemen spent the night with their families in the Bergfrieden Hotel."[19]

Straż nad Bugiem, Strażnica[20]

The title *Straż nad Bugiem* (Watch on the Bug) turned out to be unfortunate since soon after the first few issues had appeared, Soviet troops crossed the Bug River and took Chełm, where the journal was published. *Strażnica* was its continuation. The symbolic character of the name was maintained, but now, as a precaution, the place of publication was no longer mentioned.

Unlike *Przełom,* both journals appeared anonymously. Anything that would have enabled the reader to ascertain the publisher or the members of the editorial staff was carefully avoided. Similarly, articles and news agency reports were not even signed with initials. On the other hand, it was no secret that the editorial staff was looking for people to distribute *Strażnica* in the small towns. Those who were interested were to apply to the press office in Częstochowa, at Ulica Marii Panny 52, or to the *Kurier Częstochowski,* in whose printing house *Straż* and *Strażnica* were most probably printed. Thus there was little doubt who these "nameless" publishers were who, as we shall see, emphasized their affiliation with the Polish people at every turn and spoke in their name.

Straż and *Strażnica* used other arguments than *Przełom* to prove the necessity of collaborating with the Germans. They talked about the Polish government-in-exile in an almost friendly tone, declaring it the constitutional Polish representative which had been assigned the thankless task of protecting and defending the interests of the Polish people in the difficult international arena. Full of appreciation, they wrote about the efforts of the Polish soldiers abroad and the Warsaw resisters, including General "Bór-Komorowski, who has fulfilled his duty to the end."[21] There were also flattering comments about England and the United States, countries where the democratic system had proved to be positive and long-lasting thanks to the high level of civilization of their inhabitants.[22] Even the Jews, to whom all sins of this world were openly attributed, received some kind words in *Strażnica,* which offered that one could "regret their tragedy and misfortune."[23]

Both newspapers, on the other hand, assumed a slightly critical attitude toward the occupation force while avoiding any mention of a future unity with the Germans. Thus, for example, this article appeared in the issue of August 1–10, 1944:

An Important but Unpleasant Issue:
Are Roundups Really Necessary?

Recently, extensive street roundups have taken place again in Częstochowa and other locations. They are a repulsive spectacle which leads to general unrest and confusion, and whose advisability may be hard to prove. And they occurred just as the Generalgouverneur was announcing wide-ranging changes in relations toward the Polish population.

The authorities inform us of the aim of this roundup. It turns out that too few people registered for work on the fortifications; but because this work must be completed, they fell back on the tested method of the roundup.

The matter concerns this method. Could the authorities not regulate the situation with law and order instead of this kind of repression? . . . We all understand that the fortifications have to be built, that it is in our interest not to let the Bolsheviks penetrate deeper into our country.

The views and opinions implied here depict a calling card to obtain for the publishers the right to appear as defenders of the Polish cause and of western civilization broadly understood—defenders against the Red danger from the east. Germany was the natural ally in this struggle since, even though it was in its own interest, it "protects the Polish territory with all its might against Russia." Consequently, it would be political nonsense to complicate the defense of the Weichsel (Wisła) line—illogical not only from the standpoint of Polish reasons of state, but also from that of the states that had been fighting for a long time on the side of the Soviet Union. Halting the advance of the Red Army into the interior of Europe would increase both the chances and the hopes that the outcome of the war would decide what kind of Polish cause would be most desirable and necessary, not between Russia and Germany, but rather between Germany and the Anglo-Saxon world.[24] Stopping the Soviet advance would have the immediate consequence of reinforcing the authority of the Polish government-in-exile, for as long as Russia could score successes on the eastern front, increasingly extensive concessions were demanded of the Poles in London. Hence the solution given by *Straż* and *Strażnica*: To the trenches! To the shovels! To reinforcements! For the realization of every Polish demand quite simply depends on German success on the eastern front.[25]

German Pseudo-Conspiratorial Papers

A group of publications posed as underground papers but were not: *Nowa Polska: Organ Polityczny Organizacji Niepodległościowej* (New Poland: Political Organ of the Independence Organization), *Nowa Polska, Głos Polski, Gazeta Narodowa, Nowy Czas, Goniec Krakowski, Wola Ludu,* and *Informator.* Their real publisher, the Main Department of Propaganda, used various means to make the reader believe they were genuine underground papers. They took pains to mislead by their titles and subtitles, or with such statements as "members of the Polish national independence movement,"[26] "Organ of the Polish Reasons of State,"[27] "a secret organization"[28] "Voice of the Polish People in Captivity."[29] In any case, these newspapers appeared in the small format typical of the underground press[30] and carried the phrase "Pass on after reading!" They generally referred to "our own" sources, that is, to the secret transmitter Świt (Dawn), the BBC and the Polish government-in-exile, and the underground press; "colleagues from other underground editorial staffs" were also quoted. Following the model of underground newspapers, a column for coded receipts for donations from readers and sympathizers for the press fund was provided. Quite often, a publisher fell "victim" to German terror, which "because of unforseen circumstances" caused a delay or a change of place of publication, format, or layout. As *Nowa Polska* wrote in no. 3 of November 1, 1944: "We inform our readers that as a result of the arrest of a few members of the editorial committee by the Gestapo, our issue cannot appear on time. As far as possible, our newspaper will appear every Sunday in the future after vacancies on the editorial committee are filled.[31] And in an issue of *Nowy Czas*: "Honor to our heroes! Mieczysław Rzewuski, one of our colleagues, victim of a hostile attack on the editorial staff of our newspaper, succumbed to his wounds. Our colleagues Stanisław Piotrkowski, Tadeusz Ostoj-Ostaszewski, Hiero-nim Wiśniewski, Tadeusz Jaremba, and Bolesław Jarek fell in the struggle for an independent Polish republic. The memory of these heroes will always remain alive in our ranks and will be a source of strength for us in further unyielding struggles for a free fatherland."[32]

Another of the new pseudo-underground periodicals was the *Goniec Krakowski,* whose publishers wrote that "more than one difficulty and more than one danger had to be overcome" to be able to bring it out. In this case, the Germans quite simply reverted to the model of Polish underground political journalism, which could count at least four fake issues of the reptile press to its account.

Furthermore, shrewd circulation methods were designed to prove the clandestine nature of all these journals: sales under the counter in the kiosks and through collaborationist street vendors, transmission through the mail to certain addresses, and distribution at dawn at the doors of private houses and offices. They even resorted to such tricks as fake arrest of the distributor, confiscation of the edition, and temporary detainment of the vendors. It was a masterful piece of work — hardly original, but not without ingenuity and cleverness. However, close examination of the contents and political suggestions were enough to dispel any doubt as to their origin.

Appropriately for publications that wanted to be considered underground, these newspapers were notorious for their anti-Nazi tone. Sharp criticism of the Germans was not spared and did not even exclude Hitler. The Nazis were reproached for Auschwitz, Maidanek, and Dachau,[33] and it was made clear that in no other country was the German occupation as merciless as in

Poland.[34] Finally, something kept secret was spoken aloud, that the Germans had the *entire* Polish people against them.[35] Hans Frank's statements about the new line in the GG were characterized as helpless stammering or phrases with no positive political conception behind them.[36]

Press
Policy
at the
End
of the
Occupation
147

In the opinion of the publishers of these papers, nothing good was to be expected from the Germans; but what the offensive of the Russian troops brought was a hundred times worse. Saving Poland and renewing it in the old borders could be realized only by a powerful and mighty blow of the Anglo-Saxons deep into Russia. But as long as the war in the West was not decided — and that did not go as fast as was wished — the Germans should remain on Polish territory. The German army, wrote the pseudo-underground *Goniec Krakowski,* was the only large armed power fighting the "Bolshevik hordes." Therefore, and not out of any irrational sympathy for the Germans, the victory of the German army in the defense of the eastern front is in the Polish interest; therefore, in the present situation, Poles should not hinder this army in its struggle against the eastern and Jewish inundation of Poland and Europe. In the light of the Bolshevik threat, the Polish struggle against the Germans recedes, and this is clear for every nationally conscious Pole and European.

In dealing with the Polish government in London and its organizations in Poland, these newspapers took a point of view that came close to that of *Straż* and *Strażnica,* but devoted more space to these issues. Every step of the Polish government was followed attentively. Whether they wrote well or badly about them depended on the attitude of the government-in-exile vis-à-vis the Soviet Union. In this respect, the attitude of *Nowa Polska* and *Gazeta Narodowa* was characteristic. These newspapers managed to turn around their view of the Polish government and the Warsaw Uprising from one edition to the next. Thus, for example, the October 1944 issue of *Nowa Polska* sharply condemned the instigators of the Warsaw Uprising and emphasized that the vast majority of the inhabitants of the capital were against it. In the next issue, however, *Nowa Polska* also wrote: "The AK [Home Army], under its leader and supreme commander General Bór-Komorowski, acquired eternal renown through its grim and courageous struggle, which impressed the entire world and even the enemy." The September and October issues of *Gazeta Narodowa* did something similar. In September the newspaper wrote: "Thus, he [Bór-Komorowski] is directly responsible for the catastrophe of Warsaw. World opinion must condemn him along with the Germans, the powerless Allies, and the criminal and treasonous Moscovites." In the following issue, the same newspaper confirmed that Bór-Komorowski was one of the greatest heroes of this war and that he would go down in history for exemplary courage and bravery, inflexibility, firmness, and tenacity. If we overlook the obvious lack of principles in these newspapers, this sudden change of views was conditioned by the further aggravation of the Polish-Russian conflict, after the premier of the government-in-exile, Mikołajczyk, did not accept the Soviet Union's demands for a Polish National Liberation Committee during his stay in Moscow in October 1944.

What is the essential element in the new attempt of the German occupation force to influence the behavior of the Polish population? What did the differentiation of journals in the final phase of the occupation mean? And finally, what did the Germans really hope for in this campaign?

A fundamental element of press policy in this period was the change of the propaganda solution of the Polish question. The Poles, who had previously been the object of vulgar abuse in the reptile press, were suddenly promoted to Europeans and defenders of western culture; but at a certain moment the Polish question, whose solution the Germans had announced for all time, became the object of "special concern" of the occupation force. Even in the final phase of its rule, this force strove for other, more ingenious methods to transmit their propaganda. Instead of a uniform press which addressed all groups of the population in one and the same language, several diverse journals were created, each of them tuned to a different circle of readers.

Przełom was undoubtedly issued with the idea of winning over that circle of Polish society which had formerly sympathized with German fascism. But, as has already been pointed out, until 1944 the Germans sought no Polish adherents to their ideology and programs. But by the time they thought of doing so, it was too late: an insuperable barrier had emerged between Germany, then on the brink of defeat, and the pro-German and pro-fascist circles in the Polish population. On the Polish side of this barrier lay millions of human victims, ruins, and fires; on the German side was hatred for everything Polish and for the fact that the crimes committed could not be concealed.

By contrast, *Straż nad Bugiem* and *Strażnica* were written with the assumption that despite sympathy for the government in London and a decisive rejection of Nazism, the Polish population would declare itself on the German side, at least for the time being, when it faced the choice between the new line of a moderate German occupation policy and Soviet occupation.

The quasi-underground press of the German propaganda department was based on similar assumptions. The differences between *Strażnica* and *Gazeta Narodowa* or *Nowa Polska,* however, were substantive. Through the circulation of pseudo-conspiratorial newspapers, the Germans admitted that they were no longer convinced they could come to Polish society in their own name with any political proposal. Moreover, this wide circulation indicates that it was clear to the Germans that everything bearing the official stamp of the occupation force was completely unacceptable to the Poles. Styrer, chief of the Weichsel transmitter in the GG, told Frank "that the Pole in principle says the opposite of what the German side reports. And the Pole takes everything that comes from the German side as something directed against him."[37]

Press
Policy
at the
End
of the
Occupation
149

All the papers discussed above appeared in the framework of the so-called Campaign Berta. Under this code name, from February 1944 on, the Main Department of Propaganda, along with the Security Police of the GG, carried out an extensive anti-Russian and anti-Communist campaign involving twelve million brochures of various kinds and almost twenty million fliers, whose real origin was often concealed.[38] Among other things, the propaganda department circulated mass editions of a paper, *PPR: Płatne Pachołki Rosji* (Polish Workers Party — in the Pay of Russia), whose title played on the name of the party established by the Communists during the occupation, Polska Partia Robotnicza; a false speech of Roosevelt: "Poland, Don't Worry! I Entrust You to the Benevolent Protection of Stalin";[39] and the instructions of a supposed "Committee of the Friends of the Red Army" for the annexation of Poland to the Soviet Union.[40]

A German propaganda department in the GG, along with the Wehrmacht this time, was busy copying articles from the American Polish press (for example, *Ameryka Echo* of Toledo, Ohio). Along with other anti-Soviet material, this patchwork was distributed among the Polish soldiers and officers of the Polish prisoner-of-war camps (for both officers and enlisted men).[41] And finally, in Kraków, there was a center that prepared the anti-Soviet fliers supposedly signed by Polish independence organizations and dropped on Italian towns where Polish military units were concentrated. Ohlenbusch, who personally directed this campaign, emphasized at a government meeting that it gave him a special satisfaction that the Reich Ministry for Public Enlightenment and Propaganda had entrusted the job to him.[42]

In Campaign Berta, staff assemblies were organized in the GG, and compulsory meetings of official employees and schoolchildren were held to pass "spontaneous" anti-Soviet and anti-Communist resolutions. The police and the GG authorities forced the Polish population to attend these meetings, which generally concluded with pro-German speeches. But physical force was not the only means. People were brought together in large numbers by the promise of various entertainments such as concerts, small theatrical reviews, newsreels, and radio programs. The police proposed the formation of partisan units in the GG allegedly armed by Russia, "who behaved annoyingly in order to stop the population from sympathizing with the Soviets."[43] The normal reptile press was also harnessed to "Campaign Berta." All of them — *Nowy Kurier Warszawski, Goniec Krakowski, Kurier Częstochowski,* and others — stated both simply and perfidiously that they represented "the authentic interests of the Polish people." The acme of perversion was the articles that appeared during the Warsaw uprising: from the start of the uprising, on August 1, to August 20 there was not a word about the outbreak of the struggles in the capital.

Following Ohlenbusch's definition of the campaign as an attempt to allow the Poles to speak, as a first step toward creating a Polish anti-Bolshevik league, Campaign Berta was to fill various tasks, some short-range, others aimed at the future. The first group includes appeasement of territories near the front, the mobilization of a labor force for war production, the instigation of a civil war between the "London" underground and groups of the Polish Workers Party and the the People's Army, as well as the attempt to gain influence throughout the GG over the attitude of the government-in-exile toward the Soviet Union and the western allies. The second group comprises the creation of an anxiety psychosis about the Soviet army and the Lublin Poles (a pro-Soviet government was established in Lublin after the city's capture by the Red Army in July 1944) in order to alleviate the evacuation of the population and the transport of stocks. The strident descriptions of the impending danger from the East was aimed at creating an appropriate climate for a new conspiracy — this time behind Soviet army lines.

Nevertheless, the efforts of the Germans to use the Polish population in the final phase of the occupation were not goals in themselves, as indicated in the April 12, 1944, bulletin of the press information department of Armia Krajowa headquarters: "The unsubstantiated intensive anti-Soviet (and anti-English) propaganda cannot be explained as an aspiration to draw the Poles to the German side. . . . This whole violent and stubborn propaganda campaign strives only for secondary (instead of real) goals." The bulletin formulated these goals thus:

1. To stem the social power of the rebels by emphasizing the might and imperialistic tendencies of the Soviets. 2. To contribute indirectly to the reinforcement of the inflexible behavior of the country vis-à-vis Soviet claims and to the deepening of the political conflicts in the allied camp which began with [the discovery] of the Katyń graves, with its effect on the Polish population (a knockout blow for those who were resistant to German propaganda, and a clear influence on the politically inexperienced). 3. To facilitate the expected evacuation of Polish workers by rousing fear of Bolshevik terror (press, propaganda meetings for workers).[44]

The actual results of Campaign Berta, like those of the previous propaganda campaign with the motto Katyń, did not fulfill the hopes of the Nazis — as they themselves clearly recognized. Kundt, governor of the District of Radom, testified to that at a conference in Radom on May 26, 1943:

Press
Policy
at the
End
of the
Occupation
151

> The case of Katyń hardly had an effect as the result of the much too strongly noticed agitation among the population. The agitation was carried out so that the most primitive Pole had to see clearly that it was not a feeling of humanity but rather agitational material directed at foreigners. The Poles would have hardly reacted to it according to their knowledge of things.[45]

Dr. Eberhard Schöngarth, commander of the Security Police and the SD (Security Service), wrote in his report of May 31, 1943, on the situation in the GG: "The majority of the Polish intelligentsia, as always, is not influenced by the news of Katyń and rebukes the Germans for supposed similarly repulsive acts, especially Auschwitz. Among the broad masses of the Polish population, the news about Katyń does not evoke any favorable consequences for the Germans." That Frank quoted an excerpt from Schöngarth's report in his memorandum to Hitler of June 19, 1943, indicates that opinion on this issue was not monolithic.[46]

The Germans judged Campaign Berta in the same way. Governor Kundt said that politically it was completely worthless. Dr. Kurt Ludwig von Burgsdorff and Dr. Ludwig Fischer, governors of the Districts of Kraków and Warsaw, also expressed skepticism.[47] Indeed, the only one who believed that Campaign Berta exercised a "constant and successful influence on the Polish population" was Ohlensbusch, the main organizer of the whole enterprise. But when he set about to build a so-called Polish Anti-Bolshevik League, it turned out that aside from Burdecki (its chairman), Skiwski and de Nisau he could not find any other candidates.

The hopes of the occupation force for the pacification of the Polish territory were not realized either. This goal was not to be attained either by terror or by propaganda. The resistance movement that commenced in September 1939 reached its culmination precisely in the period between the spring and fall of 1944, when the big partisan fights, in which divisions numbering thousands of AK (Home Army), AL (the Communist Armia Ludowa), and BCh (Peasant Battalions) participated, were taking place on Polish territory. Furthermore, this increase of resistance activity of the entire people happened right behind the back of the German army. In practical terms, said Frank on May 16, 1944, a third of the District of Lublin was no longer in the hands of the Germans, where their administration no longer functioned and the transportation system had almost completely come to a standstill. In this area, the German police could appear only in regimental strength.[48]

Although German propaganda did not achieve the expected effect, especially in 1944, it is wrong to believe that it had no effect at all on the consciousness of the society it was intended for. To draw up an objective and documented analysis of the political and social consequences of the German propaganda campaign at the end of the occupation is unusually difficult, even largely impossible. Research on this problem is complicated not only by the fact that sources are missing, but also by the nature of the object of research: that is, the press during the occupation did not operate in a vacuum. At the same time, the Polish underground press appeared, the overwhelming majority of which adopted a decidedly negative and hostile point of view toward the Soviet Union, but also toward the Polish National Liberation Committee (PKWN, the Lublin puppet government) and the Polish Workers Party; a press which, through its link with the center of power in London, was directed by divergent conceptions of the sovereignty of the state and its constitution, as well as by a traditional aversion to the Russians and to communism. There were also underground papers that, after realizing that both Germany and Russia were the enemies of Poland, called for an immediate cessation of the struggle against Germany. But such an extreme standpoint in 1944 was taken only by the press of the far right Narodowe Siły Zbrojne. We also know that some of the armed divisions of this group, like the *Brygada Świętokrzyska,* cooperated actively with the Germans against the Soviet Union and the Communists, and left Poland with their German allies in 1945. But even in this case, it cannot be determined if German propaganda and persuasion produced that collaboration or if it is to be attributed to an independent political program. Aside from the case of the *Brygada Świętokrzyska,* German attempts failed to win over any specific groups of Polish society.

Poland was a country without a Quisling. But for the sake of historical precision, it must be said that in the course of their more than five-year rule in Poland, the Germans never seriously attempted to produce such a figure; for without some tangible concessions, including a margin of sovereignty (no matter how narrow), there was no place for Quislingism in Poland.

Conclusion

The Polish press, decimated during the war in the autumn of 1939, was completely liquidated shortly after the occupation of Poland. Never before in the history of Poland had the occupation force deprived the defeated country of the right to its own press. During the time of partition by the three powers, newspapers and journals appeared in Galicia (under Austria), in Congress Poland (under Russia), and in the Prussian part which were legal and published by Poles. Often, indeed, this was an "influenced" press, under strict censorship, and in some ways the partitioning powers wanted it to serve their purposes. Still, a Polish press did exist. This type of legal press also appeared in almost all the countries occupied by Germany during World War II, obviously under different conditions: in the Protectorate of Bohemia-Moravia, in Denmark, Norway, Belgium, Holland, France, Serbia, and Greece, and to some extent in a few occupied areas of the Soviet Union: in Lithuania, Latvia, and Estonia.

In almost all these countries, especially in Scandinavia and Western Europe, the Germans attempted in various ways to win over the local population. Hence the policy of compromise and concession, and attempts to create collaborationist governments in these countries — attempts that often succeeded. One apparent form of this policy was the relatively liberal policy toward the press and radio — more liberal than in the Reich itself.

For the historian investigating the German occupation in Poland, the extent, thematic disparity, and multiplicity in the forms of organization of the press in the other German-occupied territories must be surprising. Thus, for example, in Bohemia-Moravia, according to the statistical data of 1941, 1,733 press titles appeared, including 55 daily newspapers, as well as 350 journals devoted to culture, pedagogy, and various sciences, including health service and physical education.[1] At the same time, in occupied France, not counting the professional periodicals, about a hundred daily and weekly newspapers were published;[2] and in Athens alone, eight daily newspapers appeared, exactly as many as in the GG from 1939 to 1944.[3] In Denmark and Holland, respectively, 134 and 129 newspapers and journals were published during the German occupation.[4] Even during the war, the legal press in these countries was printed in sizable editions: in Paris, for example, the fifty newspapers appearing there reached a total edition of about three million copies.[5]

The legal press in the other occupied countries was largely a continuation of the newspapers and journals of the prewar period, politically as well as formally. Even in the war, their publishers were private persons, press agencies, and cultural, religious, professional, social, and even political organizations. In Denmark, to cite an extreme case, among the many social democratic papers an organ of the Danish Communists, *Arbejdebladet,* also appeared.[6] It was liquidated by order of the Nazi authorities only after the outbreak of the German-Soviet war in July 1941.

Moreover, in almost all the occupied countries there were federations of publishers and journalists — for example, *Národní Svaz Novinářů* in Bohemia-Moravia, *Corporation de la Presse* in France, and *Journalisten Innung* in Holland. In universities and vocational schools, the next generation of journalists and editors was trained. In many capitals, organizations of accredited foreign representatives of editorial staffs and press agencies from the Reich, neutral states, satellite states, and a few occupied countries were working, such as the federation of the foreign press in Paris, in which eighty-four journalists from twenty-seven countries were represented.[7]

Of course it was a muzzled press, subject to strict political censorship and to the pressure of the authorities and the police, and on the part of not only the occupation force but also the local collaborationist government. The right to allow a newspaper to continue appearing or to reopen was granted only to those editors who were loyal to the Germans and the government collaborating with them. Disloyalty entailed various kinds of repression: loss of the right to sell, shutting down of the publishing house, and arrest of members of the editorial staff. An equally successful measure to influence the character and direction of the legal press was the system widely used by the Germans which won "trustees" among publishers and journalists, through purchase or otherwise. Not least, the occupation force was also aided by certain extreme right-wing and fascist groups and parties who carried on an especially lively organizational and publishing activity in the territories dependent on the Germans under the new order and on a climate that was politically favorable for them.

Through a clever and supple policy, the Germans also succeeded in guaranteeing for themselves a certain amount of cooperation of the rather large number of journalists who covered the professions. František Bauer says of these journalists that despite their cooperation, their patriotism was never in doubt. For their behavior as nationally conscious citizens they often paid with their lives or were sent to a concentration camp.[8] Moreover, the printing presses and editorial staffs of the legal press often formed a technical and material reservoir for the underground press. Unlike the reptile press in the GG, the legal press outside the GG remained to some degree available for journalists to express their own views and opinions on culture, economics, morals, and customs.[9] Therefore, it was not only an instrument of propaganda in the Nazi sense but also, to a certain extent, an expression of public opinion — even if a muzzled one.

Whether it concerned the situation on the front, events in the country, or world politics, the legal press in the Protectorate, Denmark, Norway, and France informed the populace in a much more extensive and diversified way than in occupied Poland. And the population could still get news from radios, which were not confiscated, even if — as elsewhere in the Reich — listening to enemy broadcasts was threatened with harsh punishment.

The legal press in the occupied West European countries or even in the Protectorate of Bohemia-Moravia, which appeared to present reliable information, was at the same time very dangerous because it imitated a free and independent objective press and thus was actually or at least potentially capable of exercising a Nazi influence over the population of the occupied country. A large mass of clandestine writings also appeared in these countries, despite an extensive legal press and the radio. The struggle of the underground press with the propaganda of the occupation force and collaborationist circles was not simple.

The situation in the press sector that developed during the German occupation was both the result and the function of the general policy of the Third Reich toward the subjugated peoples of Europe. In the countries mentioned above, despite specific and completely different forms of government and methods at the time, the German occupation was never as ruthless and as brutal as in Poland. Only farther east, in the occupied Soviet territories in the Russian, White Russian, and Ukrainian republics, did comparably severe conditions prevail.

In Poland, terror and extermination, forced labor programs, and wholesale plunder were the expressions of an occupation policy outside recognized law and without the slightest understanding of the long-term effect. Political results cannot be insured by propaganda and naked force. This study has tried to present a picture of this singular phenomenon.

Notes

Introduction

1. *Gazeta Żydowska* was published in Kraków, in Polish, from July 1940 to summer 1942. The paper was edited by Jews connected with the *Judenraten* (Jewish councils) and served as yet another tool to mislead the Jewish population about the real Nazi plans. In 1941 and 1942 one could find in it arcticles about the development of so-called Jewish autonomy and the productivization of the Jews in the ghettos of the GG alongside Jewish achievements in Palestine. The *Gazeta Żydowska* also reprinted stories in Polish translation by classic Jewish writers like Mendele Moykher Sforim, Sholem Aleichem, and I. L. Peretz. To complete the deception, the paper introduced Hebrew lessons using the Hebrew alphabet. The Nazi Department of Public Enlightenment and Propaganda in Kraków was behind the *Gazeta Żydowska*. The paper was distributed only to people cut off from the outside world, that is, in the ghettos. When the mass extermination of Jews began, the *Gazeta Żidowska* was reduced from twelve pages to eight, then to four, and finally was discontinued altogether.

2. See *Presse in Fesseln: Eine Schilderung des NS Pressetrusts* (Berlin, 1948), 126ff., and H. Seemann, "Zeitungen für die ausländischen Arbeiter in Deutschland," in *Zeitungswissenschaft: Monatschrift für die Internationale Zeitungsforschung* 10, no. 20 (1942), 529.

3. Archiwum Głównej Komisji Badania Zbrodni Hitlerowskich w Polsce, Warsaw [hereafter cited as AGKBZH], Sign. z/OR 154, vols. 1–2; Correspondence of the Main Department of Propaganda in the GG and the District Administrators of Blachnowia and Wieluń with the editor-in-chief of the *Kurier Częstochowski.*

4. See A. Czarski, "Zajęcie drukarni 'Godziny Polski,' " *Z dziejów prasy socjalistycznej w Polsce* (Warsaw, 1919), 81: "Only after acquiring independence did the documents in the editorial office, especially the journal of Meiner, the 'official' editor of *Godzina,* confirm the full dimension of the assumption that the newspapers were subsidized by the Germans."

5. T. Cieślak, *Z dziejów prasy polskiej na-Pomorzu Gdańskim w okresie zaboru pruskiego* (Gdańsk, 1964), 10ff.; A. Wojtkiewicz, letter to the editor, *Polityka,* no. 46 (Nov. 17, 1962).

6. D. Durr, "Our Mission," *Krakauer und Warschauer Zeitung,* no. 1 (Nov. 12, 1939).

1: The First Measures

1. Erich Murawski, *Der deutsche Wehrmachtsbericht, 1939–1945: Ein Beitrag zur Untersuchung der geistigen Kriegsführung* (Boppard, 1962), 137.

2. K. M. Pospieszalski, "Hitlerowskie 'prawo' okupacyjne w Polsce," *Documenta Occupationis 5* (Poznań, 1952), pt. 2:11.

3. Deutsches Zentralarchiv I, Potsdam [hereafter cited as DZA-Potsdam], Sign. 876, vol. 34, Files of RMVP; K. Scheel, "Der Aufbau der faschistischen PK-Einheiten vor dem zweiten Weltkrieg," *Zeitschrift für Militärgeschichte* 4 (1965), 454ff.; see also A. Dresler, "Die Presse in Generalgouvernement für die besetzten Polnischen Gebiete," *Zeitungswissenschaft* 15, no. 4 (1940), 139.

4. M. Czygański, *Mniejszość niemiecka w Polsce w latach, 1918–1939* (Łódź, 1962), 55; F. Goetel, *Czasy Wojny* (London, 1955), 31; W. Czarnecki, "Wyprawa po wielki reportaż," *Wspomnienia dziennikarzy o wrześniu 1939r* (Warsaw, 1965), 21; J. Lankau, "Prasa krakowska w przełomowych dniach wrześniowych," *Prasa współczesna i dawna* 1 (1958), 79–89; *Almanach deutsches Wort im Osten: Ein Jahr Krakauer Zeitung* (Kraków, 1941), 57, 61; F. Gollert,

Warshau unter deutscher Herrschaft: Deutsche Aufbauarbeit im Distrikt Warschau ([Kraków], 1942), 271.

5. Wojewódzkie Archiwum Państwowe, Łódź [hereafter cited as WAP-Łódź], Sign. 1015/10/I, Files of the Heads of the Civilian Administration in the German Eighth Army.

6. Scheel, "Faschistischen PK-Einheiten," 455.

7. "Zeitgeschichte der Frontpresse," *Deutsche Press* 29, no. 21 (Oct. 14, 1939); *Handbuch der deutschsprachigen Zeitungen im Ausland* (Essen, 1940), 185; "Bibliographie der deutschen Feld- und Soldatenzeitungen des Zweiten Weltkrieges," *Bücherschau der Weltkriegsbücherei* 26 (1954), 428–434.

8. *Almanach deutsches Wort in Osten,* esp. 55.

9. See Roger Manvell and Heinrich Fraenkel, *Doctor Goebbels: His Life and Death* (London, 1960), 186: "Goebbels laid down a careful policy for approach to be made by Germany for the foreign listener before conquest. The first stage was to establish a friendly atmosphere — Germany the neighbour. The second stage involved criticism developing into open attack on the country and the policy of its leaders. The third stage involved the threats of violence to come and the need for the people to get rid of their leaders and capitulate. The last stage was the interim period of deliberate confusion before the Germans themselves took control of the nation's broadcasting from the home stations."

10. See Hans Frank, *Diensttagebuch* [hereafter cited as DTgb], 37:185; S. Zadrożny, *Tu — Warszawa: Dzieje radistacji powstańczej "Błyskawica"* (London, 1964), 92; and H. Heiber, *Joseph Goebbels* (Berlin, 1962), 171–179.

11. See *Ilustrowany Kurier Codzienny,* no. 249 (Sept. 11, 1939); *Express Poranny* (Sept. 20, 1939); *Dobry Wieczór, Kurier Czerwony,* no. 261 (Sept. 20, 1939); and *Dziennik Polski,* no. 252 (Sept. 14, 1939). For a detailed report of German radio sabotage during the September campaign, see M. Kwiatkowski, "Warszawska rozgłośnia Polskiego Radia we srześniu 1939," *Najnowsze Dzieje Polski: Materiały i Studia z okresu II wojny światowej* 7 (1964), 5–43.

12. DZA-Potsdam, RMVP Files, Abteilung Rundfunk, vol. 13.

13. Ibid., 23:232ff.

14. Dagobert Dürr was recalled to the RMVP on Dec. 31, 1939; DZA-Potsdam, vol. 24.

15. WAP-Łódź, Files of the Heads of the Civilian Administration in the German Eighth Army, 1015/10/I, p. 13; Teletype of SS-Stubaf Dr. Grosskopf to the leader of Einsatzgruppe 3, SS-Stubaf Dr. Fischer.

16. Thus, for example, the order of H. Rüdiger, head of the Civilian Administration in the German Tenth Army, issued on Sept. 12, 1939, concerning the confiscation of radio equipment was withdrawn on Sept. 29, 1939. For the Jewish population it continued to be valid. See AGKBZH, Files of the Bühler Trial, 24:18, 38.

17. Ibid., 55, Rüdiger's order of Oct. 1, 1939.

18. Centralne Archiwum Wojskowe, Warsaw [hereafter cited as CAW], II/17, p. 8. Similar orders for the areas integrated into the Reich came somewhat earlier. See Pospieszalski, "Hitlerowskie 'prawo,' " pt. 1:65.

19. WAP-Łódź, Files of the Head of the Civilian Administration of the German Eighth Army, 1015/9, p. 65, Order of the Day No. 15 of Oct. 23, 1939.

20. Archiwum Żydowskiego Instytutu Historycznego [hereafter cited as AŻIH], Sign. 46, Collection of R. Ringelblum.

21. S. Nawrocki, *Hitlerowska okupacja Wielkopolski w okresie zarządu wojskowego: Wrzesień-październik 1939r* (Poznań, 1966), 228.

22. Order concerning newspapers and journals. Order about confiscation of the property of printing enterprises and publishing establishments hostile to Germany. For the complete text of both documents, see Pospieszalski, "Hitlerowskie 'prawo,' " pt. 1:66, 67–70.

23. Instytut Historii Polskiej Akademii Nauk, Warsaw [hereafter cited as IHPAN], *Memoriał w sprawie strat wojennych przemysłu graficznego w Polsce z 3/I/1942r., opracowany przez Delegaturę Rządu na Kraj;* Archiwum Zakładu Historii Parti [hereafter cited as AZHP], Sign. 202/III/151, *Sekcja Zachodnia: Dotychczasowy przebieg akcji 'niemczenia' Pomorza;* Centralne Archiwum Ministerstwa Spraw Wewnętrznych, Warsaw [hereafter cited as CAMSW)], Sign. 101/III, *E., Biuletyn W[ydziału] S[połecznego],* Report "Straty kulturalne." See also J. Deresiewicz, *Okupacja na ziemiach polskich wcielonych do Rzeszy, 1939–1945* (Poznań, 1950), 266, and K. Świerkowski, "Przemiany drukarstwa polskiego z biegiem wieków," *Księga pamiątkowa związku zawodowego pracowników poligrafii, 1870–1960* (Warsaw, 1960), 18ff.

24. Memorandum Wetzel-Hecht: "Die Frage der Behandlung der Bevölkerung der ehemaligen polnischen Gebiete nach rassenpolitischen Gesictspunkten," *Biuletyn GKBZH* 4 (1948), 148. The German text is published in Pospieszalski, "Hitlerowskie 'prawo,' " pt. 1:2–28. Polish was tolerated practically only in the local official gazettes, especially in Upper Silesia and the Dąbrowa District. Orders in Polish parallel to the official German were presented in such organs as the *Verordnungsblatt der Oberbürgermeister der Stadt Sosnowitz, Amtsblatt der Stadt Dombrowa Gornicza,* and *Amtsblatt der Stadt Bendzin.* But they also quickly dispensed with the Polish version. In Pomerania and Poznań, orders usually appeared in German, even though there, too, with certain exceptions. Thus, for example, the orders of the German military and civilian authorities in the Włocławek (Leslau) area were published in the local newspaper *ABC dla Włocławka i Kujaw.* This was certainly the only case of an old Polish newspaper title being used again. Before the war, the newspaper was a local edition of the Warsaw main newspaper *ABC Obozu Narodowo-Radykalnego.* It appeared first in Polish, then bilingually (from Oct. 10 to Dec. 1939), with German and Polish titles, and finally became the German *Weichselzeitung.*

25. See Frank, DTgb, 1:4, 39, 61.

2: The Emergence of Polish Newspapers

1. L. Szczepański, "Zapiski dla użytku przysłego kronikarza: Jak żylismy pod bombami," *Dziennik Krakowski* nos. 3, 4 (Sept. 11, 12, 1939); J. Grabowski, "Zarząd Miejski w czasie okupacji," *Kraków w latach okupacji, 1939–1945: Materiały i studia* (Kraków, 1949–1957), 3 (Rocznik Krakowski 31).

2. For more details, see Lankau, "Prasa krakowski," 79–89.

3. Ibid., 84.

4. *Dziennik Krakowski* nos. 1, 3 (Sept. 8, 11, 1939).

5. Lankau, "Prasa krakowski," 84.

6. *Ilustrowany Kurier Codzienny* (Lemberg ed.), Sept. 8, 1939.

7. Ibid., Sept. 18, 1939.

8. Archiwum Sądu Wojewódzkiego w Krakowie [hereafter cited as ASW-Kraków], IV K 22/50, 5:171, Files of the Criminal Trial against F. Burdecki and E. Skiwski.

9. Lankau, "Prasa krakowski," 85.

10. According to Lankau, the conference took place Sept. 9, 1939.

11. ASW-Kraków, IV K 22/50, 5:62ff.

12. Lankau, "Prasa krakowski," 85.

13. Ibid.

14. Ibid., no. 267 (Oct. 9, 1939). Along with the change of title, a new editorial staff also appeared; one of them, Władysław Machejek, currently one of the leading writers and political journalists in the People's Republic of Poland, began his career in the reptile press. He published two short love stories, "Bożenny wina" (Oct. 12, 1939) and "Miłość na kartki" (Oct. 14, 1939).

15. S. Rybicki, *Pod znakiem lwa i kruka: Fragmenty wspomnień z lat okupacji* (Warsaw, 1965); J. Pietrzykowski, *Hitlerowcy w Częstochowie w latach, 1939–1945* (Poznań, 1959), 13.

16. Archiwum Sadu Wojewodzkiego w Kielcach [hereafter cited as ASW-Kielce], IV K, 79/49, 3:5, Files of the Criminal Case against Stanisław Homan.

17. Wilkoszewski was arrested again on June 19, 1940, in the so-called AB-Campaign (Ausserordentliche Befriedungsaktion, or Special Pacification Campaign), and imprisoned in a concentration camp, where he was killed. AGKBZH, Sign. z/OR 154, 2 (unnumbered), Correspondence and Administration of *Kurier Częstochowski,* memorandum of editor Machura to Strozyk (June 20, 1940). See also Pietrzykowski, *Hitlerowcy,* 34, 244ff.

18. AGKBZH, Files of the Bühler Trial, 24:13, Head of the Civilian Administration, Order of the Day No. 7.

19. ASW-Kielce, Files of the Criminal Case against S. K. Homan, 3:5.

20. Ibid., 319.

21. AGKBZH, Files of the Bühler Trial, 24:13.

22. They are currently in the Museum of the City of Radom.

23. A. Piwowarczyk, "Prasa nad Uherką oraz Chełmska gadzinówka: Przyczynek do lat okupacji," *Kamena* 13/14 (1961), 11, 15; ibid., 10 (1967), 10.

24. CAMSW, Sign. 210 (unnumbered), Files of the Town Major of Kielce, Propaganda Department.

25. AGKBZH 154/OR, vol. 1 (unnumbered), Memorandum of the Main Department of Propaganda to the Propaganda Department in the District of Radom, June 28, 1940; Memorandum of the Selbstschutzbereichsführer of Radomsk-Częstochowa to the editor of *Kurier Częstochowski,* Feb. 3, 1940; Memorandum of Michał Nowacki, trustee of the printing house M. & J. Pański, to SS Headquarters in Radomsk (undated; received Jan. 31, 1940).

26. As a Jewish business, this plant was given to the trustee M. Nowacki.

27. Zygmunt Klukowski, *Dziennik z lat okupacji Zamojszczyzny* (n.p., n.d.), 66.

28. See W. Bortnowski, *Na tropach łódzkiego września: Z dziejów kampanii wrześniowej na terenie województwa łódzkiego* (Łódź, 1962), 202.

29. WAP-Łódź 1015/3, 1–3; Bulletin of the Citizens' Committee of Łódź. See also M. Czygański, "Komitet Obywatelski m. Łodzi, Sept. 6–Sept. 9, 1939," *Rocznik Łódzki* 2/5 (1959), 71–90; I. Józefowiczowa, "Wspomnienia o biskupie Tomczaku," *Tygodnik Powszechny,* no. 19 (May 19, 1968).

30. Personal interview with Mieczysław Jagoszewski.

31. WAP-Łódź, 1015/3, 1, Files of the Heads of the Civilian Administration of the German Eighth Army: Memorandum of the Citizens' Committee of the City of Łódź to Major Koepp[e]l; ibid., 5, Grosskopf's remarks on the *Bulletin.*

32. WAP-Łódź 1015/10/I, Memorandum of the Head of the Civilian Administration in the Southern Army Group to the Head of the Civilian Administration of the German Eighth Army; see also Erdmann's memorandum to Fischer.

33. WAP-Łódź 1015/10/I, 118ff., Files of the Head of the Civilian Administration of the German Eighth Army, including Memorandum of the Editor-in-Chief of the German Łódź Newspaper to Grosskopf.

34. Ibid.

35. WAP-Łódź 1015/2, 10, General Memoranda of the Reichs Propaganda Office I (undated).

36. *Gazeta Łódzka,* nos. 1–42 (Sept. 22–Nov. 9, 1939); *Deutsche Lodzer Zeitung,* no. 273 (Sept. 8, 1939).

37. Most of these newspapers have survived and are now in the National Library of Warsaw and in the AZHP in Warsaw.

38. See *Polskie Siły Zbrojne w drugiej wojnie światowej,* 3 vols. (London, 1950–62), vol. 1:

Kampania wrześniowa, 1939, 1:250; Z. Zaremba, *Wojna i konspiracja* (London, 1957), 18ff.; J. Nowakowski, "7 godzin przed pierwszym nalotem: Z notatnika sprawozdawcy parlamentarnego," *Biuletyn Komitetu Obchodu 300-lecia Prasy Polskiej* 17 (1961), 7–11; W. Wagner, "Robotnik w oblężonej Warszawie: Na Wareckiej we wrześniu," *Robotnik,* no. 243/643 (Sept. 3, 1949); and W. Giełżyński, "Prasa w dniach oblężenia Warszawy," *Stolica,* no. 36 (1939).

39. See *Kronika dni wrześniowych: Zestawił Nemo* (Warsaw, 1942), 9; KOPR Publishers (pseudonym for Information and Propaganda Department of the AK, Warsaw Region); W. Giełżyński, "Dziennikarstwo warszawskie podczas okupacji hitlerowskiej," lecture to the Zespół Starszych Dziennikarzy Stowarzyszenia Dziennikarzy Polskich, typescript in IHPAN.

40. T. Tomaszewski, *Byłem szefem sztabu Obrony Warszawy* (London, 1961), 28ff.; Kwiatkowski, "Warszawska rozgłośnia," 16ff.; J. Małgorzewski, "Relacja o działalności Polskiego Radia w obronie Warszawy," *Cywilna obrona Warszawy we wrześniu, 1939* (Warsaw, 1964), 280.

41. *Cywilna obrona Warszawy,* 23, 30.

42. Kwiatkowski, "Warszawska rozglosnia," 19.

43. *Kurier Codzienny,* no. 253 (Sept. 13, 1939).

44. C. Nusbaum, *Moje wspomnienia o pracy na Ratuszu i w Biurze Prasowym Z.M. m.St. Warszawy, 1934–1939,* Archiwum Państwowe m.St. Warszawy i Województwa Warszawskiego [hereafter cited as APW], Sign. 268; *Express Poranny* (Sept. 16, 1939); *Kurier Codzienny,* no. 258a (Sept. 18, 1939).

45. For more information, see Giełżyński, "Prasa," and J. Krawczyńska, "Wapomnienia o informacji prasowej 'Biuletyn Prasowy dla użytku piam warszawskich,' " *Cywilna obrona Warszawy,* 229–237.

46. W. Dunin-Wąsowicz, "Lista strat dziennikarstwa polskiego, 1939–1945." The typescript was kindly put at my disposal by the family of the author. *Dziennik Ludowy i Powszechny* (Sept. 9, 1939); K. K. Ch., " 'Robotnik' we wrześniu, 1939," *Robotnik,* no. 328 (Dec. 1, 1947); Borowy, *Prasa,* 27.

47. *Gazeta Wspólna,* no. 1 (Sept. 27, 1939).

48. Ibid.

49. See the Order of General Juliusz Rómmel, head of Army Warsaw, concerning the signing of the surrender document, as well as the implementation regulation of Stefan Starzyński, mayor of Warsaw, of Sept. 28, 1939; AZHP 76/III/7/2, vol. 10, 214/V-12. The complete text of both documents is published in *Cywilna obrona Warszawy,* 125–129, 129ff.

50. Ibid.

51. Giełżyński, "Dziennikarstwo warszawskie," 5ff.

52. *ABC-Nowiny Codzienne,* Spółdzielna Wydawnictwa (ed. Jan Korolec); *Czas,* Spółdzielnia Wydawnictwa Czasopism (ed. Dr. Jan Moszynski); *Dobry Wieczór, Express Poranny, Kurier Czerwony,* Dom Prasy (ed. Stanislaw Cwierciakiewicz); *Goniec Warszawski,* Goniec Warszawski (ed. Marian Gregorczyk); *Ilustrowany Dziennik Ludowy,* Zespół Czasopism (ed. Szczepan Dzikowski; after Oct. 3, 1939, Zygmunt Zaremba); *Kurier Poranny,* Stołeczna Spółka Wydanicza (ed. Ryszard Pietrszyński); *Kurier Warszawski,* Konrad Olchowicz and Feliks Mrozowski, publishers (ed. Ferdynand Hoesik and Konrad Olchowicz); *Warszawski Dziennik Narodowy,* Zachodnia Spółka Wydawnicza (ed. Feliks Jordan); *Wieczór Warszawski,* Zjednoczenie (ed. Stanislaw Strzelecki).

53. Wacław Śledziński, *Biuletyn Prasowy Światowego Związku Polaków,* quoted from *Dziennik Polski* (London), no. 885 (May 29, 1945).

54. Quoted in Z. Augustyński, "Wspomnienia: Fragmenty notatek," typescript in IHPAN, Sign. A 189/63, 38.

55. *ABC-Nowiny Codzienne,* no. 263 (Oct. 4, 1939).

56. Borowy, *Prasa,* 28.

57. Including no. 7, Oct. 25, 1939, the *Dziennik Urzędowy Miasta Stołecznego Warszawy* appeared in Polish. The interim no. 8, Oct. 29, 1939, presented the text in German and Polish on the first page; and, from no. 9 on, the *Dziennik* appeared continuously in both languages. The German title was *Amtsblatt der Stadt Warschau;* in the Polish title *miasta stołecznego* (capital city) was crossed out. The *Dziennik* last appeared on Dec. 31, 1939; in all, seventeen issues were published.

58. WAP-Łódź 1015/41, pp. 5, 15, Memorandum of the Head of the Civilian Administration of Warsaw to the Head of the Civilian Administration of the German Eighth Army, Oct. 8 and 10, 1939.

59. According to other reports, the Gestapo appeared at the Publishers' Association (Związek Wydawców) and spoke with Kauzik there. See Borowy, *Prasa,* and Augustyński, "Wspomnienia."

60. *Wspomnienia i reflekse dziennikarza, 1914–1939,* AMW, Sign. 325, 83. See also A. Ziemięcki, *Strzępy pamiętnika dziennikarskiego* (n.p., n.d.), 13. K. Polack, "Tragiczne dni Warszawy (w redakcji 'Expressu Porannego),' " *Wspomnienia dziennikarzy,* 146.

61. See *Goniec Krakowski,* no. 273 (Oct. 9, 1939), and *Soldatenzeitung der Schlesischen Armee* (Oct. 7, 1939).

62. Quoted in Augustyński, "Wspomnienia."

63. The memoranda are contained in the files of the Polski Związek Wydawców for 1928–1940 and are currently in the library of the Stowarzyszenie Dziennikarzy Polskich.

64. W. Studnicki, "Z tragicznych dni: W Krakowie i Łodzi," *Wiadomości,* nos. 19, 22, 25, 28, 31, 35 (1947).

65. "W Warszawie do końca 1939r," *Wiadomości,* no. 29 (1947).

66. See *Wiadomości,* nos. 47 (1947) and 10 (1948).

67. *Pamiętnik Teatralny: Kwartalnik poswięcony historii i krytyce teatru, 45–48,* nos. 1–4 (1963), 208.

3: The Content of the Newspapers

1. By the name *Gazeta Wspólna* I indicate all Warsaw newspapers that appeared Sept. 30–Oct. 9, 1939.

2. *Dziennik Krakowski,* no. 1 (Sept. 8, 1939).

3. Quoted in *Goniec Krakowski,* no. 1 (Sept. 27, 1939). See also the report on the meetings of the council in *Goniec Krakowski,* nos. 3 (Oct. 30, 1939) and 7 (Nov. 4, 1939).

4. IHPAN, typescript, 15. See also T. Sztumberk-Rychter, *Artylerzysta piechurem* (Warsaw, 1966), 85ff.

5. C. Madajczyk, *Generalna Gubernia w planach hitlerowskich* (Warsaw, 1961), 9–34, especially the chapter "National Socialist Leadership and the Polish Question in the First Year of the War"; L. Herzog, "Czy Hitler chciał utworzyć buforowe państwo polski? Na marginesie pracy Cz. Madajczyka," *Wojskowy Przegląd Historyczny* 4 (1962), 295–316; and Madajczyk's reply: "Cele wojenne Rzeszy po upadku Polski," *Wojskowy Przegląd Historyczny* 4 (1964), 196–205.

6. W. Studnicki, "Z tragicznych dni," *Wiadomości,* no. 22 (1947).

7. See A. Weh, *Das Recht des Generalgouvernements* ([Kraków], 1941), A:100.

8. *Dziennik Krakowski,* no. 3 (Sept. 9, 1939).

9. Szczepański, "Zapiski dla użytku przyszłego kronikarza."

10. These articles carried such titles as "Minister Beck, the Gravedigger of Poland" (no. 3,

Sept. 20, 1939); "The Jews and the War," "Horrible Misery in Warsaw," and "The Dreadful Responsibility of General Czuma" (no. 4, Sept. 22, 1939); and "Polish Dignitaries Swim in Gold," "Millions for a Carefree Life," and "The Absurd Attitude of the Western Powers" (no. 6, Sept. 27, 1939). They were taken mainly from the soldiers' newspaper and were printed in Polish in *Głos Częstochowski*.

11. *Goniec Częstochowski,* no. 10 (Oct. 5, 1939).

12. From a memorandum of the Diocesan Court, Nov. 8, 1948, to the District Attorney of Częstochowa: ASW-Kielce, Files of the Criminal Case against S. K. Homan, 1:231.

13. "Appeal to the Readers," *Gazeta Łódzka,* no. 2 (Sept. 23, 1939); "Łódź Returns to Normal Life," ibid., no. 4 (Sept. 26, 1939).

14. Ibid., no. 2 (Sept. 23, 1939).

4: Aims and Organization of Press Propaganda

1. *Ilustrowany Kurier Codzienny,* no. 282 (Oct. 26, 1939).

2. *Verordnungsblatt des Generalgouverneurs für die besetzten polnischen Gebiete* [Official gazette of the generalgouverneur of the occupied Polish territories], no. 1 (Oct. 26, 1939), 8. [Change in title as of Sept. 1, 1940, to *Verordnungsblatt für das Generalgouvernement.*]

3. Frank, DTgb, 1:21–24.

4. Ibid., 18:301.

5. Ibid., 1:46.

6. The minutes of the daily discussions of the department director of the Reichs Propaganda Ministry with Goebbels present the following entry for Nov. 2, 1939: "On the basis of the Warsaw visit [although the talks took place in Łódź, as we mentioned. — L.D.], the minister gives the following guidelines for the treatment of cultural problems: a) the omission of every support of Polish cultural life and, on the contrary, b) promotion of the *Volksdeutsch* and those *Reichsdeutsch* in the former Poland who serve actively in cultural initiatives." DZA-Potsdam, Files of the RMVP, Sign. P 50.01, vol. 7.

7. Frank, DTgb, 1:23.

8. Quoted in Stanisław Piotrowski, *Dziennik Hansa Franka* (Warsaw, 1963), 289.

9. "The Situation in the Occupied Territories," National Archives, Washington, D.C., photocopy in Archiwum Wojskowego Instytutu Historycznego [hereafter cited as AWIH]. Polish sources also mention the baseless rumors then circulating throughout the country. For example, K. Irzykowski ("The news is that the English bombed German positions in Kraków, Katowice, and Dęblin"); H. Krahelska ("The Polish population, which has been cut off from the world by the confiscation of radios, without any relations to foreign countries, without a legal press, reacted quite variously. Some people, at the sight of an airplane, thought it was all English one"); L. Landau ("There are really many rumors, often they are pure fantasy, but we are gradually losing the feeling for what is still probable — as the result of the lack of a normal press and the difficulty of listening to the radio"); and report of W. S. for I. Paderewski ("I myself have heard several reports from reputed eyewitnesses about the bombing of Gdynia, Radom, Pionki, COP, etc."). See Karol Irzykowski, *Notatki z życia, obserwacje i motywy* (selected by A. Dobosz, with a foreword by S. Kisielewski) (Warsaw, 1964), 373; H. Krahelska, "Postawa społeczeństwa polskiego pod okupacją niemiecką," IH PAN, 10; L. Landau, *Kronika lat wojny i okupacji* (Warsaw, 1962), 1:55; and Archiwum Akt Nowych, Warsaw [hereafter cited as AAN], Material of I. Paderewski, Sign. 2858, 15.

10. Piotrowski, *Dziennik Hansa Franka,* 289.

11. Frank, DTgb, 18:301.

12. For more detail, see K. Skubiszewski, *Pieniądz na terytorium okupowanym: Studium*

prawnomiędzynarodowe ze szczególnym uwzględnieniem praktyki niemieckiej (Poznań, 1960), 255ff.; F. Skalniak, *Bank emisyjny w Polsce, 1939–1945* (Warsaw, 1966), 234–246; and *Goniec Krakowski,* nos. 15–18 (Jan. 19–23, 1940).

13. Frank, DTgb, 25:132ff.

14. AZHP, Sign. 386, Report of T. J. Dobrowolski (Oct. 31, 1945) for the Instytut Pamięci Narodowej, Warsaw; T. J. Dobrowolski, letter to the editor of the *Warszawski Przegląd Socjalistyczny* (Jan. 19, 1948).

15. Undated report of the writer Zofia Kossak-Szczucka about the Polish underground press during the occupation for the Instytut Pamięci Narodowej, typed copy in IHPAN.

16. See *Centralny Katalog polskiej prasy konspiracyjnej, 1939–1945,* comp. L. Dobroszycki in collaboration with W. Kiedrzyńska under the direction of St. Płoski (Warsaw, 1962); L. Dobroszycki, "Zaginiona prasa konspiracyjna z lat, 1939–1945," *Najnowsze Dzieje Polski* 7 (1963), 183–196.

17. Details of this conference of Easter 1940 are unknown. Our reference is from a report of Ohlenbusch, then head of the Propaganda Department of the Warsaw District to the District Governor Fischer, for Mar. 6-Apr. 8, 1940, Archiwum Sądu Powiatowego m.St. Warszawy [hereafter cited as ASP-Warsaw], 3:251.

18. Here, e.g., are the titles of a few brochures that appeared in 1940 from the German-established publishers *Wydawnictwo Nowoczesne:* "Crimes against Mankind: England's Great Betrayal of the Peoples of Europe" (E. Stefanski); "Attention, Attention! We Present News from the Front, Reports from Home and Abroad as well as Press and Radio"; "Betrayal and Sale: How the Polish People Were Deceived; Facts in Light of Discovered Documents" (H. Borkowski); and "Heroes or Traitors? Memoirs of a Political Prisoner" (S. Brochwicz).

19. Even before the establishment of the GG, the decision to impound privately owned Polish radios was made. See chapter I. However, the police supported the view that this action had not produced satisfactory results during the phase of the military administration. At any rate, that was expressed by the SSuPolF of Kraków, SS-Gruf Zech, who, on Nov. 2, 1939, also presented Frank with the draft of an order about the confiscation of radio receivers. After its confirmation by Frank, the order was published on Dec. 15, 1939. See VOB1 f.d. bes.poln. Territories, 225. The idea of equipping permitted radio receivers for Poles with a limited reception frequency was first expressed by Hans Kriegler, the person in charge of radios in the GG. On Nov. 16, 1939, he presented a memorandum to Frank in which he proposed the allocation of 300,000–400,000 "replacement instruments" for the Polish population. Kriegler's purely commercial calculation that the expected fees would almost cover the total expenses of the transmitter was not taken into account. Only in 1940, with the change of the propaganda line, did Frank take more pains for such standard equipment, which he saw as a means to address the Polish population quickly. The issue dragged on for two years; since the RMVP was categorically opposed, it was never realized. See AGKBZH, Files of the Bühler Trial, 103:22ff.; AAN, Sign. 653, 21–25; Governmental Files of the GG, Kriegler's Memorandum to Frank; and Frank, DTgb, 3:764, 4:1145, 11:286, 338.

20. According to statements of Feb. 5, 1943, 198 cinemas were open in the GG (half of all the cinemas in the area), 23 of them exclusively for Germans. AGKBZH, uncatalogued material of the Main Propaganda Department: existing movie theaters in the Generalgouvernement according to the situation of Feb. 5, 1943. *Mały Rocznik Statystyczny, 1939,* 347. For the theater, see *Pamiętnik Teatralny,* nos. 1–4 (1945–1948); APW, Sign. 17; and J. Dąbrowa-Sierzputowski, *Warszawski sezon teatralny, 1940–1944* (with critical comments by E. Szwankowski).

21. AWP, Sign. 2a, 52, Biennial Report of the District Chief in Warsaw for the period Oct. 26, 1939-Oct. 1, 1941.

5: Organization Scheme

1. See "Die Presse im Generalgouvernement für die besetzten polnischen Gebiete," *Zeitungswissenschaft* 15, no. 4 (1940), 138.

2. AAN Sign. 897, 19ff., Files of the Government of the GG: Memorandum from Prel to the Auditing Department of Nov. 17, 1939.

3. Ibid., Sign. 631, 1ff. A note on the preliminary discussion with the staff of the Department for Public Enlightenment and Propaganda. According to another project of Feb. 7, 1940, the Main Department was to be constructed as follows: (a) Propaganda Office: 1. Department of Active Propaganda; 2. Department of Film Propaganda; 3. Department of Radio; (b) Office for Culture, Press, and Administration. See the Draft of the Tasks and Meaning of Propaganda, as well as the Structure of the Propaganda Machinery: AGKBZH, Files of the Main Department of Propaganda.

4. AAN, Sign. 9a, 131.

5. Ibid., Sign. 1008, 12ff., Governmental files of the GG, Press Chief of the Government: Office Chart.

6. AGKBZH, Sign. 147/OR, 21; AAN, Sign. 687, 113, and Sign. 1008, 14. Government files of the GG, press department, office chart and memorandum of the director, Main Propaganda Department, Arnold, to the Finance Department, Sept. 1, 1942. In it, Arnold applies for a permanent position for a certain Bryk and comments that it was to be his "function [to research] the mood in foreign circles of the GG and to find illegal writings." Also see the organization chart on p. 53.

7. Ibid., Sign 653, 31ff., Staff situation of the Department for Public Enlightenment and Propaganda as of Jan. 20, 1940; AGKBZH, Files of the Personnel Department of the Government of the GG (uncategorized): List of staff members of Feb. 1, 1941, and Apr. 29, 1943.

8. Ibid., Apr. 29, 1943.

9. *Journalism Is a Mission,* Report of the First Congress of the Union of National Journalists' Associations (Venice, 1942), 199.

10. Frank, DTgb, 10:16ff., 34–45, 242.

11. Goetel, *Czasy Wojny,* 32.

12. Studnicki, "Z tragicznych dni," *Wiadomości,* no. 28 (July 13, 1947).

13. APW, Sign. 267, 1–22, Personnel File of Ohlenbusch.

14. Frank often emphasized that Hitler had entrusted him with the fate of the GG; Hitler had even gone so far as to forbid General Keitel and everyone else to interfere in matters of the GG. See DTgb, 9:333, 338ff., 503.

15. Frank, DTgb, 1:23. See also DZA-Potsdam, Sign. 776, Organizational Chart of the RMVP, 1940.

16. The Office of the Proxy (Dr. Wilhelm Heubert after October 1943 Taschner) consisted of four departments, including press and propaganda. They were led by Dr. Wilhelm Cuypers (Nov. 18, 1939, to the end of Jan. 1942) and then Adolf Dresler. See AGKBZH, Files of the Bühler Trial, 43:120; "Ein halbes Jahr Generalgouvernement"; A. Dresler, "Die Presse des Generalgouvernements," *Zeitungswissenschaft* 17, no. 9 (1942), 463ff.; Du Prel, "Das Deutsche Generalgouvernement Polen," ibid., 218ff.

17. Pospieszalski, "Hitlerowskie 'prawo,' " 2:36.

18. On Sept. 23, 1943, Goebbels noted in his diary: "Propaganda in the occupied territories should also be subordinate to me, not only in those territories controlled by civilian commissars, but also where military governors still control the administration. . . . I explain my ideas about the nature of propaganda to the Führer. It is my opinion that if you form a propaganda ministry, you should also subordinate to it all propagandistic, journalistic, and

cultural endeavors inside the Reich and in the occupied territories." Diary of 1942–1943, published with other documents by Louis P. Lochner (Zurich, 1948) [hereafter cited as Goebbels's Diary].

19. See Paul Schmidt, *Statist auf diplomatischer Bühne, 1933–1945* (Bonn, 1949), 468ff.: "Once again, Ribbentrop kept us busy until two o'clock in the morning. It had to do with such an infinitely important question for the outcome of the war as whether he or Goebbels should manage foreign propaganda, a subject which, throughout the war, even in the critical days, took up a substantial part of Ribbentrop's time and certainly (as a result of the persistent state of war with Goebbels) most of his nervous energy."

20. See A. Dallin, *Deutsche Herrschaft in Russland, 1941–1945* (Düsseldorf, 1958), esp. the chapter "Das Propagandaministerium, Politiker und Propagandisten."

21. See Goebbels's Diary, 334, and E. Morawski, *Wehrmachtsbericht,* 137–143.

22. DZA-Potsdam, Files of the RMVP, Sign. P 50.01 (1.b, 1.d), Minutes of the daily conferences of Minister Dr. Goebbels with the department heads.

23. See Goebbels's Diary, entries of Mar. 6, May 7, and May 10, 1942.

24. Ibid., 405.

25. Frank, DTgb, 10:15ff.

26. Ibid., 18:313.

27. Ibid., 34:pt. 1, 248.

6: The Fate of Polish Periodicals

1. Frank, DTgb, 35a:335.

2. Data for 1935.

3. See *Mały Rocznik Statystyczny, 1939,* 34; *Informator Prasowy, 1938/1939* (Warsaw, 1938), 16–19; CAMSW, Sign. 101/III, Report "Straty kulturalne," *Biuletyn Komitetu 300-lecia prasy polskiej* (Warsaw, 1961), 45–70.

4. CAMSW, Sign. 101/II/E, no. 4/44.

5. See R. Heizler, "Das Presserecht der besetzten Gebiete: Archiv für Presserecht," *Zeitungswissenschaft* 15, no. 10 (1940), 576.

6. See Order on Publishing in the Generalgouvernement, VOBIGGP 1939 (Oct. 31, 1939).

7. Second implementation regulation for the order of Oct. 26, 1939, on the publication of printed material, VOBIGG 1940, 2:487.

8. First implementation regulation for the order of Oct. 31, 1939, on publishing in the GG, VOBIGG 1940, 2:513.

9. Before implementation regulations were issued, this material was regulated through usual circulars to publishers. In Częstochowa, the editor-in-chief of the *Kurier Częstochowski* composed such a circular by order of the captain of the town militia, Marcher. The circular of Apr. 14, 1940, says that all work to be printed was to be submitted for permission; this also concerned death notices, advertising posters, and leaflets. Advertisements (posters, flyers, etc.) were not allowed to contain any trademarks, nor was a reference to the printing press allowed. AGKBZH, Sign. 154 z/OR, vol. 2.

10. As distinct from the territories annexed to the Reich, in the GG printing presses were occasionally left in Polish possession. However, the Germans had confiscated all large and medium-sized enterprises and had introduced strict supervision through police and German trustees over the rest; aside from the "general trustee for Polish printing presses," Heinz Strozyk, there were also trustees in the districts. The trustee's first official act usually was to close the printing press, which was then disbanded. The few printing presses left in operation could then accept only the rare job printing orders. According to an estimate of the Delegacy of

the government-in-exile in London, the transactions of Polish printing presses reached only about 10 percent of the prewar level. Despite strict controls by police and administration, underground newspapers were definitely also produced in the legal printing presses. The first printed edition of the *Wiadomości Polskie,* published by the ZWZ (Association for Armed Struggle), came from such a printing press on Nowy Świat Street in Warsaw: Memorandum of the *Delegatura* of the London Government-in-Exile on the war losses of the printing industry in Poland, typescript in IHPAN; Report of the Warsaw District Governor to the Government of the GG for Apr. 1942 (May 12, 1942), 20; Frank, DTgb, 8:274. J[ózef] W[ardas], "Drukarz polski w walce z okupantem," *Waidomości Graficzne: Organ Związku Zawodowego Pracowników Przemysłu Poligraficznego w Polsce,* no. 6/7 (1948), 7; Jan Rzepecki, "Zarys organizacyjny propagandy ZWZ i AK," typescript in IHPAN, 4ff.; communication of the former owner of the printing press Kazimierz Wojtyński (Hoża St., Warsaw) to the author.

11. Independent publishing by authors was the only thing that was expressly forbidden, but selling books and journals was also outlawed (see the order of the Generalgouverneur of July 10, 1940). Moreover, from 1940 to 1943 the Main Department of Propaganda annually published a "List of Polish Publications Hostile to the Germans, Harmful, and Undesired," which included both books and journals.

12. During the entire period of the occupation, censored children's books, prayer books, and other religious literature were published by Polish institutions sporadically and in limited editions. Krzyżanowski Publishers in Kraków put out three childrens' books: *Grandmother Blind Cow, When the Thermometer Was Sick,* and *The Enchanted Spinningwheel.* The "Jedność" printing press in Kielce put out *Meet Your Church!* (published by the Diocese of Kielce). On the other hand, the publications of the Wydawnictwo Polskie — founded by Wilhelm Ohlenbusch's wife Gertrud — or of the Wydawnictwo Nowoczesne Publishers can hardly be seen as Polish publications. These two publishers put out a few hundred books and brochures, most of them propaganda writings in Polish. AAN, Sign. 1172, 145, and Sign. 470 (unnumbered); CAMSW, Sign. 101/II/E, 556; *Biuletyn WS,* no. 4/44, Situation Report from Poland (Nov. 1943), 44; AGKBZH, Files of the Bühler Trial, 54:73 (Testimony of Tadeusz Zapior). See also P. Cedro, "Nauka, szkolnictwo i sztuka w Polsce po wrześniu 1939," *Wiadomoście Polski* [London], no. 39 (Dec. 8, 1940).

13. *Wiadomości Gospodarcze* 1–2 (Nov. 7, 1939).

14. Ibid., no. 5 (Nov. 28, 1939).

15. See Pospieszalski, "Hilterowskie 'prawo,' " 2:39ff. At about the same time, in other cities of the GG, official publications of the Chamber of Commerce and Industry also appeared: on Aug. 1, 1940, the *Report of the Chamber of Commerce and Industry for the District of Radom,* on Nov. 1, 1940, a similar paper in Kraków, at the beginning of January 1941 in Lublin.

16. See *Mały Rocznik Statystyczny, 1939,* 345, 354.

17. Of 2,579 clergy imprisoned in Dachau, 1,748 (68%) were Poles, 411 (16%) were Germans, and 420 (16%) were of other nationalities. In all, 1,034 clergy were killed in Dachau — 867 Poles (83%), 94 Germans (9%), and 83 of other nationalities (8%). See *Spis pomordowanych Polaków w obozie koncentracyjnym w Dachau,* (Dachau-Munich: Hochwürden Chart, Słowo Polskie Press, 1946), 288; J. Domagala, *Ci, którzy przeszli przez Dachau* (Warsaw, 1957), 391; and M. Broszat, "Verfolfung polnischer katholischer Geistlicher, 1939–1945" (unpublished typescript of 1959 at the Gutachten des Instituts für Zeitgeschichte, Munich), 83.

18. Report, "Straty kulturalne," 16.

19. Czesław, Bishop of Kielce, to the Reverend Brothers, Curates, and Beloved Believers. Issued in Kielce on the day of Saint Jan of Dukla, in the year of our Lord 1939, *Kielecki Przegląd Diecezjalny* 10 (Oct. 1939).

20. His previous pastoral letter, in the early period of the occupation (Sept. 24, 1939), says, "which does not contradict our Catholic conscience and our Polish dignity." Czeslaw, Bishop of Kielce, to all Brothers, Curates, and Beloved Believers of the Diocese of Kielce. Issued on the day of the Most Holy Virgin Mary, Champion of the Enslaved, in the Year of Our Lord 1939. The third pastoral letter quoted from the first, in the May and June editions of the *Przegląd*, however, omits the words "and our Polish dignity," inserting three dots instead.

21. *Kielecki Przegląd Diecezjalny,* no. 5–6 (1940), 55.

22. Leonard Świderski (who left the church and the priesthood after the war), the former editor of the *Przegląd*, states in his memoirs that the original version of this pastoral letter had been formulated even more sharply and, as proof of that, presents the photocopy of a galley proof with handwritten changes, commenting: "In the first version, he expressly condemned 'conspiratorial acts.' That was then softened by substituting the words 'imprudent steps,' so as not to wound too crassly the patriotic sentiments of the population. For the same reason, the passage 'or any political demonstration' was deleted from the final text." See Świderski, *Oglądały oczy moje* (Warsaw, 1963), 32ff. This interesting statement was indeed invalidated by the fact that all supposedly deleted passages were printed in the *Przegląd*. See the issue in question in the library of the Polish Society of Jesus, as well as in the National Library of Warsaw.

23. *Kronika Diecezji Sandomierskiej,* no. 1–4 (1940), 6.

24. In this issue the table of contents for 1939 was published. The anti-Nazi article by Reverend Sciskała, "Wrażenie z Niemiec" (Impressions from Germany), was, however, not detected in the list. See *Kronika Diecezji Sandomierskiej,* no. 8 (1939), 252–259.

25. Ibid., no. 11–12 (1942), 32.

26. CAMSW, Sign. 183, 28:248, Memorandum of the Propaganda Department of the District of Radom to the editorial staff of the *Przegląd*.

27. *Przegląd,* no. 8–9 (1942), 148.

28. CAMSW, Sign. 210 (unnumbered).

29. Ibid., Sign. 183, 28:248.

30. Ibid.

31. *Posłaniec Serca Jezuwego,* no. 4 (Sept. 1946), 107–110.

32. Ibid., nos. 10–11 (Oct.-Nov. 1939), and nos. 1–7 (Jan.-July 1940).

33. Ibid., no. 10 (Oct. 1939), 362.

34. Ibid., anniversary issue (Jan. 1947), 3.

35. Before the war Father Kolbe had been a missionary in Japan; moreover, he was one of the founders of the Franciscan monastery Niepokalanów in Warsaw. For his biography, see Harald Bratt, *Stille Helden, Grosstaten menschlischer Gesinnung* (Bergisch-Gladbach, 1964). In 1982 Kolbe was canonized by the Catholic church.

36. *Rycerz Niepokalanej* 1/215 (July 1945).

37. Ibid. (Dec./Jan. 1940/1941).

38. *Barykada Wolności,* no. 37; in the 1930s the order, under Father Kolbe, published a popular antisemitic daily entitled *Mały Dziennik* (The Little Daily).

39. *Rycerz Niepokalanej* 1/215 (July 1945), 7.

40. "Kościół w Polsce pod biczem swastyki" (abridged version of a lecture by Bishop Wincenty Urban), *Wrocławski Tygodnik Katolików* 38 (Sept. 19, 1965); J. Stemler, "Wspomnienie o ojcu Kolbe," *Tygodnik Powszechny* 19 (May 8, 1966).

41. S. Uhma, *Polski Czerwony Krzyż, 1919–1959* (Warsaw, 1959), 131, writes that the first issue of the *Biuletyn Informacyjny* of January 1940 is in the archive of the Polish Red Cross (PCK) executive board. Unfortunately, this issue is missing.

42. *Kommunikat* is mentioned by Adam Ronikier. An allusion to the *Informator* is in a publication of the same name, *Informator (Biuletyn Wewnętrzny Biura Informacji PCK),* Jan. 1946.

43. In *Informator* 3 (Mar. 1946) there is a general communication about the article "O

rzetelność w udzieleniu informacji," which had been published during the war in the *Biuletyn Wewnętrzny* by then-editor Emilia Grocholska. Among the materials of the PCK about the period of the war and the occupation in the executive board archive, there is also the draft of an article titled "Pamiątki po poległych," with the comment, "Article for the *Biuletyn*."

44. Evidently the local sections of the PCK also put out their own bulletins, such as the one in Lowicz, *Informator dla Placówek i Członków PCK* (1940–1941). See *Informator* 4 (1946).

45. See *Informator* 1 (Jan. 1946), 1.

46. For the total activity of the PCK and its information office during the occupation, see *Informator,* 1946–1947, and Uhma, *Polski Czerwony Krzyż,* 7–77.

47. AAN, Material RGO, Portfolio 303, vols. 1, 26, 29; memorandum of Dr. Celichowski to the Jagiellonian Library and correspondence about labor documents and exchange.

48. Ibid., specimen copy of *Wiadomości RGO.*

49. The blessing read: "I most warmly bless the charitable work of the Main Welfare Council, which is so needed today, and wish that the Central Relief Committee can fulfill its mission and render much and extensive help to the unfortunate." Ibid., 1. On Sept. 8, 1940, in the *Chronicle of Andrzej* [Kazimierz Gorzkowski], is the news that the German authorities had withdrawn permission for the RGO organ back in Sept. 1940. AZHP, Sign. 231/7.

50. AAN, Files of the Dept. I RGO (General Organization Department), 1940–1941, Sign. 106 (unnumbered).

51. Froehl was an official of the Central Department of Population and Welfare in the government of the GG.

52. Here are a few typical deletions [the text is in brackets]: "According to its regulations, the Main Welfare Council is primarily concerned with maintaining a legal framework to guarantee the organization [a Polish character and] the possibility of extensive generosity in its work. To describe the conditions under which the work occurs, we need only mention that the number of incoming proposals and counterproposals [from the German authorities] amounted to 28 before the Main Welfare Council in the above-mentioned meeting decided to depart from the final text of the statutes. [German authorities were notified that the discussions would be conducted in Polish, according to the statutes of the organization.]"

53. "Straty kulturalne" (24ff.) contains the following data on clergy imprisoned and killed in the GG: in Częstochowa, 50 imprisoned, 6 killed; in Kielce, 30 imprisoned, 7 killed; in Kraków, 100 imprisoned, 1 killed; in Lublin, 200 imprisoned, 24 killed; in Łomza, almost all clergy imprisoned, 2 killed; in Podlasie, 40 imprisoned, 2 killed; in Sandomierz, 19 imprisoned, 7 killed; in Warsaw, 250 imprisoned, 8 killed.

54. Library of the Polish Association of Journalists, Files of the Polish Association of Newspaper and Journal Publishers, Minutes of the Meetings of the Board of Governors. Akta Związku Wydawców Dzienników i Czasopism, 1939–1940, w Bibliotece Związku.

55. VOBIGG 1940 1:225.

56. Appeal to the industrial law of the Second Polish Republic was certainly only a tactic. We cannot know how far Polish journalistic circles considered it successful.

57. Library of the Polish Association of Journalists, Files of the Polish Association of Newspaper and Journal Publishers, Memorandum of S. Kauzik, Akta Związku Wydawców Dzienników i Czasopism, 1939–1940, w Bibliotece Związku.

58. CAMSW, Sign. 101/II/E, 551, *Biuletyn WS* 4/44, 36.

7: The Polish-Language German Press

1. AGKBZH, Sign. 154 z/OR, vol. 2 (unnumbered).

2. The number of newspapers in Poland had been larger a century before. See S. Dziki, "Przegląd statystyczny prasy polskiej (do 1918r)," *Zeszyty Prasoznawcze* 1–2 (1961), 140–161.

3. Even after the closing of all Polish publishers, the RMVP granted an exemption for the sale of two Polish-language newspapers in the annexed areas. The first was the *Dziennik Poranny;* the second, *Nowy Czas,* was explicitly for areas annexed to the Reich, the former district of Warsaw (Płońsk, Płock, Ciechanów, Pułtusk, Maków, Ostrołęka, Mława, and Przasnysz), and was published in Allenstein. In the summer of 1942, the *Dziennik Poranny* was stopped; in its place, *Dziennik Ogłoszeń dla powiatów Bendsburg, Bielitz, Blachstädt, Ilkenau, Krenau, Sosnowitz, Warthenau* appeared in Katowice. In this change, the policy of territorialization and Germanization, which was carried out very intensively at that time in Upper Silesia, was expressed particularly clearly. Instead of a newspaper substitute, which the *Dziennik Poranny* was, the Polish population now obtained an advertising paper with a list of all official communications, orders, and slogans. The publishers formulated the task of this new *Dziennik Ogłoszeń* bluntly: "The present new paper, which will appear twice a week from today, August 1, 1942, does not aim at the dissemination of any opinion, but wants to inform the Polish population objectively about all legal, official, and semi-official orders, about announcements of the government, the administration, and the public service, as well as about every event that every citizen should know." See AGKBZH, Sign. Z/OR (unnumbered), Memorandum of the District Administrator of Blachstädt, Aug. 22, 1940, to the Editor-in-Chief of the *Kurier Częstochowski,* and *Dziennik Ogłoszeń,* no. 1.

4. Along with the journals sold in the GG, from July 1940 on, the occupation force published a biweekly propaganda news sheet for the rural population: the *Ścienna Gazetka dla Wsi Polskiej.* It was sold, or rather posted, through administrators who also bore responsibility for the newspaper being posted publicly and visibly (walls near the church, central places in the village) in all villages. Later they were supplied for such purposes in the villages at so-called "points of communal life." See *Służba Informacyjna dla wójtów* 2 (June 5, 1940).

5. In addition, various order papers in Polish, or Polish and German, were published, e.g., *Dziennik Rozporządzeń dla Generalnego Gubernatorstwa, Dziennik Rozporządzeń Dystryktu Radomskiego,* as well as the official papers of various authorities, e.g., *Wiadomości Urzędu Patentowego.*

6. From time to time this caused a curtailment in the level of circulation as well as the number of pages of the individual journals. See CAMSW, Sign. 210, Memorandum from Reisch (Apr. 16, 1941) to all governors.

7. Before the war, a newspaper cost 10–25 groszy, a journal 30 groszy–1 złoty. In the GG, the corresponding prices were 10–30 groszy and 25 groszy–3 złoty.

8. The data are from *Zweieinhalb Jahre Pressearbeit im Generalgouvernement* (Mar. 1942), 9; Frank, DTgb, 3:154, 25:132, 34:267.

9. According to *Ala−Zeitungkatalog* (1941), 157, 238; AGKBZH, unsorted files of the Department of Propaganda.

10. Frank, DTgb, 30:1272ff.; CAMSW, Sign. 101/III; "Straty kulturalne," 19.

11. Frank, DTgb, 25:138.

12. *M[eldunek] O[kresowy]* of Kraków (1944), 25.

13. Based on the lists of such staff members of the occupation press and Telepress in the files of the trials of occupation-press staff: ASW-Kraków, IV:22/50, VII:85/A6, Criminal Case against F. Burdecki, E. Skiwski, and S. Wasylewski; ASW-Kielce, IV k/49, Files of the Criminal Case of S. Homan; ASP-Warsaw, Files of the Criminal Case of H. Wielgomasowa. Information was also collected by the illegal Polish organizations and by the underground press. AZHP 203/III-126, Report of Department II of the AK. IHPAN, Material of the information center CIN of the Delegacy of the Polish Government-in-Exile; *Biuletyn Informacyjny, Wolna Polska, Barykada Wolności, Biuletyn Informacyjny Ziemi Czerwieńskiej, Agencja Prasowa.*

14. Studnicki, "Z tragicznych dni," *Wiadomości,* no. 22 (June 1, 1947).

15. Order on Cultural Activity in the Generalgouvernement, Second Executive Order to the Order of Mar. 8, 1940 (Oct. 18, 1940).

16. Persons who registered had to fill out a form, the so-called "Application for a Permit to Exercise a Profession as . . ." After an examination of the facts of the application, the "permit" was issued by the Propaganda Department and the Sicherheitsdienst (SD, or Security Service).

17. During the occupation, in Warsaw alone about six hundred members remained in the former journalists' association. See Dunin-Wasowicz, "Lista strat dziennikarstwa polskiego," 3.

18. AWP, Sign. 2a, 53; *Zweijahresbericht des Warschauer Distriktchefs.*

19. *Dziennik Ustaw Rzeczypospolitej Polskiej,* the organ of the first *delegacy* of the Polish government-in-exile, allegedly managed by Ryszard Świętochowski, printed an order about the press published by the occupation force in the edition of Aug. 20, 1940. Paragraph 1 of the order: "According to Article 5 of the Secret Decree of July 15, 1940, about the sphere of activity of the Propaganda Ministry (DzURP no. 1a, Section 3), I order the following: (1) Polish citizens are forbidden to participate in the editorial work of newspapers, periodicals, or any printed material with political, cultural, social, economic content, published in Polish or a foreign language by the German and Russian occupiers. This ban does not affect newspapers and printed material with nonpolitical content." We may assume that this order of the journalists was well known, since S. Kauzik, the former director of the Association of Newspaper and Journal Publishers and later head of the Information Department of the real governmental *delegacy* also belonged to Świętochowski's self-styled *delegacy.* The statement "prominent positions in the country" (i.e., Poland) of Apr. 4, 1941, about the writers, which was published in the secret *Biuletyn Informacyjny* of May 23, 1941, is also interesting: "The cooperation of Polish writers, book and professional authors, and informational writers in the so-called *Wydawnictwo Polskie* is inadmissible; for it means cooperation with an agency of the German occupation force. Writers and authors who violate this order will be treated as persons who, during the occupation and in the face of the harsh crimes the Germans commit against the Polish people and their culture, did not refrain from cooperation with the Germans." Almost the entire underground press presented numerous articles on this subject.

20. AGKBZH, 154 z/OR, vol. 2 (unnumbered). See also CAMSW, Sign. 120 (unnumbered), Memorandum of the head of the Propaganda Department in the District of Radom, Huhn, of Sept. 7, 1942, to the mayor of Kielce.

21. From the testimony of S. J. (education: 7 years of grammar school): "In 1941, when I was in Kraków, I bought the Sunday edition of the *Kurier Częstochowski.* After I had leafed through it and read the articles with religious content, I thought that this newspaper by the Paulist Fathers was published with permission of the German authorities. Convinced of the Catholic character of the paper, I wrote to the editor of the *Kurier Częstochowski* and asked if I might write something for the newspaper. I soon received an answer that I could send in my work, but only on religious life; I was to omit political events. This answer confirmed me even more in my conviction that the paper was published by clergymen. . . . Soon afterward, I also sent the *Kurier* my first work in verse: 'Month of Mary. Roses of the Most Holy Virgin Mary.' I wrote this poem with the intention of encouraging the Polish people spiritually and bringing the Polish people closer to God in this very difficult time." ASW-Kielce, IV:79/49, 317.

22. Stanisław Wasylewski cites the assignment of the group Konfederacja Narodu, for whom he was to collect information on the press company Lemberger Zeitung (a branch of the Kraków-Warsaw newspaper publishers) and the activity of the editor Lehman on the *Gazeta Lwowska.* Zdzisław Stanisz cited the assignment of the organization *Polski Związek Wolności.* Wasylewski also excused his work on the *Gazeta Lwowska* in consideration of a "well-understood national interest," "for the welfare of Polish culture, otherwise Lwów would have

been flooded by a wave of Ukrainian culture." See A. Wyleżyńska, *Dziennik,* Biblioteka Narodowa, Zaklad Rękopisow; AZHP, Sign. 231/a, 48 (Feb. 5, 1942), Handwriting Department of the National Library no. 6456 (Aug. 18, 1943), 262.

23. Stanisław Płoski, as director of the Instytut Pamięci Narodowej, who testified as an expert in the trial against occupation-press personnel, stated: "If an underground organization placed its people in the German press to get certain secret information, it selected them from technical personnel. In no case were they allowed to work as Polish editors." The second expert, Professor Stanisław Lorentz, explained further: "The underground organizations carried out educational work in German propaganda offices, including the Polish-language German press. This educational activity was supported by those technical Polish staff members employed by this press who belonged to the independent organizations. It was not usual for a journalist, writer, or employee writing for the occupation press to be delegated. On the other hand, it did happen, but also not very often, that illegal authorities used the information of the Polish members of the editorial staff. . . . They normally tried to give the appearance in certain circles that they were actually working with this press on orders or rather by an agreement with the underground movement. They did that so as not to be boycotted." ASW-Kielce, IV K 79/49, 2:326; ASP-Warsaw IV, K, 1:37.

24. ASP-Warsaw IV K, 4:441, Statement of M. K., former employee of the *Nowy Kurier Warszawski.*

25. ASW-Kraków, IV K 22/50, 2:41, Testimony of S. J.; also VIII K 249/250, minutes of the trial, memoranda of a former staff member of Telepress to S. Płoski.

26. The names of a few Polish physicians who collaborated on the German journal *Zdrowie i Życie,* "either thoughtlessly or consciously," were divulged by the underground journal *Abecadlo Lekarskie.* After the war they were published in the journal *W Służbie Zdrowia,* nos. 7, 8, 17–18 (1947), 9–10.

Chapter 8: The Press System in the Third Reich and the Generalgouvernement

1. In recent years many works on this subject have appeared. I can mention here only the most important of them: J. Wulf, *Presse und Funk im Dritten Reich* (Gütersich, 1964); O. J. Hale, *The Captive Press in the Third Reich* (Princeton, 1964); Z. A. B. Zeman, *Nazi Propaganda* (London, 1964); E. K. Bramsted, *Goebbels and National Socialist Propaganda, 1925–1945* (Lansing, Mich., 1965); Karl-Dietrich Abel, *Presselenkung im NS-Staat: Eine Studie zur Publizistik in der nationalsozialistischen Zeit* (Berlin, 1968); Jürgen Hagemann, *Die Presselenkung im Dritten Reich* (Bonn, 1970); Henning Storek, *Dirigierte Öffentlichkeit: Die Zeitung als Herrschaftsmittel in den Anfangsjahren der nationalsozialistischen Regierung* (Opladen, 1972); Elke Fröhlich, "Die Kulturpolitische Pressekonferenz des Reichspropagandaministeriums," in *Vierteljahrshefte für Zeitgeschichte* 22 (1974): 347–381; Fritz Sänger, *Politik der Täuschungen: Missbrauch der Press im Dritten Reich; Weisungen, Notizen, Informationen, 1933–1939* (Vienna, 1975). In Polish, F. Ryszka appears to be the only one who has dealt with the problem of Nazi propaganda: see *Noc i mgła: Niemcy w okresie hitlerowskim* (Wrocław, 1962) and *Państwo stanu wyjątkowego: Rzecz o systemie państwa i prawa Trzeciej Rzeszy* (Wrocław, 1964).

2. Ryszka, *Noc i mgła,* 238.

3. See *Presse in Fesseln,* 104, 177.

4. See Wulf, *Presse und Funk,* 72ff.

5. Ibid., 107.

6. Horst Hano, *Die Taktik der Pressepropaganda des Hitlerregimes* (n.p.,n.d.), 7.

7. Wulf, *Presse und Funk,* 86–105.

8. Willi A. Boelke, *Kriegspropaganda, 1939–1941: Geheime Ministerkonferenzen im Reichspropagandaministerium* (Stuttgart, 1966), 131.

9. Frank, DTgb, 18:302; Piotrowski, *Dziennik Hansa Franka,* 150.

10. Memorandum, AGKBZH, SIGN. 154 Z/OR, 2 (UNNUMBERED). SEE *Goniec Krakowski* and *Kurier Częstochowski* (both Apr. 8, 1940) and *Nowy Kurier Warszawski* (Apr. 6/7, 1940).

11. Compare the text of a flier of the propaganda department in Radom announcing the appearance of the *Kurier Kielecki:* "Farmers! The normalization of social, economic, and cultural life in the Generalgouvernement is making rapid progress. The extensive orders of the Generalgouverneur, Dr. Frank, especially insofar as they concern the country, have changed our life and aimed at making the Polish land more productive. To get an idea of what is happening, to be able to keep up with the new time, one must know everything. Therefore, a new Polish press, cleansed of Jewish elements [*Judenrein*], has been built; it informs its Polish readers precisely and honestly, and presents only the pure truth. The great information paper *Kurier Kielecki* was created for the Kielce region and will present the latest and truthful information every day." CAMSW, Sign. 210 (unnumbered).

12. See *Goniec Krakowski,* no. 259 (Dec. 16, 1941), and *Dziennik Radomski,* no. 294 (Dec. 17, 1941).

13. Dec. 6/7, 1941: "Rostow and Moscow: Circles in Berlin on the Situation."

14. The *Kurier Częstochowski* was considered by its publisher the only Catholic newspaper for the entire GG. "As a Catholic newspaper," the editor-in-chief, Georg Aurel Machura, said on one occasion, "this newspaper may not use Warsaw jargon." In practice, the *Kurier Częstochowski* was written like the rest of the occupation press, with the single difference that it also presented texts with church and religious content, published next to such decidedly profane articles as "Money and Love: The Peculiarity and Greed of American Millionairesses" and "How Can Men Be Made to Like Women? (What to Do to Strike the Taste of Men? How Does One Acquire Beauty and Slimness?)," ASW-Kielce, Files of the Criminal Case against S. K. Homan, 3:6; AGKBZH, Sign. 154/OR, vol. 1, Correspondence and Administration of the *Kurier Częstochowski; Kurier Częstochowski,* nos. 36 (Feb. 11, 1942) and 55 (Mar. 5, 1942); see also nos. 37 and 38.

15. AAN, Administration Files of the GG, 1171:83; Dąbrowa-Sierzputowski, *Warszawski sezon teatralny,* 27.

16. Hans Frank (DTgb, 18:305) testifies that the private lives of the Polish editors were also under strict surveillance. The security police had been asked to make reports of possible violation of the law.

Chapter 9: The Content

1. *Gazeta Rolnicza,* no ?

2. See also "Congress Confirms Roosevelt," in *Nowy Kurier Warszawski,* no. 4 (Jan. 8, 1941).

3. Ibid., no. 6 (Jan. 10, 1941).

4. Ibid.

5. Ibid., no. 230 (Sept. 29, 1941).

6. Ibid., no. 5 (Jan. 9, 1941).

7. Ibid., no. 242 (Oct. 11, 1941). See also in *Nowy Kurier Warsawski,* "Roosevelt Demands Dictatorial Powers: Criticism on the Bill for Aid Provisions" (no. 10, Jan. 13, 1941); "American Loan for England in the Sum of $425 Million" (no. 172, July 23, 1941); "Declaration of Roosevelt's Son: The U.S. Is Ready to Be Involved in the War; Although the United States Has Not Yet Sent Any Troops, It Is Already in a State of War" (no. 11, May 12, 1941).

8. Ibid., no. 146 (June 23, 1941).

9. Ibid., no. 149 (June 26, 1941).

10. Ibid., no. 165 (July 15, 1941).

11. Ibid., no. 178 (July 30, 1941).

12. Ibid., nos. 193 (Aug. 16/17, 1941) and 231 (Sept. 30, 1941).

13. Ibid., nos. 37, 108, 111.

14. Ibid., nos. 39 (Feb. 15/16, 1941), 209 (Sept. 4, 1941), and 222 (Oct. 19, 1941).

15. Special supplements of the *Nowy Kurier Warszawski* were devoted to the Swedish neutrality (Apr. 19, 1940), the blockade of England (Aug. 18, 1940), and the separation of Yugoslavia from Greece and the capture of Belgrade (Apr. 9 and 13, 1941); of the *Nowy Głos Lubelski* to the occupation of Denmark and Norway by German troops (n.d.). The *Krakauer und Warschauer Zeitung* also published special supplements in German and Polish devoted to, among other things, the occupation of Denmark and Norway and the attack on the Soviet Union.

16. The following are additional points of the program for the celebrations worked out by the Main Propaganda Department:

Description of the course of the rally 'Moscow Conquered!' on the Adolf Hitler Square [the Kraków marketplace]. Units of the Wehrmacht, SS, police, Sonderdienst, Eastern Railroad, etc., line up according to the plan of Party Member Stahl. The German population is outside the formation (determine if the balconies on the west side in the first floor of the Cloth Hall [Sukienniki] can be made available for spectators).

Honored guests (as few as possible) take their places on the stand.

The Generalgouverneur appears with high officials and sets off for the stand.

March of the standard-bearers (line up on the stand). On the speakers' platform the head of propaganda Party Member Ohlenbusch. He opens the rally. The Generalgouverneur speaks. The Generalgouverneur Director Schalk pays homage to the Führer. German anthem and Horst-Wessel song.

Moscow Conquered. Program for Kraków.

1. Poster: See general sketch.

2. Rally on Adolf Hitler Square.

Decoration of the east side of the square: mayor.

Installation of the podium, microphone and loudspeaker: radio department.

Orders and measures for closing the streets: SS and police.

Planning of the course of the rally: Party Member Stahl.

Music: Party Member Teuchert.

Decoration of the stand: Party Member Heinsohn.

Radio reporting: Party Members König and Jansen.

Newsreel: Party Member Guttenberg.

Press report: Party Member Stuckmann.

Photo reporting: Party Member Rosner.

Program: Party Member Gauweiler.

17. See "Berlin on the Military Situation in the East," *Goniec Krakowski,* no. 41 (Dec. 16, 1941).

18. *Nowy Kurier Warszawski,* no. 27 (Jan. 31/Feb. 1, 1942); *Kurier Częstochowski,* no. 27 (Feb. 1, 1942).

19. *Nowy Kurier Warszawski,* no. 252 (Oct. 25, 1942).

20. Ibid., nos. 253–259 (Oct. 26-Nov. 2, 1942).

21. Ibid., no. 260 (Nov. 3, 1942).

22. On Nov. 6, 1942, aside from information that the German troops had retreated to positions that were even farther west, the *Nowy Kurier Warszawski* also presented the article "Where Are Ours, Where Are the Enemy's? Eleven Days of Grim Battle at El-Alamein." Among other things, it said: "On November 4, the frontlines were cut into deep wedges. . . . To get out of this confinement, the German-Italian troops retreated from individual sections to prepared positions."

23. After the defeat of Stalingrad, the underground *Biuletyn Informacyjny* (no. 8/163, Feb. 25, 1943) wrote: "Thus the awful night is past. Our most dangerous enemy has been taking one blow after another for four months. We no longer need imagine this defeat. We already see this defeat."

24. *Nowy Kurier Warszawski,* no. 277 (Nov. 20, 1942).

25. Ibid., no. 302.

26. Ibid., nos. 21 (Jan 25. 1943) and 22 (Jan. 26, 1943).

27. Ibid., no. 15 (Jan. 18, 1943). In an editorial of Jan. 28, 1943, the *Nowy Kurier Warszawski* used a formulation previously uncommon in the occupation press. Here are a few interesting excerpts: "Everyone who knows the nature of Bolshevism is uneasy about the latest news from the eastern front, news we have grown accustomed to count as bad. . . . We have known for some time that since November 20 attacks of the Red Army have been in progress on the eastern front and have not been getting weaker. German military reports indicate the loss of [Velikie Luki] and the evacuation of [Voronezh], as well as the shift of the Caucasian front from the Kuban area. . . . The German army has gone over to a mobile defense; for the possession of a few hundred or a few thousand square kilometers does not have much significance in this boundless country. . . . The Bolsheviks have succeeded in outflanking and enclosing advanced German positions here and there. That mainly concerns Stalingrad."

28. Ibid., nos. 28–30, 32 (Feb. 2–4 and 6/7, 1943).

29. Among other things, it was declared that the news that Stalin had appealed to the Pope could not be published in the press for Poles (see *Nowy Kurier Warszawski,* no. 78, Apr. 1, 1942, and *Kurier Częstochowski,* no. 81, Apr. 5, 1942) since "Nazism represents the view that Bolshevism is the enemy of the Church." Similarly the report of the *Daily Express* that the English information on the sinking of ships and submarines did not agree with the German. However, protests were especially sharp against information that appeared in the press about the Polish government-in-exile (below). See Frank, DTgb, 18:299ff.

30. Ibid.

31. For comparison, I have examined the military reports of the OKW in the Kraków newspaper and in *Nowy Kurier Warszawski* for the period Jan. 1–Mar. 31, 1942, as well as in the German *Allgemeinen Zeitung* and the *Goniec Krakowski* for the period July 1–Dec. 31, 1944. In these periods, the Wehrmacht suffered major defeats, but the text of news reports is the same everywhere, down to the last detail.

32. Here is an egregious example of the mendacity of the Wehrmacht reporting of the OKW during the Polish-German war. On Sept. 2, 1939, the OKW announced the sinking of a Polish submarine; on Sept. 6, two more; and on Sept. 8, a fourth. The Polish navy, however, had five submarines, three of which (*Sęp, Ryś,* and *Żbik*) were interned in Sweden, while two (*Orzeł* and *Wilk*) were able to break through to England that month. See "Tak kłamać może tylko niemieckie Oberkommando," in the underground *Dwa Dni,* no. 159 (July 20, 1942), and "Druga wojna światowa," *Informator* (Warsaw, 1962), 407.

33. In *German Radio Propaganda* (London, 1944) Ernst Kris and Hans Speier cite the following data from a New York newspaper in September 1941 on the credibility of war reports of the various countries from the beginning of World War II up to the invasion of the USSR (quoted in Erich Murawski, *Wehrmachtsbericht,* 121): German reports, 100% true; Radio

Stockholm, 75% true; French General Staff, 20% true; Reuters Agency, 0% true. Although this list does not lack exaggeration, it does convey the war reporting of the time on the British and French sides quite strikingly. See also L. Dobroszycki, "Prasa polska w okresie kampanii wrześniowej (1–28 września 1939)," *Rocznik Historii Czasopiśmiennictwa Polskiego* 5, no. 1 (1965), 151–166.

34. The press for Poles took pains to say as little as possible about the Allied air raids in the Reich. In the first phase of the war the occupation press, unlike the newspapers published in Germany, printed only the tersest reports. It was always emphasized that the objects of the air raids were hospitals, churches, social institutions, or such, but never military targets. Later, they stopped giving news about the air raids altogether in the "Polish" press. The Main Department of Propaganda did not receive air war reports from the Reich after 1943. See AGKBZH, Sign. 147/OR, 98, Memoranda of the Main Department of Propaganda to the Department in the District of Radom.

35. *Zachodnia Straż Rzeczypospolitej,* no. 1 (July 7, 1943).

36. It was also mentioned there that Hitler, in his speeches of Sept. 19 and Oct. 6, 1939 (both published in the *Ilustrowany Kurier Codzienny*), did not describe the Polish question as finally solved; this is indicated by the sentences about the creation of a Reich border that would correspond to historic, ethnographic, and economic conditions, and about the establishment of a Polish state whose government was to offer a guarantee that it would pose no new danger to Germany and the Soviet Union.

37. See *IKC* and *Goniec Częstochowski.*

38. Madajczyk, *Generalna Gubernia w planach hitlerowskich,* 59.

39. Poland and the Soviet Union, until the German-Russian war of June 1941, did not have diplomatic relations. After the alliance between England and the USSR, the Polish government-in-exile was pressured to establish friendly relations with Russia. This was the essence of the Sikorski-Majski accord. At that time Majski was the Soviet ambassador to England. For the Polish-Soviet accord of July 30, 1941, see the General Sikorski Historical Institute's *Documents on Polish-Soviet Relations,* vol. 1: *1939–1943* (London, 1961), 141ff.

40. *Goniec Krakowski* and its offshoot, *Kurier Kielecki,* as well as *Dziennik Radomski,* presented this news item on p. 2.

41. The centers directing the underground movement in Poland from London anxiously followed the attacks of the occupation press on the government and the émigrés. Their main concern was that the press could count on a wide readership if it dealt with the émigrés, their internal conflicts, and the position of the government-in-exile. AZHP, Sign. 203/VII-42, Material AK, Report "Stimulation of Propaganda of the Occupation Press" (Sept. 19, 1941).

42. *Kurier Częstochowski,* no. 216.

43. *Nowy Kurier Warszawski,* no. 263. See *Gazeta Lwowska,* no. 83 (Nov. 13, 1941).

44. *Nowy Kurier Warszawski,* no. 304.

45. In *Gazeta Lwowska* it was titled "A Critical Assessment of General Sikorski's Pact with the USSR"; in *Kurier Częstochowski* and *Goniec Krakowski,* "Experiences or Hopes."

46. Frank, DTgb, 18:309.

47. See *Nowy Kurier Warszawski,* nos. 121 (May 23/24, 1942) and 222 (Sept. 20, 1942). The Katyn massacre will be discussed in a later section of this book.

48. ASK-Kraków, Sign. IV K 22/50, 3:27, Files of the Criminal Case against F. Burdecki and E. Skiwski, Testimony of Bronisław Król; J. Jarowiecki, "Eugeniusz Kolanko — poeta konspiracji," *Kwartalnik Rzeszowski* (1966), no. 2, 76–85; S. Sierotwiński, "Kolanko nie Kolankowski," *Dziennik Polski* (Feb. 2, 1966).

49. The views of Germans and the commentary of German authors were published mainly in the German-language papers, e.g., in the *Krakauer und Warschauer Zeitung.*

50. For example, a series of forty-eight articles entitled "The Sold-off Wings," allegedly a memoir by Major Kazimierz Kubala, who had been on the staff of the *Głos Częstochowski* before the war; *Kurier Częstochowski* (Jan.-Mar. 1941).

51. Editorial, "Zastanówmy się," *Nowy Kurier Warszawski*, no. 199 (Aug. 23/24, 1941). See also letter to the editor, *Goniec Krakowski*, no. 11 (Jan. 15, 1941): "We want to be spokesmen of Polish society, mediators, translators, and commentators of the wishes of the Polish nationality vis-à-vis the authorities."

52. *Nowy Kurier Warszawski*, nos. 19 (Jan. 23, 1940) and 175 (July 27/28, 1940).

53. Ibid., no. 169 (July 20/21, 1940).

54. Ibid., nos. 85 (Apr. 11, 1941) and 108 (May 9, 1940).

55. Thus *Nowy Kurier Warszawski*, no. 85 (Apr. 11, 1940), published the letter "Once more about the [Polish] legion" by Master of Philosophy Sójkowski. Sójkowski, head of the chemical laboratory of the AK and even during the war a liberal, naturally would never have written to the occupation press (communication of Colonel Dr. Jan Rzepecki to the author). Sójkowski's laboratory was mentioned by R. Fleszarowa, "Nauka o ziemi i nauki biologiczne," *Walka o oświatę, naukę i kulturę w latach okupacji* (Warsaw, 1967), 667.

56. See Borowy, *Prasa*, 31. Certain additional details about the case of Brochwicz are presented in the underground journal *Kronika Okupacji* (no. 6, 12) in its report on the period Nov. 16–Dec. 31, 1940. According to this source, Brochwicz was arrested in June 1939 on suspicion of spying and was condemned to death in September. German troops released him from prison, where he was awaiting execution. In early 1940 he was arrested by the Germans for obscure reasons and imprisoned in Warsaw on Daniłowiczowska Street. The renowned theater director Arnold Szyfman, who shared a cell with him for a time, reports: "Brochwicz told us in great detail about his alleged relationship with the commander-in-chief of the Wehrmacht, General von Brauchitsch, who had not only the same coat of arms but also the same name except in German spelling. He, Brochwicz, had been imprisoned only because of a misunderstanding, which would soon be cleared up, especially since he was engaged to marry the sister of a party leader. He never spoke of Hitler except as 'our Führer.' He denigrated and disparaged Poland. . . . The presence of a provocateur bothered all of us." *Moja tułaczka wojenna* (Warsaw, 1960), 70ff.

57. See chap. 4, n. 18.

58. *Nowy Kurier Warszawski* (Oct. 11–Dec. 15, 1940). The titles of individual articles were: I. Introduction; II. German Tactics; III. Officers; IV. Organization; V. Western Powers; VI. Geographical Situation; VII. Propaganda; VIII. President and Government; IX. Politics; X. Śmigły-Rydz; XI. Summary.

59. See Borowy, *Prasa*, 31.

60. See *Nowy Kurier Warszawski*, no. 288 (Dec. 7, 1940), with the statement by Maria Maciejewski, "I was never the director of the 'Seepewe' of Colonel Rtd. Henryk Weiss"; no. 302 (Dec. 24/25, 1940): Michał Pietrusiński, "Sosnkowki had his own regiment"; and no. 5 (Jan. 1941): W. S., "Frau Maria Beck and her maiden name."

61. Here are some characteristic dissenting voices: "Let it be condemned when the time has come for that and the accused can defend themselves. . . . Zrąb took the material for his articles from uncertain sources" (Jerzy Konarzewski, *Nowy Kurier Warszawski*, no. 298, Dec. 18, 1940); "Must this dirty linen be washed right now? Is today the right time for it? Could these scandals, which, with small differences, are the same in the governing circles of other states, or these disclosures yield any advantages for us in world opinion?" (no. 287, Dec. 6, 1940); "And if a new Congress of Vienna sits down at the round table and the fate of our fatherland is put on the agenda, won't the diplomats of all countries pick up your [Zrąb's] article translated into all languages, with all the commentaries and documents? Will that help us?" (Hofmoll-Ostrowski, Jan. 1, 1941).

62. One reader proposed: "(1) Public notification of what punishments those persons mentioned in Zrąb's article deserved. (2) An opinion poll in which 'the entire friendly society' was to express whether those concerned are guilty or not. (3) Public judgment, a judgment of 'historical significance.' " Letter of S. D. W., *Nowy Kurier Warszawski,* no. 298 (Dec. 18, 1940).

63. Adam Pragier, *Czas przeszły niedokonany* (London, 1966), 265ff.

64. "To Speak or Be Silent: Reply to Mr. Jerzy Konarzewski," *Nowy Kurier Warszawski,* no. 2 (Jan. 2, 1941).

65. Reply to Mr. Mirosław Skarzyński, ibid., no. 13 (Jan. 16, 1941).

66. Ibid., no. 26 (Jan. 26, 1941).

67. See Borowy, *Prasa,* 32.

68. *Nowy Kurier Warszawski,* no. 112 (May 14, 1940).

69. See also "The Marshall's Torn-up Will," *Gazeta Lwowska,* no. 51 (Oct. 7, 1941); "An Historical Moment: The Beginning of a New Epoch in the Former Poland," *Goniec Krakowski,* no. 10 (Nov. 8, 1939); and "You Know That?" *Wiadomości Chełmskie,* no. 5 (Nov. 23, 1939).

70. *Biuletyn Informacyjny* (July 3, 1941).

71. CASW, Material Gendarmerie Lublin, 119:74.

72. *Nowy Kurier Warszawski,* nos. 221 (Sept. 18, 1941), 223 (Sept. 21, 1941), and 226 (Sept. 24, 1941).

73. See, e.g., Professor von Loesch, "Volkische Flurbereinigung im Osten," *Krakauer Zeitung,* no. 37 (Feb. 16/17, 1941).

74. *Nowy Głos Lubelski,* no. 11 (Mar. 22, 1940); *Goniec Krakowski,* nos. 191 (Aug. 8, 1940), 214 (Sept. 14, 1940), 237 (Oct. 11, 1940), and 252 (Oct. 29, 1940).

75. Thus the editorial of the *Goniec Krakowski,* no. 238 (Oct. 12, 1940), on Frank's speech at the ceremonial opening of the autumn fair in Radom: "The word loyal should not be misunderstood. It does not mean servility and subjection in private interests. . . . To be loyal means to be orderly, straightforward, and conscientious. To be loyal means to have the wish to adapt to the larger community and to be loyal means, finally, that I want to earn my bread with my own hands, or rather with my own mind."

76. See "The Poles and the New Order in Europe," *Goniec Krakowski,* no. 160 (July 13, 1940), and "The Gateway to the New Europe," ibid., no. 167 (July 21, 1940).

77. Frank, DTgb, vol. 33.

78. See Editorial, "Our Złoty," *Goniec Krakowski,* no. 14 (Jan. 18, 1940), and issues of Jan. 19, 26, 23, Feb. 1, and Oct. 27, 1940.

79. "The Polish Building Service Works for the Better Future of All Inhabitants of the GG," *Goniec Krakowski,* July 30, 1941; "The Important Work of the Polish Building Service," *Nowy Kurier Warszawski,* no. 64 (Mar. 16, 1942).

80. "Two Years of the Generalgouvernement," *Kurier Częstochowski* (Oct. 26, 1941), and all other newspapers.

81. Health and social welfare were favorite subjects of the reptile press.

82. *Nowy Kurier Warszawski,* no. 3 (Jan. 3/4, 1942).

83. *Kurier Częstochowski,* no. 82 (Apr. 7, 1942). See also "Forestry of the District of Radom Takes New Paths," ibid., no. 80 (Apr. 5, 1942).

84. *Goniec Krakowski,* nos. 263 (Nov. 10, 1941) and 276 (Nov. 23, 1941).

85. Editorial, *Goniec Krakowski,* no. 48 (Mar. 1, 1940).

86. "Work as the Content of Current Life: What Do the Clerk, the Worker, the Manicurist, the Shop Assistant, the Entrepreneur Say?" *Goniec Krakowski,* no. 59 (Oct. 16, 1941).

87. *Krakauer und Warschauer Zeitung,* no. 147 (June 23/24, 1940). But in this semi-official German-language publication of the Generalgouvernment we can also read an interview with Warsaw district governor Fischer: "The greatest success of the German reconstruction in the

Warsaw district. The Poles have more confidence in the German administration than previously in the regime of Beck and Rydz-Śmigły" (no. 70, Mar. 24/26, 1940). This needs no comment.

88. Landau, *Kronika,* 2:311, 448, 512.

89. Ibid., 198.

90. K. Wyka, *Życie na niby: Szkice z lat, 1939–1945* (Warsaw, 1957), 65.

91. ASW-Kielce, IV K. 79/49, Files of the Criminal Case against S. K. Homan.

92. S. Srokowski, *Zapiski z lat, 1939–1944* (Archive of the Polish Academy of Science, III-22), 30; AZHP, Sign. III-22; B. Dudziński: Reports (for the article "Polityka prasowa hitleryzmu"), *Kuźnica* 7 (1945); Adam Próchnik, *Kronika okupacji,* Nov. 3, 1939.

93. Frank, DTgb, 18:306.

94. "Fantasies and Hopes," *Goniec Krakowski,* Nov. 10, 1939.

95. Work was a major subject of the reptile press. The articles or exhortations quoted here come from *Kurier Częstochowski, Nowy Głos Lubelski, Goniec Krakowski,* and *Nowy Kurier Warszawski.* Letters of Polish forced laborers in Germany or interviews with them were presented just as often. In Frank, DTgb, there is often talk of the need to publish such material.

96. See *Nowy Kurier Warszawski,* no. 235 (Oct. 5/6, 1940). Reprinted from *Krakauer und Warschauer Zeitung.*

97. Thus, in the *Nowy Kurier Warszawski,* the week of Feb. 9–15, 1942, we find the following articles and news items: "With a Snowball He Puts Out His Fiancée's Eye," "Scuffles and Brawls," "Bestial Murder and Robbery," "Wife and Son Destroyed by Hatchet Blows," "Stepdaughter Breaks Stepmother's Hands with a Wooden Stool," "Male Bodies Found," and "Poisoned Vodka." These all from a single weekly issue.

98. The editorial staff of the occupation press organized special writing competitions to promote these ideas. The first was announced by *Kurier Częstochowski* in 1941. See also *Goniec Krakowski,* no. 155 (July 7, 1940).

99. The reptile press served as a source for the Pamiętnik Teatralny, which was devoted to the legitimate theater of the years 1939–1945.

100. *Nowy Kurier Warszawski,* nos. 282 (Nov. 30/31, 1940) and 304 (Dec. 28/29, 1940); *Kurier Częstochowski,* nos. 133 (June 6, 1942), 53 (Mar. 3, 1942), 147 (Apr. 26, 1942), 184 (Apr. 8, 1942), and 75 (Mar. 28, 1942); *Nowy Kurier Warszawski,* nos. 152 (July 1, 1941) and 15 (Jan. 15, 1941).

101. The guidelines of the Main Office of Propaganda of the GG of 1940 for Polish cultural life (in Pospieszalski, "Hitlerowskie 'prawo,' " 2:408ff.): Obviously no German authority may support Polish cultural life in any form; on the other hand, at the present no cause exists to suppress the cultural life of the Poles; hence the leading circles should allow the Poles cultural activity as long as this serves a primitive need for enjoyment and diversion. Similar formulations are found in reports of Warsaw district chief Fischer for the period Oct. 26, 1939 Oct. 1, 1940. APW, Sign. 3, 4.

Chapter 10: German Professional Journals in the Polish Language

1. A complete collection of the *Ilustrowany Kurier Polski* is in the National Library in Warsaw.

2. AAN, uncatalogued material.

3. *Biuletyn GKBZH* 4 (1948), 123.

4. *M[eldunek] O[kresowy] z Krakowa, 1944,* 26.

5. See the underground *Kronika okupacji,* no. 6 (Nov. 16–Dec. 31, 1940), 11.

6. AAN, Sign. 664 (unnumbered), Government Files of the GG, Memorandum of Dec. 9, 1942.

7. For more detail, see L. Dobroszycki, "Konspiracyjne 'Abecadło Lekarskie," *Polityka* (1962).

8. "Twelve Journals with Special Subjects Give Advice: The Development of the Professional Press in the GG," *Kurier Częstochowski,* no. 232 (Sept. 30, 1942).

Chapter 11: The Press and Its Readers

1. "The Duty to Fight Hostile Propaganda," *Barykada Wolności,* no. 57 (July 27, 1941).

2. From the instructions of the *Kierownictwo Walki Cywilnej* of the AK in *Biuletyn Ziemi Czerwieńskiej,* no. 15/16 (May 4, 1942).

3. Klukowski writes in his diary: "The Polish-language newspapers from Warsaw, Kraków, and Lublin are even worse than the German ones because of their bias. I do not read or buy these newspapers on principle, for I feel an invincible disgust for them" (153).

4. "Instead of being boycotted, the reptile press is sold out; and as if that's not enough, people generally pay a higher than normal price for it" (*Barykada Wolności,* no. 57, July 27, 1941); "Because of the small edition, people pay even 1 Zł. for the Gestapo newspaper *Nowy Kurier,* and there are even lines at the vendors" (*Znak,* no. 35, July 25, 1941); "The reptile press still sells well" (*Biuletyn Informacyjny,* Feb. 13, 1941); "The price of the *Kurier Częstochowski* already reaches 2 Zł. Now it can be bought for 1 Zł. and even for 66 gr. . . . While one previously got the newspaper as a regular customer at his kiosk, now one can buy it easily at any time" (*Meldunek Terenowy* of Kraków, May 16, 1944); "Yesterday the newspaper was published after a delay of several hours because of a speech by Hitler, translated and trimmed for us. Only after three hours did the newspaper vendors stop announcing their newspapers. I go to a small boy who demands 80 gr. Someday he'll be a good tradesman. I didn't buy a newspaper" (Wyleżyńska, *Dziennik,* 221, Oct. 3, 1942).

German testimonials: "We warn all our readers not to pay more than 30 gr. for the *Nowy Głos Lubelski,* according to the indication of price on page 1" (*Nowy Głos Lubelski, no. 12, Mar. 28, 1940); "The Ilustrowany Kurier Polski, 7 Dni,* and *Fala* are sold in the District of Galicia at black market prices" (*Gazeta Lwowska,* no. 75, Nov. 4, 1941). For the proceedings of a denunciation that kiosk owners were selling the *Kurier Częstochowski* with a 25 percent surcharge, see AGKBZH, Sign. 154/OR, vol. 1 (Files of the editorial staff of the *Kurier Częstochowski*). "The *Nowy Głos Lubelski* quickly disappears from the kiosks" (AGKBZH, Sign. 147/OR, Main Office of Propaganda, Weekly Report of the Districts, Jan. 1944); "Five Zł. and even more are paid for the *Nowy Głos Lubelski*" (AWIH, Microfilm from Alexandria, Va., Reports of the Main Office of Propaganda GG to the RMVP, Weekly Report for the period Apr. 28–May 5, 1942, vol. 21384).

5. Under the headline "What Is Allowed — What Is Not Allowed" in advertising in the reptile press, *Głos Polski i Komunikat Informacyjny Podubki* wrote: "For patriotic reasons, advertising in the daily reptile press like *Nowy Kurier Warszawski, Goniec Krakowski,* etc., is undesirable. One should instead use other means of publicity which do not serve the enemy. In a few cases, however, one may be forced for important reasons to soil one's name or address by publishing in a rag. Hence we warn every Pole who decides to place such an announcement that he has possibly made himself responsible to the Polish authorities in the future. Nothing and no one, however, will be able to justify advertisements appearing in the periodicals of the reptile press. . . . These journals may not even be bought on any pretext, much less may advertisements be published in them. Persons who violate this prohibition break the solidarity of the Poles and print their own death sentence with the advertisement" (no. 134, Oct. 13, 1942). *Głos Polski* then printed a list of names of such advertisers.

6. In the early period of the occupation, until Dec. 18, 1940, a few obituaries contained information from which the cause of death, such as execution in prison and concentration camp, could be inferred: e.g., "died suddenly," burial of the "urn" (instead of the body), etc.

The long interval between the date of death and the date of the notice was also eloquent. The obituaries of Janusz Kusociński and Stanisław Ludwig Poraj-Różecki, who were shot on July 21, 1940, appeared in the *Nowy Kurier Warszawski* ("they died") on Mar. 10, 1941. But the underground press was also strongly opposed to publishing such announcements. For example, the *Biuletyn Informacyjny* of Feb. 13, 1941, wrote: "We have already indicated to our readers that it is inappropriate to publish obituaries in the reptile press. These appear daily and degrade the esteem of good Poles who are often enough murdered by German executioners. Recently, in a funeral announcement published in *Nowy Kurier Warszawski* for a general of the former Polish army, a requiem mass was announced which is simply an incomprehensible offense to the memory of the deceased." See also the underground *Znak*, no. 23 (Oct. 17, 1940). Aurelia Wyleżyńska writes of it in her diary: "To put an obituary in the *NKW* or not? Maybe I should consult Włodzimierz, my cousin, who passed away, in case we later meet in the other world" (*Dziennik,* entry of Feb. 28, 1941). In view of the request on the part of the underground press not to insert such announcements, the following editorial comment was possibly a pointed reaction: "In the coming days, we shall also accept obituaries under private headlines in the local chronicle. We are convinced that this innovation will meet with the approval of our readers, and request family members of the deceased who wish to announce the death of their loved ones *gratis* [my emphasis] to call at the editorial offices daily between 10 and 11 o'clock" (*Kurier Częstochowski,* no. 97, Apr. 24, 1942). The *Goniec Krakowski* had introduced an obituary column even earlier.

7. *Biuletyn Informacyjny* (Jan. 9, 1941).

8. AWIH, Microfilm 24, 21460, Weekly Report for the period Dec. 16–22, 1941.

9. Ibid., 21454, Weekly Report for the period Jan. 5–12, 1942.

10. Ibid., 21369, Weekly Report for the period Nov. 2–9, 1942.

11. Ibid., 21381, Weekly Report for the period Nov. 21–28, 1942.

12. AGKBZH, SIGN. 147/OR, 2, SITUATION REPORT FOR THE MONTHS DEC. 1942 AND JAN. 1943.

13. FRANK, DTGB, 33:42/97, 24/266, 25/267.

14. RYSZKA, *Noc i mgła,* 238.

15. In a study done by the Sekcja Zachodnia Departamentu Informacji DRz entitled "Principles of Polish Propaganda," there is an interesting comment on the subject of Nazi propaganda in Poland: "Although Hitler had worked out the principles of propaganda aimed at his own people, it seems uncertain that he had also done it for the peoples in the occupied territories." German propaganda was "not well received among the Polish people; that is to be attributed not only to our mental force of resistance but also to the inability of the measures employed which, instead of breaking our resistance, had precisely the opposite effect" (AZHP, Sign. 202/III, unnumbered).

16. *Barykada Wolności,* no. 57 (July 27, 1941). See also "The Poisoning by the Reptile Press, or the Reich's Press Progresses Very Slowly," *Jutro,* no. 23 (Apr. 27, 1942).

17. ASW-Kielce, IV K 79/49, 2:326. Jacek Wołowski said in the Warsaw trials: "As an experienced journalist, I was aware that even such incompetent propaganda as the German, if it is used constantly and systematically, must have a certain influence on society."

18. Bolesław Dudziński, "Polityka prasowa hitleryzmu," *Kuźnica* 4/5 (1945), 37.

19. Antoni Szymanowski, "Generalgouvernement — uwagi o niemieckiej polityce okupacyjnej," *Strażnica Zachodnia* ½ (1946), 26.

20. "Dni zgrozy i walki o wolność," *Pamiętniki robotników z czasów okupacji* (Warsaw, 1949), 31–38.

21. I dealt with the attitude of the Polish clandestine Press toward the destruction of Jews under the Nazi occupation in an essay, "The Jews in the Polish Clandestine Press, 1939–1945,"

Notes to
Pages
114–118
181

in *The Jews in Poland,* ed. Andrzej K. Paluch (Kraków: Jagiellonian University, 1992), 1:289–297.

22. Irzykowski, *Notatki z życia,* 369.

23. Landau, *Kronika,* 1:607, 621.

24. AZHP, Sign. 231/8, *Kronika Agaty i informacje Sabiny,* 159.

Chapter 12: The "New Polish Policy" of the Occupation Force

1. Frank, DTgb, 26:350.

2. "The New Political Line and Our Answer," *Biuletyn Informacyjny,* May 20, 1943.

3. See Frank's speech to the NSDAP leaders of the GG (Dec. 14, 1942) and at the meeting on issues of police and security (Jan. 25, 1943). *Logbook of the German Generalgouverneur in Poland, 1939–1945* (Stuttgart: W. Präg and W. Jacobmeyer, 1975), 590ff, 598–612.

4. For more detail, see A. Dallin, *Deutsche Herrschaft in Russland* (Düsseldorf, 1958), and Goebbels's diary.

5. Frank, DTgb, 25:135.

6. Typical excerpts from the DTgb of Hans Frank: "On the other hand, no other policy can be carried out in the Generalgouvernement except that which is directed at making the strength of the people useful in the service of victory. . . . One cannot change the fact that 12 million Poles live in the Generalgouvernement who cannot possibly all be exterminated. The foreign population, therefore, must also be fed adequately to some extent" (July 9, 1943, 28:663, 785). "What happens with this people after the victory is at present insignificant, but what happens now is important. . . . We all know that this country will someday be German, that we will not endure the Polaks here. But that is for when we have won the war" (Aug. 2, 1943, 28:785). "Thus, every means that keeps this territory quiet and orderly, that brings the Polish farmer to the harvest, the Polish worker to the machine, transport, railroads, is more important than the anticipation of a conclusion which in any case we will attain only by the coming victory" (Oct. 23, 1943, 29:1097). "My goal is completely clear: for me, the Poles we shot don't count, but only the Poles we have brought to work. As long as the war lasts, the treatment of the conquered territories must finally be subordinate to the principle of introducing the territory to achievement" (Dec. 14, 1943, 30:1339). "If I came to the Führer and told him: Mein Führer, I report that I have annihilated another 150,000 Poles, he would say: Fine, if it was necessary; but unfortunately, the trains aren't moving, the whole country is full of sabotage, another assassination is committed every day — that can't go on. So, I prefer to say: the factories are working, the farmers come with their harvest, food production is up because we have followed a reasonable human European popular policy in this country. I know that we have been suspected, especially me, of being friendly to the Poles. I am and remain what I always was: an old National Socialist comrade-in-arms of the Führer. From the beginning, he has depended on me to guarantee this country for the duration of the war, which I estimated from the outset as longer than only one or two years. That requires us to take good care of the country. We can demand from a cow either milk or meat; if I want milk, I have to keep the cow alive. The same is true of the conquered country" (Mar. 18, 1944, 33:171).

7. C. Madajczyk, *Generalna Gubernia w planach hitlerowskich* (Warsaw, 1961), 145ff. See also M. Broszat, *Nationalsozialistische Polenpolitik, 1939–1945* (Stuttgart, 1961), 188.

8. For the complete text of the memorandum, see *Trial of the Major War Criminals before the International Military Tribunal. Official Text* (Nuremberg, Government Printing Office, 1947–1949), 16:15–37.

9. The report appeared in the *Nowy Kurier Warszawski* on Apr. 14, 1943, and in the *Goniec Krakowski* the following day.

10. *Trial of the Major War Criminals,* 16:25.

11. Broszat, *Nationalsozialistische Polenpolitik,* 190.

12. Frank, DTgb, 34:pt. 1, 235–252, entry on his conversations with Hitler.

13. For the order about the protection of the seizure of the harvest and the guarantee of food in the fiscal year 1943–1944, see *Documenta Occupationis,* 6:487ff., and *Goniec Krakowski,* no. 181 (Aug. 6, 1943).

14. APW, Sign. 17, 2ff., *Informacja Bieżąca,* no. 18/142 (May 6, 1944); J. Dąbrowa-Sierzputowski, "Warszawski sezon teatralny, 1940–1944."

15. *Goniec Krakowski,* nos. 324 (Oct. 7, 1943) and 252 (Oct. 28, 1943); IHPAN, *Materiały DI DRz: M[eldunek] O[kresowy] z Krakowa* (Oct. 31, 1943).

16. For the order, see *Documenta Occupationis,* 6:516ff., and *Goniec Krakowski,* no. 244 (Oct. 19, 1943).

17. Broszat, *Nationalsozialistische Polenpolitik,* 192.

18. *Goniec Krakowski,* no. 254 (Oct. 30, 1944): "The Polish question will be decided here in the country. Declaration of the Generalgouverneur to Representatives of the Foreign Press." The clandestine *Iskry* (issued by the Delegacy in the Kraków District) wrote: "German functionaries have recently hinted in private conversations that a generous autonomy will be introduced into the GG on the model of the Baltic states. It is also naturally emphasized that such autonomy would be granted only to a few districts, obviously not including the District of Warsaw."

Chapter 13: Change of Press Policy: Planning and Failure

1. Frank read these seven points of the circular to the conference on press issues of Feb. 23, 1943: AGKBZH, Files of the Bühler Trial, 10:168 (copy in IHPAN).

2. Frank, DTgb, 25:118.

3. AGKBZH, Sign. 34 x, Document 367.

4. Frank, DTgb, 25:132–142; AGKBZH, Files of the Bühler Trial, 10:162–170.

5. Frank, DTgb, 25:134.

6. Heim gives a somewhat different order of speakers. He writes not very precisely that before they got to the issue, Frank read aloud secret memoranda by Goebbels presented to him by Ohlenbusch, which had arrived the same day.

7. According to Heim's description.

8. Ibid. Frank says, on the other hand, "At the suggestion of Editor-in-Chief Fenske . . . in the Berlin Office of the deputy" (DTgb, 25:139).

9. Frank, DTgb, 25:138. After the Soviet Union occupied eastern Poland, the Soviet security forces executed about 15,000 Polish officers, who had been taken from Soviet prisoner-of-war camps, and buried them in various places, including Katyn forest, near Smolensk. After the Nazi invasion of the Soviet Union on June 22, 1941, Katyn fell under German control. In April 1943 the Nazis announced that they had discovered in the forest a mass grave of 4,443 men, mostly Polish officers. Although it was obvious from the beginning that the Katyn massacre had been perpetrated by the Soviets, only under *perestroika* and then after the demise of the USSR did the Russians publicly admit responsibility.

10. Thus according to the DTgb. According to Heim's description, Frank attacked the expulsion policy in the territory of Lublin especially sharply and stated that he was willing to "grant wide-ranging freedoms" to the Poles in the context of Goebbels's order. He also spontaneously canceled the still-valid ban on dealing with issues of the Polish government-in-exile and Sikorski personally, and agreed to move Poles into administrative functions of the press.

11. Frank, DTgb, 25:143.

12. CAMSW, Sign. III/B/1, vol. 4, *Pro memoria o sytuacji w kraju.*

13. AGKBZH, Files of the Bühler Trial, 10:170.

14. Right after the first failures and defeats on the eastern front, Goebbels expressed the idea that it was necessary to revise the policy in the occupied territories of the Soviet Union. His diary entry for Feb. 24, 1942, reads: "In the East, we must undertake a change in our propaganda and policy — this has already been coordinated with the Führer. The previous propaganda and policy was directed toward occupying the East very quickly. This hope has not been filled. Thus, we must adjust to a longer campaign and are obliged to change our speech and our policy in basic things. It may even be necessary to introduce puppet governments into the occupied countries." Contrary to Goebbels's entry, however, Hitler was ready neither to give in nor to allow a revision, and Goebbels himself admits this in later diary entries. For more detail on the differences in occupation policies, see Dallin, *Deutsche Herrschaft in Russland,* 188–192.

15. Typically, the questionable Goebbels edict of Feb. 2, 1943, was passed over in silence in this memorandum. When Frank learned of the negative attitude of party headquarters toward it, he informed all participants in the conference of Feb. 23, 1943 that the meeting was secret.

16. AGKBZH, uncatalogued material of the Main Office of Propaganda.

17. Goebbels's diary, (Apr. 4, 1943). Hano testifies that Katyń was the main subject of Reich propaganda in the period Apr. 14–July 7, 1943. *Die Taktik der Presapropaganda,* 83. Rudolf Semler states that by Goebbels's order every newspaper at that time had to print articles on the subject of Katyn at least three times a week. *Journal du secrétaire de Goebbels* (Paris, 1948), 102ff. (Apr. 16, 1943).

18. Frank, DTgb, 32:37.

19. Ibid., 33:24, 256.

20. Ibid., 32:37.

21. Ibid., 32:42.

22. Just as previously, the GG press was concerned with the Polish government-in-exile almost exclusively in the context of the Polish-Soviet conflict (future borders, Katyń, the disruption of diplomatic relations). The first news about the Polish government-in-exile after the one-year ban appeared in an editorial of Mar. 8, 1943, in *Nowy Kurier Warszawski:* "England Washes Its Hands in Innocence." Afterward, the government-in-exile was one of the major subjects of the reptile press.

23. See *Goniec Krakowski,* Mar. 15, 16, Oct. 27, 30, 1943.

24. See *Nowiny Literackie* 6 (1948).

25. In the last weeks of the occupation, Dec. 1944–Jan. 1945, the illustrated newspaper *Na Szańcach,* which was for youth employed in fortifications, was published in Kraków. On the other hand, other titles were canceled: from the beginning of the Warsaw Uprising of 1944, *7 Dni* was stopped, and even earlier *Fala* and *Co Miesiąc Powieść* had been discontinued. *Gazeta Lwowska* ceased publication when the Red Army took Lwów.

Chapter 14: Nazi Press Policy at the End of the Occupation

1. Madajczyk, *Generalna Gubernia w planach hitlerowskich,* 165.

2. Frank, DTgb, 37:188.

3. The first issue was dated Apr. 17, 1944, but appeared for general sale only in the second half of May 1944, since the Main Department of Propaganda held it up for reasons that are not clear; the final issue is dated Jan. 1945. Publisher and editor in chief (without the usual emphasis on this double function) was Dr. Feliks Burdecki. *Przełom* appeared in Kraków, although Racławice, Wieliczka, Warsaw, Warsaw-Kraków and Kraków appeared in a row on the masthead. The meaning of the printer's mark is not clear; only the post office box was named for correspondence. According to Polish underground reports, initial circulation was

30,000 copies. According to German sources, the issue of Dec. 14, 1944, had a circulation of 200,000 copies. Sixteen issues appeared (three double issues, 5/6 and 7/8 of 1944 and 1/2 of 1945) and a special supplement dated "end of August 1944," which contains the full text of the speech of the editor in chief of *Przełom* in the Weichsel broadcast on the Warsaw Uprising. See *Informacja Bieżąca*, no. 19/143 (May 13, 1944); IHPAN, Materials BIP, KG AK; *Informacja W* 1 27/44, July 6, 1944, 7; and AGKBZH, uncatalogued files of the Propaganda Main Office, Spengler's memorandum (Dec. 29, 1944), as well as the complete collection of *Przełom*.

4. IHPAN, *Materiały DI Drz, dok. Centrala Stem* (May 14–18, 1944). The other points of the dispatch were omitted since they did not relate to the subject.

5. AGKBZH, Files of the Bühler Trial, 134:77; "Ideas for a Curriculum in the History of Culture and Economics in the Schools of the Polish Generalgouvernement," *Dziennik* (entry of Oct. 31, 1941, Jan. 3, 1942, Apr. 20, 1943); *Kronika Agaty i informacje Sabiny*, pt. 2:17; AZHP, Sign. 231/III-1, 13, *Kartki z pamiętnika, 1939–1945*.

6. *Nowy Kurier Warszawski*, no. 92 (Apr. 17, 1943); *Goniec Krakowski*, no. 96 (Apr. 24, 1943); *Kurier Częstochowski*, no. 100 (Apr. 27, 1943).

7. AGKBZH, Files of the Bühler Trial, 134:77–84.

8. For a time, Jerzy de Nisau was editorial secretary of *Robotnik* (communication of Tadeusz Szturm de Strzem). Moreover, he was also said to have directed the work of the general secretariat of the military section of the PPS in the Polish-Russian war of 1920. See "The Third Possibility and the PPS in View of the Bolshevik Attack of 1920," *Przełom*, nos. 11, 12. In the material of the PPS (in AZHP, Folio 137) there is an activity report of the military section signed by Jerzy de Nisau as "Aide to the Secretary [Aleksander Dębski]."

9. W. Studnicki, *Irrwege in Polen: Ein Kampf um die polnisch-deutsche Annäherung* (Göttingen, 1951), 105. The Polish publication of the memoirs in the *Wiadomości* (London) has already been mentioned at various points.

10. *M[eldunek] O[kresowy] z Krakowa* 42/S II (May 6, 1944).

11. Along with Burdecki's appeal "Farmers!" and Skiwski's "Price of Blood" in *Przełom*, no. 1, these are the most important articles: no. 2 (1944), "Our Voice" (S); no. 3 (1944), "Political Imagination" (S), "For Our Cause" (B); no. 4 (1944), "Our Struggle" (B); no. 5/6 (1944), "Parliamentarianism and Democracy" (S), "German Propaganda" (B); no. 7/8 (1944), "August 1920-August 1944" (B), "Gradual Deceit" (S); no. 9 (1944), "Tragic Truth" (S), "Sources of pro-British Disappointment" (B); no. 10 (1944), "Before a New Start" (B), "The Liberator" (S), "When They Lose" (S); no. 11 (1944), "The Jewish Question" (S); no. 12 (1944), "Eyes on the Future" (B); no. 13 (1944), "The Paths of Polish Misfortune" (B); no. 14 (1944), "Pathos and Stupidity" (S); no. 1/2 (1945), "The Look Back."

12. See *Przełom*, the above-mentioned articles in nos. 2, 3, 12, and 13.

13. Ibid., no. 1.

14. Ibid., no 9

15. Ibid., no. 2.

16. Ibid., no. 10.

17. This statement, however, was complemented by the following commentary: "We must be aware that the course of action of the Germans toward us was and is provoked to a great extent by our often unconsidered and simply suicidal behavior, as well as by the circumstance that the attention of the Germans is totally concentrated on the world struggle currently being played out." "For Our Cause," *Przełom*, no. 3. See also the article signed by Stanisław Kościelski, "The Polish People Will Live" (no. 5/6).

18. See "August 1920-August 1944" and "After the Assassination Attempt" [on Hitler], in no. 7/8.

19. Frank, DTgb, 37:382.

20. *Straż nad Bugiem* appeared every fifteen days (no. 1 presumably on Mar. 1, 1944);

Strażnica appeared every ten days (no. 1 in Sept. 1944). The issues of both newspapers were not numbered consecutively.

21. "From Warsaw's Heroic Days of Struggle," *Strażnica* (Nov. 1–10, 1944).

22. "The Great Test of Democracy," *Strażnica* (early Dec. 1944). For comparison, here is what Skiwski wrote in his article "Political Imagination" on the Anglo-Saxon democratic system (*Przełom*, no. 3): "These two states are in a crisis of democracy, with all their phenomena of disease, from which they have found no way out, feverishly occupied as they are with testing half measures so typical of this period of dissatisfaction and fermentation." See also Skiwski's diatribe "Parliamentarianism and Democracy," *Przełom*, no. 5/6.

23. "The Jews in Light of Their Religious Convictions," *Strażnica* (late Oct. 1944).

24. "The Bulwark against Inundation," *Straż nad Bugiem* (Apr. 16, 1944); "The Most Important Order for the Moment," *Strażnica* (Oct. 1944).

25. "The Demands of the Soviets on the Poles," *Straż nad Bugiem* (Mar. 1, 1944).

26. "At an Historical Turning Point," *Gazeta Narodowa*, no. 1 (Sept. 1944).

27. "Political Ceasefire?" *Głos Polski*, no. 3 (Dec. 1944).

28. AZHP, Sign. 214/IX-2, Copy of *Nowy Czas* (Nov. 23, 1944). This newspaper was produced by the publishers of the *Litzmannstadter Zeitung* in Łódź and was primarily for areas already liberated from the German occupation.

29. "Here Speaks the Polish Underground: The Voice of the Polish People in Captivity," *Goniec Krakowski*, no. 205 (Sept. 2, 1944).

30. Exceptions were *Gazeta Narodowa* and the pseudo-underground *Goniec Krakowski*.

31. The statement is entitled "For the Knowledge of Our Readers."

32. AZHP, Sign. 114/IX-2. See also *Informator*, no. 10 (May 15, 1944), with the editorial staff's warning, "Careful in passing on!"

33. "Dangerous Game," *Nowa Polska*, no. 3 (Nov. 1, 1944); "At an Historical Turning Point," *Gazeta Narodowa*, no. 1 (Sept. 1944); "A Policy of Vacillation or a Policy of Principles?" *Gazeta Narodowa*, no. 2 (Oct. 1944).

34. "The New Year," *Głos Polski*, no. 5 (New Year 1945).

35. "On the Threshold of the Sixth Year of War," *Goniec Krakowski*, no. 205 (Sept. 2, 1944).

36. "At an Historical Turning Point," *Gazeta Narodowa*, no. 1 (Sept. 1944); "Fair Distribution of Rights and Duties," *Nowa Polska*, no. 2 (Oct. 1, 1944); "Political Ceasefire?" *Głos Polski*, no. 3 (Dec. 1944).

37. Frank, DTgb, 37:185 (entry of Oct. 17, 1944).

38. Ibid., 38:63ff.

39. On May 25, 1944, the Main Department of Propaganda sent the following telegram to all propaganda offices of the GG: "A few days ago, leaflets entitled 'Roosevelt's Message' were sent by special courier. They also contained yellow labels with the stamp PPR and a supplementary Polish text which said . . . 'Paid Mercenaries of Moscow.' This label should be distributed as an underground publication." AAN, uncatalogued files of the Main Department of Propaganda in the government of the GG/Propaganda Group. See also the guidelines of the director of the propaganda department in the District of Radom of May 19, 1944: AGKBZH, SIGN. 147 Z/OR, 217–233.

40. *Małopolska Agencja Prasowa* (underground), no. 1 (Jan. 5, 1944).

41. AZHP, Sign. 202/III/26, 8; 202/III/22, 69, Report for the period Oct. 1-Dec. 20, 1944; *M[eldunek] T[erenowy] z Krakowa* 34-S II (Apr. 4, 1944).

42. Frank, DTgb, 38:100ff.

43. Ibid., 36:197.

44. *Informacja Bieżąca*, nos. 14/138–15/139.

45. Frank, DTgb, 26:341. Here is a much more informative excerpt from the report of the

director of the propaganda department of the District of Radom to the Kraków central office: "The propaganda wave based on the murder at Katyń has evoked not only a strong interest in the Polish population but also a strong counterpropaganda which is concerned with German concentration camps, especially Auschwitz. The current anti-Bolshevik and antisemitic wave of propaganda meets with practically no interest in the Polish population. . . . I have found posters of this campaign torn down in many places." AGKBZH, Sign. 147/OR, 38, Report for Apr.–May 1943.

46. *Trial of the Major War Criminals,* 16:15–37.
47. Frank, DTgb, vol. 38.
48. Ibid., 35a:564.

Conclusion

1. *Drei Jahre im Reich: Protektorat Böhmen-Mähren* (Prague, 1942), 35; L. Mareda, "Organizacja i struktura prasy czechoslowackiej," *Kwartalnik Prasoznawczy* 1 (1957), 102ff.

2. H. Teipel, "Die Presse im besetzten Frankreich," *Zeitungswissenschaft* 16, no. 4 (1941), 212–218 (with bibliography).

3. "Griechenland," *Zeitungswissenschaft* 16, no. 10 (1941), 471ff (with bibliography).

4. L. Bindslov Frederiksen, *Pressen unter Besoettelsen* (Aarhus, 1960), 519ff (app. 1); *Handbuch der Auslandspresse* (Bonn-Köln-Opladen, 1960), 166.

5. G. Walter, *La vie à Paris sous l'occupation, 1940–1944* (Paris, 1960), 10.

6. Frederiksen, *Pressen,* 519.

7. "Organisation der Presse — Besetzte Gebiete," *Zeitungswissenschaft* 16, no. 1 (1941), 35.

8. F. Bauer, "České noviny za valky," *Šest let okupacy Prahy* (Prague, 1946), 71–80. Bauer was the director of the Press Department in the Information Ministry in the Beneš government.

9. Typical in this respect were Hitler's instructions to Joachim von Ribbentrop. When Hitler looked through *Paris-Toujours,* published in occupied France, he noticed that it was insipid, unlike the previous French magazine of that name, which was known for its distinguished illustrations. He thought it was the result of the intervention of German offices, which, in a "typical German way," interfered in things that were none of their business. He added that a few old generals were probably sitting around somewhere who saw their mission as robbing the French of the entertaining illustrations and forcing them to follow their own morals. It was not good, he said, that this journal was subsidized by the German embassy. Hitler thought the French must be diverted from politics, but that it was absurd for a German office to bother about the French morals. As far as he was concerned, German intrusion into French press politics should be limited to assuring that no publisher employed Jews; that journals that allowed themselves to make adverse and hostile comments about Germany and the occupation troops be threatened with closure; and that jokes and caricatures in French newspapers be in the German spirit. Hitler further declared that German offices should not be concerned with journals that do not deal with politics. See Rudolf Morsey, "NS-Pressepolitik im besetzten Frankreich," *Publizistik* 2 (1960), 107–11.

Index

Europe, 142
Express Ilustrowany (Illustrated Express), 22
Express Lubelski (Lublin Express), 22
Express Poranny (Morning Express), 29
Extraordinary Pacification Campaign (Aktion AB), 105

Fala, 108, 113, 131, 184*n25*
Fenske, Karl, 67, 96, 130
Ferou, Bernard, 79
Fischer, Ludwig, 24, 46, 49, 58, 151, 179*n87*
Fitzner, O., 14
Flach, Józef, 16, 17, 42
Food quotas, 109, 116
Forced labor, 58, 118–19, 144–45
Forster, Albert, 52
France: news coverage on, 88, 90; occupied, publishing in, 153, 154, 155, 187*n9*
Frank, Hans: and identity of reptile press producers, 3; diary of, 6, 55, 67, 117, 143, 182*n6;* appointment as governor-general for Poland, 45; requirement of approval for publishing, 45, 56, 57, 65; conference with Goebbels on propaganda policy, 45–47, 54; and German policy toward Poles, 46, 103, 106, 125, 126, 127, 134–35, 140, 178*n75,* 182*n6,* 183–84*n10;* establishment of Propaganda Department, 50, 51, 54; in Nazi internal power struggles, 54, 55, 165*n14;* requirement of registration for professionals, 71, 173*n16;* and content of news coverage, 93, 96; and labor recruitment in Poland, 106, 109, 182*n6;* and *1943* Goebbels edict on press reform, 125–26, 127, 129–32, 136; and Katyń massacre, 127, 133–34, 151; evacuation of Poland, 143; pseudo-clandestine papers and, 147, radio confiscation order, 164*n19*
Freie Presse (Free Press), 22, 24
French General Staff, 175–76*n33*
Front Ludowy, 74

Galicia, 1, 51
Gassner, Emil, 46, 48, 54; conflicts with Ohlenbusch, 55, 81; and Polish government-in-exile, 94–95, 96; and *1943* press policy reforms, 130, 131, 136
Gaulle, Charles de, 90
Gazeta Codzienna (Daily Gazette), 1–2

Gazeta Krakowska (Kraków Gazette), 16
Gazeta Łódzka, 24–25, 30, 31, 35, 41–42, 101
Gazeta Lwowska, 84, 85–87, 184*n25*
Gazeta Narodowa (National Gazette), 5
Gazeta Narodowa (pseudo-conspiratorial), 136, 145, 147–48
Gazeta Wspólna, 28–29, 30, 35
Gazeta Żydowska, 157*n1*
Gdyby Hitler zwyciężył (If Hitler Had Won; Kułakowski), 111
Generalgouvernement (GG): documentary sources, 5–6; publishing restrictions, 45, 50, 51, 55, 56–57; establishment of, 45, 108; Nazi policy toward, 47, 54–55, 103, 125–28; professional registration requirement, 71–73; official news sources, 80–81; news coverage on, 94, 103–4; press reforms of *1943,* 129–32, 134, 136. *See also* Poland
Generalgouvernement Polen (du Prel), 52
Geneva Convention, 65
German-language press, 1
German News Agency (Deutsche Nachrichtenbüro, DNB), 78–79, 93, 95, 127, 133
German Press Service, 51
German Propaganda Ministry. *See* Reich Ministry for Public Enlightenment and Propaganda
German Radio Propaganda (Kris and Speier), 175–76*n33*
Germany: annexed territories of Poland, 1–2, 11, 14, 45; invasion of Poland, 11, 12, 35, 102; military administration in Poland, 11, 45; propaganda policy in, 11, 77; Polish propaganda policy, 11–12, 48–49, 94, 130, 132–33, 148–50; confiscation of radio equipment, 13–14; liquidation of Polish press, 14–15, 31–32, 56–57, 153; occupation of Poland, 37–38, 94, 103–5, 117, 121, 125, 127–28, 155; war with Poland, 38, 40, 175*n32;* war with Soviet Union, 51, 84, 85, 90–91, 92–93, 125, 127, 145, 147, 154; Nazi internal power struggles, 54–55; press restrictions in, 77–80; credibility of war reporting, 93–94, 175–76*n33;* terrorism in Poland, 105–6, 125, 126–28, 132; labor recruitment in Po-

Świętochowski, Ryszard, 171*n19*
Świt (Dawn), 146
Św. Wojciecha (St. Adalbert) publishing
house, 15
Szafrański, A., 61
Szaniec: Narodowe Siły Zbrojne (Entrench-
ment: National Armed Forces [under-
ground]), 120
Szczepański, Kazimierz, 16, 17
Szczepański, Ludwik, 16, 17, 38
Szyfman, Arnold, 177*n56*
Szymanowski, Antoni, 118
Szymanowski, Karol, 107
Szymanowski, Stasiek, 119
Szymański, Felek, 119
Szymczak, Kazimierz, 119

Teatr Rozmaitości (Warsaw), 128
Telepress, 51, 71, 76, 80–81, 84, 86, 93, 95
Tempo Dnia (Daily Rhythm), 16
Tomczak, Kazimierz, 23
Trud, 2
Twardowski, Julian, 36
Twórczość Gospodarcza, 111

Ukrainian-language press, 1
Umiastowski, Roman, 25
Underground press, 2, 121, 155; hostility to
reptile press, 3–4, 113, 114–15, 171*n19;*
propaganda masquerading as, 5, 145–49;
Nazi propaganda and, 48, 51–52, 102; war
coverage, 89; anti-Semitism in, 119–20;
hostility to Soviet Union, 152; printing of,
166–67*n10;* and publication of obituaries,
181*n6. See also* Polish resistance; *Agencja
Prasowa; Barykada Wolności; Biuletyn
Informacyjny; Biuletyn Informacyjny
Ziemi Czerwieńskiej; Dziennik Ustaw
Rzeczypospolitej Polskiej; Głos Polski i
Komunikat Informacyjny Pobudki; Infor-
macja Bieżąca; Małopolska Agencja
Prasowa; Na Ucho; Polska Żyje*
(Kraków); *Polska Żyje!* (Warsaw);
*Szaniec; Walka; Wiadomości Polskie;
Wolna Polska; Znak*
Union of National Journalists' Associations,
52
Union of Warsaw Journalists, 27
United States, 88, 89–90

United States Congress, 89
Unzer Express (Yiddish), 27
Upper Silesia, 14, 159*n24,* 170*n3*

Versailles, Treaty of (*1919*), 102, 142
Volksfreund (Friend of the People), 22
Volkszeitung (People's Newspaper), 22

Waffen-SS, 121
Walka (Struggle [underground]), 120
Walter, Michał, 24, 42
Warsaw, 104, 106; radio broadcasts, 13, 26;
uprising of *1944,* 13, 147, 150; surrender
of, 14, 28, 29; newspapers, 15, 25–34; un-
derground press in, 48; professional regis-
tration in, 73
Warsaw Chamber of Commerce and Indus-
try, 57–58
Warsaw Dom Prasy (Press House), 66
Warszawski Dziennik Narodowy (Warsaw
National Newspaper), 29
Warthegau [Wartheland], 2, 14–15, 45
Wasylewski, Stanisław, 7, 74, 140, 171–
72*n22*
Wehrmacht, 88, 120–21, 125, 147; propa-
ganda program, 11, 136, 149, 175*n32. See
also* Oberkommando der Wehrmacht
Weterynaryjne Wiadomości Terapeutyczne
(Veterinary Therapeutic News), 4
Wiadomości Aptekarskie, 111
Wiadomości Chełmskie, 35, 40
Wiadomości Gospodarcze (Economic
News), 57–58, 65
*Wiadomości Międzywiązkowej Spółdzielni
Powierniczej* (Communication of the
Trustee Society), 4
Wiadomości Polskie (Polish News), 48, 166–
67*n10*
Wiadomości RGO (News of the Main Wel-
fare Council), 63–64
Widera (editor), 131
Wieczór Warszawski (Warsaw Evening), 28,
29
Wielgomasowa, Helena, 6–7, 74
Wierzynski, Hieronim, 29
Wilkoszewski, Franciszek D., 19, 160*n17*
Wirtschaft und Handwerk (Economics and
Trade), 66
Wiśniewski, Hieronim, 146